...FOR DUMMIES®

COMPUTER BOOK SERIES FROM IDG

References for the Rest of Us!®

Are you intimidated and confused by computers? Do you find that traditional manuals are overloaded with technical details you'll never use? Do your friends and family always call you to fix simple problems on their PCs? Then the *...For Dummies* computer book series from IDG Books Worldwide is for you.

...For Dummies books are written for those frustrated computer users who know they aren't really dumb but find that PC hardware, software, and indeed the unique vocabulary of computing make them feel helpless. *...For Dummies* books use a lighthearted approach, a down-to-earth style, and even cartoons and humorous icons to diffuse computer novices' fears and build their confidence. Lighthearted but not lightweight, these books are a perfect survival guide for anyone forced to use a computer.

> *"I like my copy so much I told friends; now they bought copies."*
>
> **Irene C., Orwell, Ohio**

> *"Quick, concise, nontechnical, and humorous."*
>
> **Jay A., Elburn, Illinois**

> *"Thanks, I needed this book. Now I can sleep at night."*
>
> **Robin F., British Columbia, Canada**

Already, hundreds of thousands of satisfied readers agree. They have made *...For Dummies* books the #1 introductory level computer book series and have written asking for more. So, if you're looking for the most fun and easy way to learn about computers, look to *...For Dummies* books to give you a helping hand.

IDG
BOOKS
WORLDWIDE

by Viraf D. Mohta

IDG
BOOKS
WORLDWIDE

IDG Books Worldwide, Inc.
An International Data Group Company

Foster City, CA ♦ Chicago, IL ♦ Indianapolis, IN ♦ Southlake, TX

The World Wide Web For Kids & Parents™

Published by
IDG Books Worldwide, Inc.
An International Data Group Company
919 E. Hillsdale Blvd.
Suite 400
Foster City, CA 94404
http//www.idgbooks.com (IDG Books Worldwide Web Site)
http://www.dummies.com (Dummies Press Web Site)

Library of Congress Catalog Card No.: 96-79269

ISBN: 0-7645-0098-8

Printed in the United States of America

10 9 8 7 6 5 4 3 2 1

1E/RR/RS/ZW/IN

Distributed in the United States by IDG Books Worldwide, Inc.

Distributed by Macmillan Canada for Canada; by Contemporanea de Ediciones for Venezuela; by Distribuidora Cuspide for Argentina; by CITEC for Brazil; by Ediciones ZETA S.C.R. Ltda. for Peru; by Editorial Limusa SA for Mexico; by Transworld Publishers Limited in the United Kingdom and Europe; by Academic Bookshop for Egypt; by Levant Distributors S.A.R.L. for Lebanon; by Al Jassim for Saudi Arabia; by Simron Pty. Ltd. for South Africa; by Pustak Mahal for India; by The Computer Bookshop for India; by Toppan Company Ltd. for Japan; by Addison Wesley Publishing Company for Korea; by Longman Singapore Publishers Ltd. for Singapore, Malaysia, Thailand, and Indonesia; by Unalis Corporation for Taiwan; by WS Computer Publishing Company, Inc. for the Philippines; by WoodsLane Pty. Ltd. for Australia; by WoodsLane Enterprises Ltd. for New Zealand. Authorized Sales Agent: Anthony Rudkin Associates for the Middle East and North Africa.

For general information on IDG Books Worldwide's books in the U.S., please call our Consumer Customer Service department at 800-762-2974. For reseller information, including discounts and premium sales, please call our Reseller Customer Service department at 800-434-3422.

For information on where to purchase IDG Books Worldwide's books outside the U.S., please contact our International Sales department at 415-655-3172 or fax 415-655-3295.

For information on foreign language translations, please contact our Foreign & Subsidiary Rights department at 415-655-3021 or fax 415-655-3281.

For sales inquiries and special prices for bulk quantities, please contact our Sales department at 415-655-3200 or write to the address above.

For information on using IDG Books Worldwide's books in the classroom or for ordering examination copies, please contact our Educational Sales department at 800-434-2086 or fax 817-251-8174.

For press review copies, author interviews, or other publicity information, please contact our Public Relations department at 415-655-3000 or fax 415-655-3299.

For authorization to photocopy items for corporate, personal, or educational use, please contact Copyright Clearance Center, 222 Rosewood Drive, Danvers, MA 01923, or fax 508-750-4470.

is a trademark under exclusive license to IDG Books Worldwide, Inc., from International Data Group, Inc.

About the Author

Viraf D. Mohta

One thing that you'll realize about Viraf Mohta if you hang around him for a day is that he loves kids. That's why he couldn't have been happier that his first book is for them. And about computers. What a great combination. In addition to entertaining kids with computers, he teaches them martial arts and is also a volunteer with the Special Olympics.

Viraf strongly believes that kids are the future of any society and that teaching them to do the right thing will only make the world a better place. Besides, some day these very kids will be passing laws that'll affect us all, he says. Scary thought, huh? And an incentive, to nurture them.

Viraf's 9-to-5 job is with an educational research organization where he's a systems analyst. He also acts as technology consultant for other organizations. He holds an MBA in Management Information Systems. He's also an entrepreneur and the 1992 World Champion in Full-Contact Stickfighting. When he finds time, he runs marathons. His goal is to run his next one in under three hours.

ABOUT IDG BOOKS WORLDWIDE

Welcome to the world of IDG Books Worldwide.

IDG Books Worldwide, Inc., is a subsidiary of International Data Group, the world's largest publisher of computer-related information and the leading global provider of information services on information technology. IDG was founded more than 25 years ago and now employs more than 8,500 people worldwide. IDG publishes more than 275 computer publications in over 75 countries (see listing below). More than 60 million people read one or more IDG publications each month.

Launched in 1990, IDG Books Worldwide is today the #1 publisher of best-selling computer books in the United States. We are proud to have received eight awards from the Computer Press Association in recognition of editorial excellence and three from *Computer Currents*' First Annual Readers' Choice Awards. Our best-selling *...For Dummies*® series has more than 30 million copies in print with translations in 30 languages. IDG Books Worldwide, through a joint venture with IDG's Hi-Tech Beijing, became the first U.S. publisher to publish a computer book in the People's Republic of China. In record time, IDG Books Worldwide has become the first choice for millions of readers around the world who want to learn how to better manage their businesses.

Our mission is simple: Every one of our books is designed to bring extra value and skill-building instructions to the reader. Our books are written by experts who understand and care about our readers. The knowledge base of our editorial staff comes from years of experience in publishing, education, and journalism — experience we use to produce books for the '90s. In short, we care about books, so we attract the best people. We devote special attention to details such as audience, interior design, use of icons, and illustrations. And because we use an efficient process of authoring, editing, and desktop publishing our books electronically, we can spend more time ensuring superior content and spend less time on the technicalities of making books.

You can count on our commitment to deliver high-quality books at competitive prices on topics you want to read about. At IDG Books Worldwide, we continue in the IDG tradition of delivering quality for more than 25 years. You'll find no better book on a subject than one from IDG Books Worldwide.

John Kilcullen

John Kilcullen
President and CEO
IDG Books Worldwide, Inc.

Eighth Annual Computer Press Awards ≥1992

Ninth Annual Computer Press Awards ≥1993

Tenth Annual Computer Press Awards ≥1994

Eleventh Annual Computer Press Awards ≥1995

IDG Books Worldwide, Inc., is a subsidiary of International Data Group, the world's largest publisher of computer-related information and the leading global provider of information services on information technology. International Data Group publishes over 275 computer publications in over 75 countries. Sixty million people read one or more International Data Group publications each month. International Data Group's publications include: **ARGENTINA:** Buyer's Guide, Computerworld Argentina, PC World Argentina; **AUSTRALIA:** Australian Macworld, Australian PC World, Australian Reseller News, Computerworld, IT Casebook, Network World, Publish, Webmaster; **AUSTRIA:** Computerwelt Osterreich, Networks Austria, PC Tip Austria; **BANGLADESH:** PC World Bangladesh; **BELARUS:** PC World Belarus; **BELGIUM:** Data News; **BRAZIL:** Annuário de Informática, Computerworld, Connections, Macworld, PC Player, PC World, Publish, Reseller News, Supergamepower; **BULGARIA:** Computerworld Bulgaria, Network World Bulgaria, PC & MacWorld Bulgaria; **CANADA:** CIO Canada, Client/Server World, ComputerWorld Canada, InfoWorld Canada, WebWorld; **CHILE:** Computerworld Chile, PC World Chile; **COLOMBIA:** Computerworld Colombia, PC World Colombia; **COSTA RICA:** PC World Centro America; **THE CZECH AND SLOVAK REPUBLICS:** Computerworld Czechoslovakia, Macworld Czech Republic, PC World Czechoslovakia; **DENMARK:** Communications World Danmark, Computerworld Danmark, Macworld Danmark, PC World Danmark, Techworld Denmark; **DOMINICAN REPUBLIC:** PC World Republica Dominicana; **ECUADOR:** PC World Ecuador; **EGYPT:** Computerworld Middle East, PC World Middle East; **EL SALVADOR:** PC World Centro America; **FINLAND:** MikroPC, Tietoverkko, Tietoviikko; **FRANCE:** Distributique, Hebdo, Info PC, Le Monde Informatique, Macworld, Reseaux & Telecoms, WebMaster France; **GERMANY:** Computer Partner, Computerwoche, Computerwoche Extra, Computerwoche FOCUS, Global Online, Macwelt, PC Welt; **GREECE:** Amiga Computing, GamePro Greece, Multimedia World; **GUATEMALA:** PC World Centro America; **HONDURAS:** PC World Centro America; **HONG KONG:** Computerworld Hong Kong, PC World Hong Kong, Publish in Asia; **HUNGARY:** ABCD CD-ROM, Computerworld Szamitastechnika, Internetto online Magazine, PC World Hungary, PC-X Magazin Hungary; **ICELAND:** Tolvuheimur PC World Island; **INDIA:** Information Communications World, Information Systems Computerworld, PC World India, Publish in Asia; **INDONESIA:** InfoKomputer PC World, Komputek Computerworld, Publish in Asia; **IRELAND:** ComputerScope, PC Live!; **ISRAEL:** Macworld Israel, People & Computers/Computerworld; **ITALY:** Computerworld Italia, Macworld Italia, Networking Italia, PC World Italia; **JAPAN:** DTP World, Macworld Japan, Nikkei Personal Computing, OS/2 World Japan, SunWorld Japan, Windows NT World, Windows World Japan; **KENYA:** PC World East African; **KOREA:** Hi-Tech Information, Macworld Korea, PC World Korea; **MACEDONIA:** PC World Macedonia; **MALAYSIA:** Computerworld Malaysia, PC World Malaysia, Publish in Asia; **MALTA:** PC World Malta; **MEXICO:** Computerworld Mexico, PC World Mexico; **MYANMAR:** PC World Myanmar; **NETHERLANDS:** Computer! Totaal, LAN Internetworking Magazine, LAN World Buyers Guide, Macworld Netherlands, Net, WebWereld; **NEW ZEALAND:** Absolute Beginners Guide and Plain & Simple Series, Computer Buyer, Computer Industry Directory, Computerworld New Zealand, MTB, Network World, PC World New Zealand; **NICARAGUA:** PC World Centro America; **NORWAY:** Computerworld Norge, CW Rapport, Datamagasinet, Financial Rapport, Kursguide Norge, Macworld Norge, Multimediaworld Norge, PC World Ekspress Norge, PC World Nettverk, PC World Norge, PC World ProduktGuide Norge; **PAKISTAN:** Computerworld Pakistan; **PANAMA:** PC World Panama; **PEOPLE'S REPUBLIC OF CHINA:** China Computer Users, China Computerworld, China InfoWorld, China Telecom World Weekly, Computer & Communication, Electronic Design China, Electronics Today, Electronics Weekly, Game Software, PC World China, Popular Computer Week, Software Weekly, Software World, Telecom World; **PERU:** Computerworld Peru, PC World Profesional Peru, PC World SoHo Peru; **PHILIPPINES:** Click!, Computerworld Philippines, PC World Philippines, Publish in Asia; **POLAND:** Computerworld Poland, Computerworld Special Report Poland, Cyber, Macworld Poland, Networld Poland, PC World Komputer; **PORTUGAL:** Cerebro/PC World, Computerworld/Correio Informático, Dealer World Portugal, Mac*In/PC*In Portugal, Multimedia World; **PUERTO RICO:** PC World Puerto Rico; **ROMANIA:** Computerworld Romania, PC World Romania, Telecom Romania; **RUSSIA:** Computerworld Russia, Mir PK, Publish, Seti; **SINGAPORE:** Computerworld Singapore, PC World Singapore, Publish in Asia; **SLOVENIA:** Monitor; **SOUTH AFRICA:** Computing SA, Network World SA, Software World SA; **SPAIN:** Communicaciones World España, Computerworld España, Dealer World España, Macworld España, PC World España; **SRI LANKA:** Infolink PC World; **SWEDEN:** CAP&Design, Computer Sweden, Corporate Computing Sweden, Internetworld Sweden, it branschen, Macworld Sweden, MaxiData Sweden, MikroDatorn, Nätverk & Kommunikation, PC World Sweden, PCaktiv, Windows World Sweden; **SWITZERLAND:** Computerworld Schweiz, Macworld Schweiz, PCtip; **TAIWAN:** Computerworld Taiwan, Macworld Taiwan, NEW ViSiON/Publish, PC World Taiwan, Windows World Taiwan; **THAILAND:** Publish in Asia, Thai Computerworld; **TURKEY:** Computerworld Turkiye, Macworld Turkiye, Network World Turkiye, PC World Turkiye; **UKRAINE:** Computerworld Kiev, Multimedia World Ukraine, PC World Ukraine; **UNITED KINGDOM:** Acorn User UK, Amiga Action UK, Amiga Computing UK, Apple Talk UK, Computing, Macworld, Parents and Computers UK, PC Advisor, PC Home, PSX Pro, The WEB; **UNITED STATES:** Cable in the Classroom, CIO Magazine, Computerworld, DOS World, Federal Computer Week, GamePro Magazine, InfoWorld, I-Way, Macworld, Network World, PC Games, PC World, Publish, Video Event, THE WEB Magazine, and WebMaster; online webzines: JavaWorld, NetscapeWorld, and SunWorld Online; **URUGUAY:** InfoWorld Uruguay; **VENEZUELA:** Computerworld Venezuela, PC World Venezuela; and **VIETNAM:** PC World Vietnam. 10/22/96

Dedication

This book is dedicated to my family. To my mother Freny, from whom I get my endurance and zest for life. (Thanks Ma! Couldn't have run the marathons without you.) To my father Dali, who instilled in me the fine virtues of sacrifice and charity. (Good goin,' Dad!) And to the most precious person in my life, my sister Binaifer. (Life wouldn't be worth living without you.)

Author's Acknowledgments

I have always read with interest the acknowledgments that authors give in their books, never once thinking I would one day do the same.

First, I would like to thank Mary Bednarek who believed in the concept of this book even though others thought, "It's a great idea, but . . ." Thanks, Mary. (When's your next trip back East? We gotta do lunch.) Thanks to the IDG management team, Diane Steele, Judi Taylor, and Seta Frantz.

Barb Terry, my patient project editor, was a pleasure to work with, even though I probably drove her up the wall sometimes. Sorry, Barb. But let's do it again. 'Twas a pleasure working with you.

Joyce Pepple worked tirelessly to obtain permission for all the software you see on the CD. Thanks, Joyce. Thanks also to Kevin Spencer whose technical expertise got the CD together.

Thanks to Mike Thompson at Connectix, and to Amy Martin and Mark Franklin at Wilson McHenry Company, for making the QuickCam available at such short notice. Great product. I love it.

Special thanks to my friend John Gorman who stopped by to give me well-deserved breaks (and pep-talks) during those 48-hour writing sprees. And to Darius Stafford for always being ready on the other side of the Web to test every gadget I pulled out of my bag of tricks. Thanks, Darius. ("Can you hear me? Is that better?")

Thanks to Frankie and Lisa Pane for bringing the kids over for the "photo shoot" and to Mariel Fink, my tough little martial artist for testing the instructions in the book. (Sorry for missing the classes, Mariel. I'll let you beat me up a little extra for all that I've missed. Ouch!) Thanks also to Mr. Rooney and his English students at Christian Brother's Academy in Lincroft, NJ. Hope your Web pages turn out way cool.

Lastly, thanks to my family and friends for putting up with my crazy schedule during this period, and also to Linda Greb and Kathy Novak for shouldering the burden at the office while I was out on vacation.

Publisher's Acknowledgments

We're proud of this book; please send us your comments about it by using the Reader Response Card at the back of the book or by e-mailing us at feedback/dummies@idgbooks.com. Some of the people who helped bring this book to market include the following:

Acquisitions, Development, and Editorial

Project Editor: Barb Terry

Assistant Acquisitions Editor: Gareth Hancock

Product Development Manager: Mary Bednarek

Permissions Editor: Joyce Pepple

Copy Editors: Robin Drake, Joe Jansen

Technical Editor: David S. Karlins, Kevin Spencer

General Reviewers: Mrs. Smith, Mr. Rooney and his English students, and Mariel Fink

Editorial Manager: Seta K. Frantz

Editorial Assistants: Chris H. Collins, Michael Sullivan

Production

Project Coordinator: Valery Bourke

Layout and Graphics: Brett Black, Linda Boyer, Elizabeth Cardénas-Nelson, J. Tyler Connor, Maridee Ennis, Angie Hunckler, Drew Moore, Brent Savage, Michael A. Sullivan

Proofreaders: Rachel Garvey, Nancy Price, Dwight Ramsey, Robert Springer, Carrie Voorhis, Karen York

Indexer: Richard Shrout

Special Help: E. Shawn Aylsworth

General and Administrative

IDG Books Worldwide, Inc.: John Kilcullen, CEO; Steven Berkowitz, President and Publisher

IDG Books Technology Publishing: Brenda McLaughlin, Senior Vice President and Group Publisher

Dummies Technology Press and Dummies Editorial: Diane Graves Steele, Vice President and Associate Publisher; Judith A. Taylor, Brand Manager

Dummies Trade Press: Kathleen A. Welton, Vice President and Publisher; Stacy S. Collins, Brand Manager

IDG Books Production for Dummies Press: Beth Jenkins, Production Director; Cindy L. Phipps, Supervisor of Project Coordination; Kathie S. Schutte, Supervisor of Page Layout; Shelley Lea, Supervisor of Graphics and Design; Debbie J. Gates, Production Systems Specialist; Tony Augsburger, Reprint Coordinator; Leslie Popplewell, Media Archive Coordinator

Dummies Packaging and Book Design: Patti Sandez, Packaging Assistant; Kavish+Kavish, Cover Design

◆

The publisher would like to give special thanks to Patrick J. McGovern, without whom this book would not have been possible.

◆

Contents at a Glance

Table of Contents

· ·

Introduction

Welcome to the wonders of the World Wide Web. (Let's drop the *World* and the *Wide* and just call it the Web, okay?) Are you ready to go on a spectacular journey to faraway lands? If you are, then be prepared to see amazing things at every stop. *The World Wide Web For Kids & Parents* takes you to places where you're guaranteed to have nothing but fun, fun, fun.

Are the Internet and the Web the Same Thing?

No, the Internet and the Web are not the same thing. The Web is a part of the Internet — the easiest and most widely used part of the Internet. The good news is that you don't have to be a computer geek to browse the Web — which explains why kids as young as eight years old use it with just a few basic instructions.

But what exactly is the Web? The Web is a group of computers connected to each other, spread out all over the world, speaking the same language. And why is this group called the World Wide Web and not the Big Bread Basket or the Horribly Hideous Hive or something like that? First, the Web covers almost the whole wide world. Second, the computers are connected to each other like the strands that make up a spider's web.

What You Can Expect to See on the Web

You can see *and* hear things on the Web. Ever wonder what radio stations in other countries sound like? Do they play the kind of music you like? Would you like to listen to song-clips from your favorite band's newly released CD without having to buy it? How about being able to watch your friend as the two of you talk on the phone? Or watch a preview of a movie before going to the theater and wasting eight bucks? How about discussing fashion trends with kids your age in other countries? Or playing games with kids in other parts of the world? (Now do you see why it's called the *World* Wide Web? It stretches around the entire world.) Wouldn't it be cool to get tips on beating that new computer game you just bought? Or trade tips with others who play the game, too? How about making friends in countries you've never been to? These are only a handful of really neato things you can do on the Web.

But wait, there's more. The Web has museums and shopping malls, libraries and laboratories, restaurants and recipes, and lots of other stuff that'll blow you away. And all you have to do to get to them is turn on your computer, do some typing and click on the mouse button.

Who Should Read This Book?

This book is for two kinds of kids and their parents:

- Those who've never been on the Web yet
- Those who've already been there and want to use nifty new gadgets to do way cool things

You don't have to be a computer nerd to use this book or the Web. Even if you know very little about computers, fear not. You'll get good at it really fast. A week or so with this book, and it'll be perfectly normal for your parents to carry you kicking and screaming from the computer.

What You Can Expect from This Book

I wrote this book with only one purpose — to show you how much fun the Web can be. The Web is filled with plenty of fun stuff, but try finding easy instructions for using the stuff. The snazziest and hippest electronic gadgets are totally useless if nobody uses them. Right? I'll show you how to use cameras to see people in other parts of the world and how to talk to people without using your telephone. I'll take you to places where you can get stuff for free, and, best of all, I explain all this in plain and simple English. No technobabble here. Cross my heart.

What You Need to Get on the Web

To get on the Web, you need at least the following:

___ **A computer.** Duh! You need a Mac or at least a 486 IBM-compatible computer with 8MB of RAM. Anything slower than a 486 is too slooooooooow.

Because of the wide variety of computer systems used by kids at home and in schools, the figures in this book aren't limited to one computer system. The figures show screen shots of Windows 95, Windows 3.1*x*, or Macintosh systems.

___ **Windows.** If you use an IBM-compatible PC, you need at least Windows 3.1*x*, but preferably Windows 95.

___ **A modem.** A *modem* is a device that allows your computer to talk to another computer. The faster your modem, the better. The commonly used modems these days are called 14.4 and 28.8 modems. (I've purposely left out the true technical terms for them.) A 28.8 modem is much faster than a 14.4 modem. Although you can use the Web with a 14.4 modem that costs about $50, I recommend that you spend about $125 and get a 28.8 modem. I do so because some of the stuff on the Web doesn't work well with slow modems.

___ **A sound card and speakers**. Although a sound card and speakers aren't absolutely necessary, they are great to have — especially since you can travel to places where you can listen to music on the Web. You also need them when you talk to friends on the Web. A sound card and speakers usually cost between $150 and $160. Macintosh computers come equipped with sound features, so, Mac users everywhere, thank Apple for saving you some bucks.

___ **A browser.** A browser is special software you need to get on the Web. Some of the commonly used browsers are Netscape, Mosaic, and Internet Explorer. The examples in this book use either Netscape or Internet Explorer. But if you want to use another browser, that's fine, too, because they all work about the same way on the Web — kind of like cars. A Ferrari gets you where you want to go in much the same way a BMW does. They both use the same highway, and the drivers follow the same traffic rules.

___ **An Internet Service Provider.** An *Internet Service Provider* (ISP) is a company that makes it possible for users like you and me to connect to the Web. ISPs are like the phone company for the Internet. You first have your computer dial the number of the ISP computer, and then the ISP computer lets you jump onto the Web. (Of course, you don't need to know *how* any of this actually happens.) AT&T WorldNet Service, America Online, CompuServe, and Prodigy are a few of the numerous ISPs out there. The CD in the book comes with AT&T WorldNet Service. I've been using AT&T WorldNet Service for a few months now, and I've been thoroughly satisfied with the service. Not only can I connect to their computers without a problem, I can reach their technical support staff fairly easily, too.

Things to think about if you haven't selected an ISP

Just in case you decide not to enroll in AT&T WorldNet Service, you ought to know a few things before you sign up with an ISP. You can spend many, many hours on the Web — which could cost you mucho, mucho bucks in connection fees. But that is only if the ISP you select does not have a flat fee monthly rate. The flat rate is usually between $15 and $25. I recommend that you choose an ISP that charges a flat monthly rate because you can stay on the Web as long as you like. But you should remember one thing: a low monthly fee isn't necessarily all you should look for in an ISP. A low fee does not always translate to high quality service. Sometimes it's better to pay a little extra for that extra help you might need from the ISP technical support staff.

How do I separate the good ISPs from the bad ones?

The best way to find out about an ISP is to talk to your friends who already are on the Web and ask them about their experiences. You should ask these questions:

✔ Was the software easy to install?

✔ How good is the technical support service of the ISP?

✔ Do you have a hard time connecting to the ISP in the evenings? You're wondering why am I concerned with evenings in particular, right? Because that's when everybody and his or her brother are using the Web. If you can connect to the ISP easily at such peak usage times, then the ISP has the capability to handle a large number of users, which is good.

✔ Do you get a discount if you sign up for a year? Most ISPs give you a break if you do. But a word of caution here. Signing up for a year is not a good thing to do if you don't know anything about the ISP. The service may be horrible, and once the ISP has your money, it's a pain trying to have their billing department close your accounts — unless, of course, you like classical music and don't mind being kept on hold for an hour or so. My advice is try before you buy.

How to Use This Book

The World Wide Web For Kids & Parents is written so that even if you skip from one chapter to another, you can make perfect sense of what you're reading. It's not like your Math workbook, which you have to follow page by totally stimulating page. In this book, if you don't like what you read in Chapter 5, go to Chapter whatever. Nobody's stopping you. Skip forward, jump back, move sideways, hop around . . . uh, you get the picture. But if you've never used the Web, you may want to start with the first few chapters and get the hang of browsers before you venture off into the unknown.

When you see weird letters and numbers like `www.dummies.com`, you're looking at the special language of the Web. When you're asked to type that kind of stuff, don't faint. Just be sure to match exactly what you see in the book — small letters, capital letters, dots (.), slashes (/ or \) and no spaces. No big deal.

How This Book Is Organized

This book contains six major parts, plus two appendixes *and* a CD.

Part I: Catch a Ride on the Web

This part takes you directly to the Web. I show you how to get on the Web, move around on it, jump from one place to another, and go back to where you started. I show you the ins and outs of the two most popular browsers — Netscape Navigator and Internet Explorer. You can start surfing after reading just one chapter about the browser of your choice and then return later for some more tips on using it.

Part II: Browse Around the Web

In this part, I show you some of the weird and wacky sites on the Web. You won't believe how easily you can get to them. But what if you can't find what you want in my chapter on Web sites? Hold on to your britches! The next chapter shows you how to search the Web on your own. You can find sites for havin' fun or sites for finding information you can use to impress your teachers.

Part III: Travel the Net

In this part, I show you how to use the Web to get to other parts of the Internet. I show you how to use electronic-mail (e-mail) and other ways to get in touch with kids who share interests similar to your own.

Part IV: Welcome to Funtasia

Here's where I show you the really fun stuff. First, I reveal to you a treasure chest filled with neat software and show you how to look for cool games that you can use on your own computer. Then you listen to the radio, watch videos, call friends long distance without paying a penny, see friends on the computer as you chat with them, and play interactive games with kids in other countries.

Part V: Building Castles in the Air

In this part, I help you create your own home page, where friends can see what you look like, what your pets look like, what you like doing, and the kind of music you listen to. If you feel like making your home page really fancy, I help you with that, too.

Part VI: The Part of Tens

The chapters included in this part can be read top to bottom during those boring TV commercials. They include tips on the *do*'s and *don't*s for Internet-surfing and a list of parents' frequently asked questions.

The Appendixes

Appendix A is a For Parents Only section. In it is information about installing software for making certain that kids have safe WebVentures.

The World Wide Web For Kids & Parents comes with a CD filled with interesting software. The CD includes most of the software discussed in the book, and Appendix B discusses how to install the software. Parents should be aware that, unless specified, this software is shareware. *Shareware* means that if you decide to use the software beyond the trial period, you must pay the software author or manufacturer. The software provides the details about the trial period and the payment.

Icons Used in This Book

This book has all kinds of icons in the margins. Pay attention to them. They're in the book to make your reading easier. The icons point out when you need to get help, stuff you can skip if you're a lazy reader or in a hurry, what to do if you messed up and more — and you don't have to pay extra for them! What a bargain.

You've read this before in this Introduction, but I'll say it again. *The World Wide Web For Kids & Parents* comes with a CD. You won't find your favorite group on the CD, but you will find cool software for browsing the Web and roving the Internet.

This icon is the friendliest one in the book. Read the tip to make surfin' the Net and browsin' the Web easier.

When you see this icon, get out your pencil 'cause a list is approaching. You can actually check off the items in the list or do a mental inventory to see whether you have what you need to complete the steps in the chapter. If you're missing some software or hardware, start saving those pennies. Before long, you'll have the equipment you need to join in the fun.

Big Trouble lurks ahead if you don't watch out! Follow the advice at the Warning icon before you get yourself into hot water.

Okay, you did everything the way the instructions said, but somehow things got messed up. Read the text beside this icon and find your way back. (Hey, how *did* the author know that would happen anyway? Could it be that he did it, too?)

Hey, parents! When you see this icon, an adult needs to take over and do the dirty work that the kids might have difficulty doing on their own.

The World Wide Web For Kids & Parents contains trivia. No, you didn't read that sentence carefully enough. I didn't say that the book is trivia — only the questions and answers marked by this icon!

School and the Web? Yes, teachers can use the Web in a classroom setting. This icon marks neat computing-things a teacher can do to bring the world into the classroom.

This icon is a tip for parents. Duh! Kids don't need to read the tip, but, if they do, they won't self-destruct.

Danger zone! A humongous word is approaching. Fortunately, a simple definition always follows, too.

No, this icon doesn't refer to a Big Mac attack. Macs just work a little differently than PCs, and this icon reminds Mac users that they need to ignore the PC steps and do things the Mac way.

Houston, We're Ready for Lift-Off

You're now on the launching pad to the adventure of your life. Ready for lift-off? Ready to join the millions of others who've made Web-surfing their favorite pastime? Before you know it, you'll be addicted to it and wonder why you didn't start earlier. You'll also know what those slashes and dots and `coms` mean in those TV ads. You'll finally be able to convince your friends that those weren't hidden messages to the aliens among us.

Before you leave this introduction, I want to invite you to visit the *World Wide Web For Kids & Parents* Web site at `www.dummies.com/bonus/www_kids` It has lots of goodies for you to check out.

Enjoy!

PART I

Catch a Ride on the Web

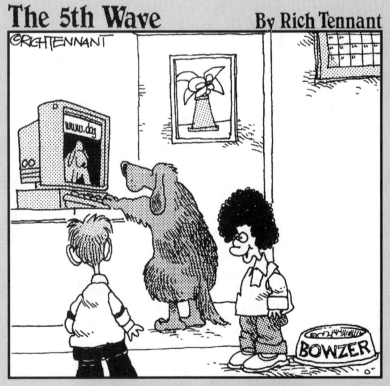

The 5th Wave   By Rich Tennant

"He's our new Web Bowzer."

In this part . . .

*B*efore you start flying through cyberspace at warp
speed, you need to be able to control your flying
machine. The flying machine is your Web browser, and, in
this part, you're introduced to two such browsers —
Netscape Navigator and Internet Explorer. The look and
feel of the two are different, but, other than that, they
perform remarkably similarly. Take your pick, fire up your
engines, and you're ready to go.

Chapter 1

Look Out, Web! Here I Come — via Netscape Navigator

. . . .

. . . .

1 know you're itching to blast off into Cyberspace, so I'll keep you waiting no more. Let's go!

Hello, I'm Netscape! I'll Be Your Navigator

Netscape Navigator (we'll call it just Netscape from now on) is a wonderful browser. Browser? Huh? Yeah, browser. You see, cruising the Web is a lot like going to a mall. You do a lot of window shopping at the mall. You "browse" a lot. You go to one store, you look, you go to the next, you look, and so on. Netscape is software that lets you go from one "shop" on the Web to the next. The "shops" are called *Web sites* or *home pages*. Netscape lets you look around — *browse* around — a Web site and even leave a marker for a site so that you can come back to it directly rather than have to go through all the "shops" again to find what you were looking for. People sometimes use the word *cruising* or *surfing* instead of *browsing,* but they all mean the same thing.

Netscape is easy to use, and it does a whole bunch of neat things. How it works is not what you need to be concerned with. Do you care how your TV works? Nosiree Bob! As long as you get *Friends, Saved by the Bell,* and

Baywatch, you're happy as a pig in mud. Not clean, but happy. So let's skip the boring stuff, which we don't need anyway, and get to the heart of the matter.

Web surfers all over the world use Netscape — even those who don't speak English. How? Don't ask! That's one of the things only Web geeks want to understand — besides, we have better things to do. We're goin' surfin'.

Question: Who's the computer geek-turned-multimillionaire who created Netscape Navigator?

Answer: Marc Andreessen. Marc is 24 years old and has more than a million bucks for each of his 24 years. Duuuuuude! Being a nerd ain't all that bad, huh?

The many forms of Netscape

Marc Andreessen (the millionaire nerd) and his friends at Netscape have developed different versions of Netscape for the Mac, Windows 95, and Windows 3.1*x,* all versions look and work very much alike. This book uses Version 3.0. If you already use an earlier version of Netscape, you'll notice that Version 3.0 doesn't look much different. But, like the big bad wolf, looks are deceiving. Trust me, Netscape 3.0 is different. It can do a whole lotta stuff that the older versions couldn't do.

People use a wide variety of computer systems to surf the Web: Windows 3.1*x* systems, Windows 95 systems, Mac systems, and many more. They all work the same for the most part, but their Netscape screens look slightly different. Just to be fair to all, I've used screenshots from the three most commonly used systems — Windows 3.1*x,* Windows 95, and Mac. In any example, if your screen looks a little different from the one shown in the book, fear not. The figure is just from one of the other systems.

Where can I get a copy of Netscape 3.0?

You can get Netscape 3.0 from many places.

- ✔ Buy it at a store for about 50 bucks.
- ✔ Copy it from Netscape's Web site (called *downloading* by the Web geeks).
- ✔ Ask your Internet Service Provider (ISP) for it. (If you don't know what an ISP is, refer to the Introduction.) Most (but not all) ISPs use it. But getting it can take a long time!

Installing Netscape

Since software installation is never much fun, let your parents take care of it. After all, you're allergic to work, and that's what parents are for anyway, right? Absolutely! So this is where you yell, "MOM! Look what I found." (Yelling "DAD" works fine, too.) When a parent-type person comes over, you point to the paragraph below and say, "I'll be back in a second," and slide away like you have something really important to take care of. Get it? Good. Now yell.

Note: If you already have Netscape 3.0 on your computer, leave your parents alone. They deserve a break! You just skip on ahead to the section "Using Netscape."

Your kid didn't just find a ten-dollar bill. Surprised? What she or he did find, though, was something fun for you to do — installing the Netscape software. Since you need to do this installation before your kid can get on the Web, it's important that you dads stop baking those cookies. Moms, stop watching football *right now*. Take the phone off the hook. We all have priorities, and I'll set yours for now. This is important. This is number one. Numero uno. What's that? You're not technical enough? Here's a test to see if you are. You have 15 minutes, starting . . . NOW!

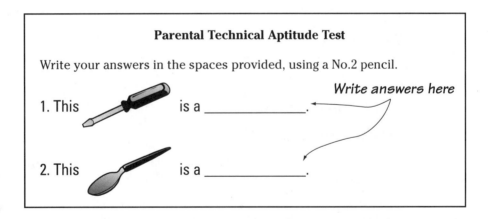

Parental Technical Aptitude Test

Write your answers in the spaces provided, using a No.2 pencil.

Write answers here

1. This ✏ is a _____.

2. This 🥄 is a _____.

Congratulations! You passed the test. Now go straight to Appendix B. Do not pass GO! Do not collect $200. You'll find instructions for using the CD there. Oh, and please let your kid know when you're done. Much appreciated.

Hey, kids, it's safe to come back now. Your parents have so graciously installed Netscape, and a "Thank you" is in order. So get the pleasantries outta the way, and continue where you left off.

Using Netscape

Now that Netscape has been installed, you're ready to begin using it.

1. **Start your computer if you haven't already.**

   It really doesn't matter whether you have a Mac or a Windows-based PC. You already know how to start it, I'm sure.

2. **Double-click on the Netscape Navigator icon shown in Figure 1-1.**

Figure 1-1:
The
Netscape
Navigator
icon.

You may not see a Netscape Navigator icon in some cases. For example, if you're using AT&T WorldNet Service you have a Service icon. Double-click on that.

You just opened Netscape and brought up its opening window, shown in Figure 1-2.

Let's take a look at the window, one part at a time.

A toolbar even Tim "The Toolman" Taylor would love

The *toolbar* shown in Figure 1-2 is what I refer to as Netscape's joystick — you know, like the ones they use in the fighter planes. Using a few joystick buttons, you can fire missiles, launch grenades — and activate the ejection seat of the person seated next to you. (You wish!) But I want you to think of the Netscape toolbar as the joystick: It gives you really easy access to the things you want to do with Netscape, such as printing what you see, moving from one place to another, or finding something on a page. I refer to the things you do with software as *commands,* but you probably are already familiar with another type of commands, aren't you? Carry out the trash! Clean up your room! Please be QUIET!

Toolbar
Menu bar   Location text box   Logo box

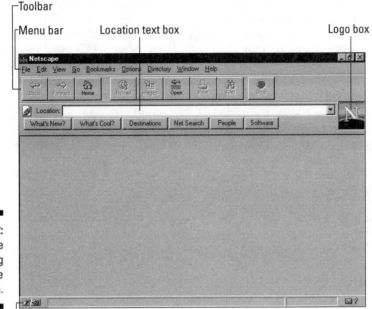

Figure 1-2:
The
opening
Netscape
screen.

Status bar

May I have the menu, please?

The *menu bar* is another version of the toolbar, but the menu bar lets you do everything the toolbar does and many more things too, such as changing the way Netscape looks and works, copying stuff from Netscape to your hard drive, making other software work with Netscape, and getting help from Netscape. Chapter 2 looks more closely at the menu bar.

Do I need a Web map to find an address?

To get anywhere on the Web, you need to know the *address* of the place you want to visit. It's like wanting to talk to someone on the phone. Unless you know the phone number of the person you want to talk to, you can't call him or her. Like, duh! The address of the place you're visiting goes in Netscape's *Location text box*, much like the telephone number of a person you're calling appears on your screen, if you have Caller ID.

Now you're wondering if there's a way of looking up someone's Web address, like you can look up a person's phone number, right? Well, although there isn't a directory like a phone book that lists people's Web addresses, there are many search techniques you can use to find all kinds of information on the Web. Chapter 6 discusses search techniques in detail.

What's with all the dots and coms?

The technical term for an address on the Web is *URL — Uniform Resource Locator.* (In this book, I use *URL* and *address* to mean the same thing.) Most URLs (or addresses) look like a meaningless, jumbled mess of letters; they make absolutely no sense. Imagine a postman trying to deliver a letter with nothing but `dfr.cc.com` written on it. To Netscape, however, such a salad of letters makes a lot of sense. Let's see how.

Usually the address tells you the name of the company (or person) the address belongs to. For example, you can probably tell from the following addresses what companies the addresses belong to:

Web Address	Company
www.microsoft.com	Microsoft Corporation
www.ibm.com	IBM Corporation
www.nbc.com	NBC Corporation

Not all Web addresses have `www`, but it is becoming a standard. And not all addresses have `.com` at the end. That dot and the three letters `com` tell us that the address belongs to a *com*mercial organization, meaning a company like IBM, Microsoft, AT&T, or Pizza Hut. Every address has one of the three-letter codes in it, but they aren't all `com`. Some other three-letter codes and the types of organizations the letters stand for are

Code	Type of Organization	Example
.edu	Educational (colleges and universities)	www.ucla.edu
.org	Non-profit	www.ets.org
.gov	Government	www.whitehouse.gov
.mil	Military	www.navy.mil
.net	Internet Service Provider	www.worldnet.att.net

Sometimes a dot and a two-letter code, such as `uk` or `in`, follow the three-letter organization code. This abbreviation is the country code, telling you that you're looking at the address of an organization in a particular country. For example, `www.ibmpcug.co.uk` is the address of PC User Group in the United Kingdom.

If you don't know the address of a company you want to visit, just add www. (including the dot) in front of the name of the company, followed by .com, as in www.disney.com. That works in most cases. If you want a college or university, use .edu instead of the .com.

Freddy Krueger's favorite — slashes

Freddy would have a ball on the Web. The Web has slashes all over the place. He'd probably call it the Blood Wide Web. But why all these slashes? Aren't the dots and coms enough? Well, not really. The slashes make traveling the Web very specific. They make it easier to get to exactly where you want to go, like putting a very specific address on a letter. Isn't it easier for the postal carrier to deliver a letter if the name, street, town, state and ZIP code appear in the address (Kathy Smith, 123 Alphabet Street, New York, NY 12345-1234) than if the address is too simplified (Kathy Smith, New York)? Can you imagine how long it would take you to find the right Kathy Smith in New York if you didn't have the street address?

Following are some URLs for typical Web sites:

URL for the opening screen or Page 1	www.companyname.com
URL for the Marketing Department	www.companyname.com/marketing
URL for the Software Department	www.companyname.com/software

Get the picture? If you know the URL of the Marketing Department within the company, you can go there directly without having to go through the company's main URL. That way you save at least one step and you're always looking to save time, aren't you? There are only so many Web sites you can visit in one day. You want to get to as many as you can.

May I please start cruising now?

Ooooooookay! I know you're itching to blast off into Cyberspace, so I'll keep you waiting no more. Let's go!

1. Click on the Open button on the Netscape toolbar.

Netscape displays the Open Location dialog box shown in Figure 1-3.

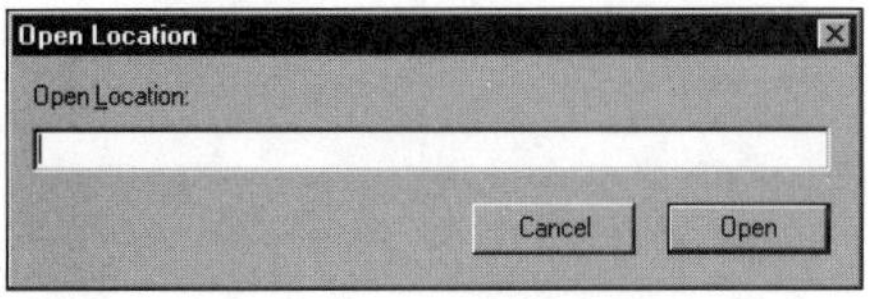

Figure 1-3:
The Open
Location
dialog box.

Open Location	✕
Open Location:	
	Cancel Open

2. **Type a URL in the Open Location text box.**

   For example, I typed www.worldnet.att.net.

3. **Press Enter.**

   Netscape starts transferring information (called *downloading*) from the Web site to your screen. While Netscape does this, pay close attention to the bottom line of the Netscape window (the *status bar*) and everything in the logo box (see Figure 1-4).

Your own play-by-play commentary — the status bar

The status bar at the bottom of the window tells what's happening as you're downloading information — how much information Netscape has downloaded and how much remains. After Netscape downloads the entire page, the status bar says, "Document Done." Well, the status bar can't talk, but that's the message it gives you.

Logo box

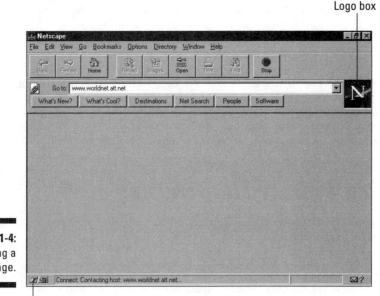

Figure 1-4:
Loading a
Web page.

Status bar

The status bar sometimes tells you the speed at which the information is being sent to your computer, and that's important to know. If you're using a 28.8 modem, a good connection should result in speeds of around 2.5KB per second. But sometimes even a fast modem will just crawl, and the plant in the corner of your room will grow six inches or more before Netscape downloads all the information. That's when you hit the brakes and tell Netscape to *STOP* it.

Stop it. Stop it now!

The Stop button on the menu bar automatically lights up as soon as you connect to a home page. When you click on the Stop button, you end the connection you just made to that address. Why would you want to do that? I have a number of reasons:

- You have a sloooooooow connection. You want to get on with your life, so you stop the downloading and try another address.

- You realize that the address you're connecting to isn't the address you really wanted.

- Sometimes the entire page has been downloaded with the exception of one measly little piece of information, but you can't tell this since your screen is blank even after what seems like ages. This slowness usually happens when the URL you have connected to has a counter on it that counts the number of people who stop by there. By clicking on the Stop button, you tell Netscape, "I don't care about that piece of information. Just give me what you've downloaded so far," and Netscape obeys.

Pressing the Esc key does the same thing as clicking on the Stop button.

Screen frozen — How can I thaw it?

When everything in the Netscape logo box freezes in space for a few seconds, the information is downloading slowly. On the other hand, if everything stays frozen for, say, five minutes, you have a problem. You should exit Netscape, start it again, come back to the opening window, and try the address one more time. Sometimes the entire screen freezes, preventing you from exiting Netscape the normal way. At such times, it's not wise to use a hammer to test how solid your monitor is. Instead, gently turn the machine off and switch it back on again. That works much better.

We know that you can type fast, but can you type correctly?

If you get the message shown in Figure 1-5, check whether you've typed the address correctly. As you can see in the figure, I mistyped the address by leaving out one of the *w*'s in the www portion of the address.

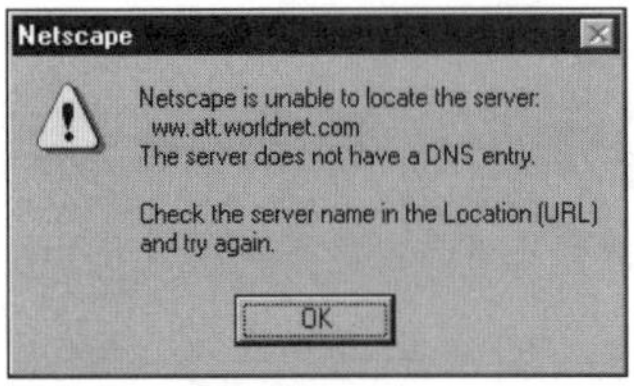

Figure 1-5:
The error
message
that means,
"Excuse me
please, but I
think you
typed the
address
wrong —
you doo-
doo!"

> **Netscape**
>
> ⚠ Netscape is unable to locate the server:
> www.att.worldnet.com
> The server does not have a DNS entry.
>
> Check the server name in the Location (URL)
> and try again.
>
> [OK]

Problems that need a hammer

The message shown in Figure 1-6 means that you could have any one of a number of problems.

Figure 1-6:
The error
message
that means,
"Sorry, but
this
situation is
a little more
serious."

> **Netscape**
>
> ⚠ A network error occurred:
> unable to connect to server (TCP Error: No route to host)
> The server may be down or unreachable.
>
> Try connecting again later.
>
> [OK]

The most common reason for this problem is usually not yours at all. It's your Internet Service Provider's computers. However, rather than begin by bugging your ISP, make sure that everything is okay on your end.

First, maybe you don't have enough *free* memory on your computer, especially if you're using Windows 3.1*x*. You may have way too many software applications open right now. Close those applications that you don't need right now, go back into Netscape, and then try to connect to the address again. If the problem persists, follow these steps:

1. **Close all applications.**

2. **Exit your computer.**

3. **Restart your computer.**

4. Start Netscape, and try to connect to the address again.

If the problem *still* persists, call your Internet Service Provider to see whether the ISP is experiencing problems on its network.

If you see a hand, it's a link

After Netscape completely loads a Web page, you may notice that some of the words are a different color. The color can indicate that you're looking at a *link*, an address to another location on the Web. Sometimes the location is right next door; at other times, it's half a world away. To find the links on a Web page, follow these steps:

1. Move the mouse pointer over one of those different-colored words.

The pointer changes from an arrow to a little hand with a pointing index finger. This little hand, shown in Figure 1-7, means that the word has a link to another page with more information.

The hand points to a link

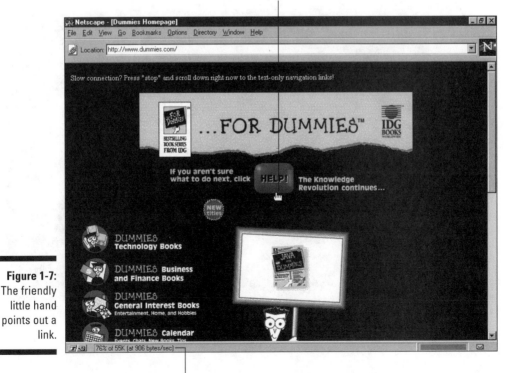

Figure 1-7:
The friendly little hand points out a link.

The address for the link

Even pictures can connect you to different pages. All you have to do is move the mouse over the picture. If the pointer changes to a hand, it's a link. Go ahead, try it.

2. **Look at the status bar at the bottom of the page.**

   Netscape displays the URL for that link in the status bar.

3. **Move the pointer to another picture or different-colored word.**

   The URL in the status bar changes again (see Figure 1-8).

4. **Click on the link you're pointing to.**

   Your page goes blank within a few seconds, the Stop button lights up again, and information from the new URL starts streaming to your computer. Netscape is flying you to the page that's linked to the word you clicked on.

5. **Watch the changes in the status bar and the Location text box as the new page loads.**

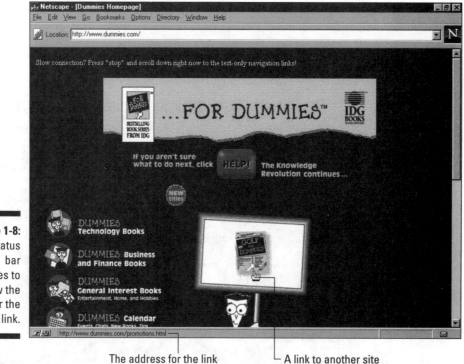

Figure 1-8:
The status
bar
changes to
show the
URL for the
link.

The address for the link   A link to another site

The secret behind links is something called *HTTP — HyperText Transfer Protocol,* a set of rules that allows information to be moved from one computer to another, as long as both computers use the same rules. On the Web, all computers use HTTP. Essentially, HTTP tells your browser, "Yo, Netscape! If someone clicks on a linked word, go to the URL to which it's linked and fetch the information," to which Netscape replies, "Your wish is my command," and hurries along to get the information.

Question: Who invented HTTP and where?

Answer: Tim Berners-Lee invented HTTP at CERN, the European Laboratory for Particle Physics, in Switzerland.

You don't need to wait for a page to completely download before you can click on a link. As the links become visible on your screen, you can click on them. The page stops downloading immediately and tries to connect to the linked page.

I'm lost and I wanna go back

Remember the story of Hansel and Gretel, the children who left a trail of bread crumbs in the forest to help them find their way home? Netscape leaves a trail too, only without bread crumbs; otherwise, you'd find a pile of crumbs at every site — and a sign that says, "Your mother doesn't work here, so clean up after yourself." Keep following links for a few minutes longer, and, before you know it, you'll be far away from where you started. Netscape has a very easy way to retrace your steps:

1. **Click on the Back button on the toolbar.**

   If you click on the Back button once, Netscape takes you to the previous URL.

2. **Click on the Back button again and again to retrace your steps.**

   You don't have to wait for the previous page to display completely before you click on the Back button.

3. **Click on the Home button on the toolbar to go all the way home — to your starting point.**

   Netscape takes you back to your starting point in one quick step.

Oops. I went back too far!

When you want to listen to a song over and over and over again on your Walkman, you hit the Reverse button endlessly. But getting to the exact place where the song begins isn't easy. Sometimes you go too far back. When that happens, you press the Forward button to quickly move ahead, right? Netscape's Forward button does the same thing when your speedy little mouse finger clicks on the Back button too many times.

Footprints in space — History

Instead of using the Back button to retrace your steps, you can use Netscape's History feature to take you back to a URL in one jump. Follow these steps:

1. **Press Ctrl+H, or choose Window⇨History.**

   Netscape lists the pages you've been to, as shown in Figure 1-9.

   The links in the history file get deleted every time you exit Netscape. When you start a new Netscape session, a new history file is set up for that session, containing only those sites you go to during that session.

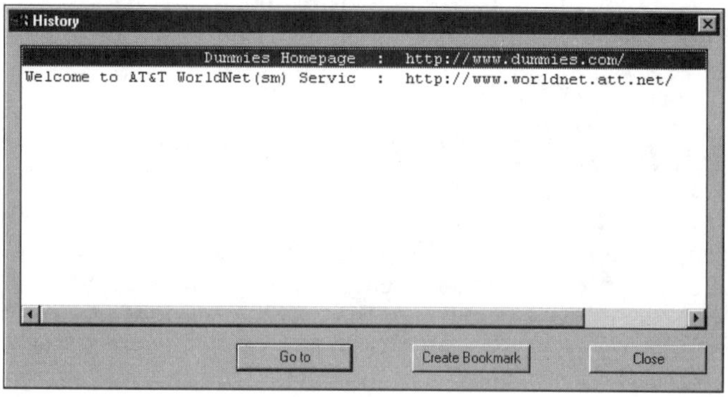

Figure 1-9:
The list of
the pages
I've been to
in this
session.

```
History                                                              ×
        Dummies Homepage    :   http://www.dummies.com/
Welcome to AT&T WorldNet(sm) Servic  :   http://www.worldnet.att.net/




◄                                                                    ►
           Go to            Create Bookmark              Close
```

2. **Select the page you want to jump to.**

3. **Click on Go to.**

   This displays the page you selected.

4. **Click on Close in the History window.**

   The History window closes.

Leave a mark — a bookmark

In the course of your WebVentures, you may come to a page that will make you shout out, "COOOL! Let me write down the URL of this page. I'll be coming back here often." So you look for a paper and pencil to write down the URL. When you find an itsy-bitsy piece of paper and a really, really blunt pencil, you scribble the URL in handwriting that your teachers say could easily pass as Greek. You then stash the itsy-bitsy piece of paper away in this thing you call a "desk drawer," which everyone knows has an invisible hole through which everything vanishes. A week later, you look for that itsy-bitsy piece of paper, and Ta Da! It's still there. Must be your lucky day. But your excitement turns to despair when you realize that you don't read Greek anymore. You can't make heads or tails of what you've written. You wonder if you're looking at a slash or a one, a zero or an oh! You try every combination of characters and slashes, but you can't connect to the site. Sad, isn't it? But worry no more. I have a solution to that problem. Actually, I have two. First, stop writing in Greek. Second, use Netscape's bookmarks.

To mark the currently displayed page for later reference, *bookmark* it by doing any of the following:

- ✔ Press CTRL+D. Voilà! Your page is now bookmarked, in English too!
- ✔ Choose Bookmarks⇨Add Bookmark.
- ✔ Press the right button on your mouse and click on Add Bookmark.

Reload often

When you press the Reload button on the toolbar, you tell Netscape, "Connect to the URL displayed on my screen and get the most recent information available." Some Web sites, such as those providing news reports, update the information on their pages on an hourly basis. Reloading ensures that you get the latest information.

A picture is worth a thousand words

On the Web, a picture is probably worth *ten thousand* words. Graphics take a long time to download, and on a slow connection, even longer. If you don't want to see the pictures and want to see text only on the page you're viewing, you can use the Images option to ask Netscape not to load the pictures. Follow these steps:

1. Choose <u>O</u>ptions from the menu bar.

The Options menu shown in Figure 1-10 appears.

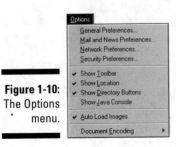

Figure 1-10:
The Options
menu.

2. Click on <u>A</u>uto Load Images until you don't see a check mark in front of the option.

A check mark next to <u>A</u>uto Load Images means that image-display is turned on. No check mark means image-display is turned off.

Now every page you download will display a blank square or rectangle where the image was supposed to be, as shown in Figure 1-11. Even though you don't see the images, the links still work if you click on the text within the box where the image is supposed to be. To turn on image-display again, repeat the preceding steps, but make sure that the option has a check mark in front of it.

To turn on image-display temporarily — just for the page you're looking at — click on the Images button in the toolbar. Netscape reloads the page and displays all the images on it. Image-display for future pages still stays off until you turn on Auto Image Display.

To see any one particular picture only, click on the broken mosaic within the square. Netscape displays only that image. Figure 1-12 shows a page with lots of broken mosaics and a single picture displayed.

Boxes where images usually appear are called broken mosaics

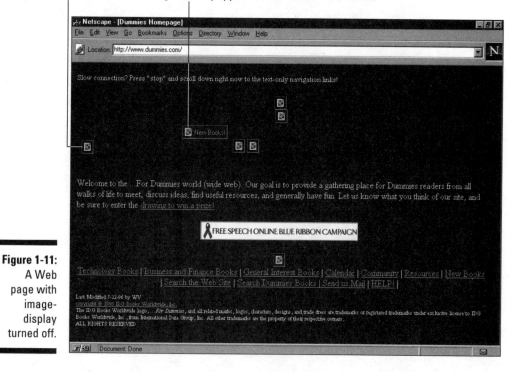

Figure 1-11:
A Web
page with
image-
display
turned off.

Image displayed

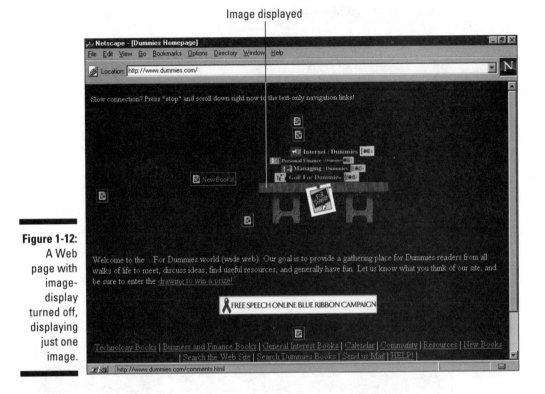

Figure 1-12:
A Web
page with
image-
display
turned off,
displaying
just one
image.

I wish I could print that

Printing is a pretty straightforward matter in Netscape. All you do is click on
the Print button when you want to print the current page. Just remember
that the printed copy won't turn out as fancy as what you see on the screen.
If you have a dot-matrix printer, I don't recommend that you print any page
with graphics on it. If you still insist on doing so, you may want to take out
the garbage, feed the dog, do the dishes, and clean your room in the time
your printer takes to print the page.

The binoculars

The toolbar button with binoculars is the Find button. With it, you can look
for a particular word on the page being displayed. This button is especially
handy if the page you're viewing is very long, and scrolling down takes
forever. To find a word on that page, follow these steps:

1. Click on the Find button.

The Find dialog box appears (see Figure 1-13).

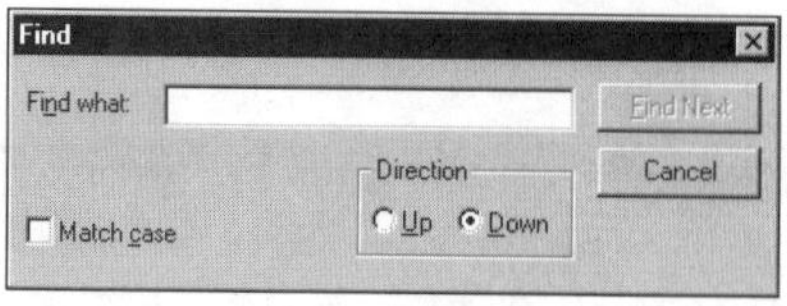

Figure 1-13:
The Find
dialog box.

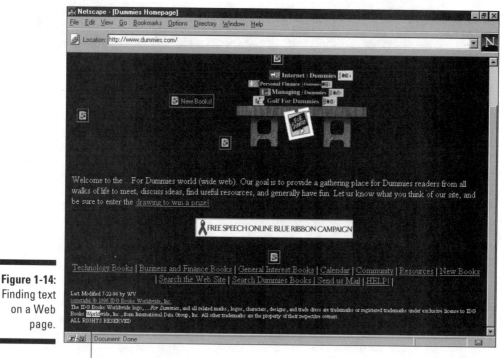

2. **Type the word you're looking for in the Find what text box.**

3. **Click on the Match case option if you want Netscape to find the word capitalized exactly the way you typed it.**

4. **Click on Find Next.**

   If Netscape finds the word in the page, it will be highlighted. (You may have to drag the Find dialog box to one side to view the found word.)

5. **Click on Cancel to close the Find window.**

   Figure 1-14 shows highlighted text found with the Find dialog box. Notice that you don't have to search for whole words; in this example, I just searched for the letters *world* to find *Worldwide*.

Figure 1-14:
Finding text
on a Web
page.

Here's the highlighted word

If Netscape doesn't find the text you're looking for, you see the `Search String Not Found` message shown in Figure 1-15. Click on OK to continue. You can then try looking for another word or close the Find window by clicking on Cancel.

The Find button finds text only on the page being displayed. This kind of finding is not the same as searching for information on the Web, which is discussed in Chapter 6.

What's new? What's cool?

The What's New? and What's Cool? buttons right under the Location text box take you to a collection of — ready for this? — new and cool sites. Duh! You wouldn't have guessed, right? The folks at Netscape put together these lists of new and cool sites and update them about once a month. The lists are a collection of funny, educational, scientific, helpful, and sometimes totally weird sites. Give 'em a try.

Ready to Leave?

After you've had enough and are ready to say goodbye to Netscape for the day, choose File➪Exit to close Netscape.

To return to Netscape, double-click on the Netscape icon. Your bookmarks will be waiting for you.

Chapter 2

Getting to Know Netscape Better

· ·

In This Chapter

▶ Downloading multiple pages simultaneously

▶ Sharing URLS

▶ Making more bookmarks

· ·

*I*n this chapter, you uncover Netscape's hidden gems, the ones that aren't visible on the surface. You specifically look at some of the commands on the menu bar. Saddle up — you have a lot of exploring to do.

You Get a Bigger Selection at the Menu Bar

If the toolbar is the cockpit, the menu bar is the command center for flight operations — like the place where Capt. Kirk, Capt. Picard, or Capt. Janeway sits and oversees everything that goes on. From the menu bar, you can control exactly how Netscape looks on your screen, how it behaves, and what other computers it connects to. Everything that you can do with the toolbar, you can also do from the menu. But the menu has tons more options than the toolbar does. All the major controls for Netscape are on the menu bar.

You may never need to use some of the options on the menu. They're set during the installation process and rarely if ever have to be modified. But you can use other options to do some really cool things — like being at two Web sites at the same time, or saving a home page to your hard drive. Read on and discover how to use Netscape to the max.

Oh, just a word of caution first. The figures in this chapter show Netscape running on a Windows 3.1 system (see Figure 2-1). These figures may look a little different from the version of Netscape that you use, but the appearance is the only difference.

Toolbar

Menu bar

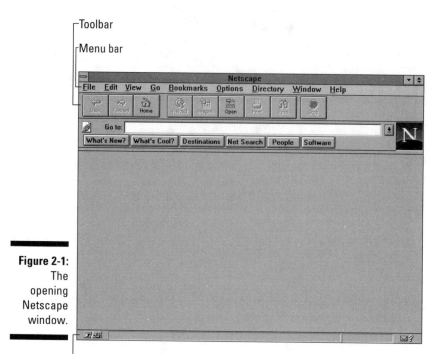

Figure 2-1:
The
opening
Netscape
window.

Status bar

Wanna See Two Pages at a Time?

Sometimes watching a page download to my computer is like watching grass grow. Very exciting! So instead of staring at the screen twiddling my thumbs, I fire up a second copy of Netscape — from within Netscape. This way, while Netscape downloads the first page, I can start downloading a second page. This feature works great if I know that the first URL I have connected to is usually slow and gets a lot of visitors. While the first copy of Netscape is connecting to this slow URL and downloading information from it, I ask Netscape to start working on a second page. You can do the double-download too by following these steps:

1. **Click on Open in the toolbar.**

   The Open Location dialog box appears (see Figure 2-2). No more watching grass grow — whoa!

Figure 2-2:
The Open
Location
dialog box.

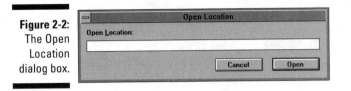

2. **Type the URL of the slow site in the Open Location text box and then click on Open.**

   Netscape downloads that site, in slow-mo.

3. **Choose File⇨New Web Browser.**

   This action brings up a new Netscape screen, which automatically starts loading the very first page you loaded since you logged on to the current Netscape session. Obviously you don't want to see this first page again. So click on the Stop button in the toolbar. Screeeech! Those were the brakes being applied to the page, stopping it from being loaded.

4. **Click on Open on the toolbar.**

   The Open Location dialog box shown in Figure 2-2 appears — again.

5. **Type the second URL that you want in the Open Location text box and then click on Open.**

   This loads the second page. Now you can feast your eyes on two pages. How can one person handle so much excitement?

No matter how many pages you load this way, they all share the one history file. In earlier versions of Netscape, opening a new browser didn't automatically load the first home page of the current session. Also, both browser windows didn't share the same history file. Each had its own file. If you used an earlier version of Netscape, you should be aware of the difference.

Switching between pages

Have you ever tried stuffing your mouth with two sandwiches at a time? Not a good idea, right? But you certainly can take a bite of one, and then the other. When you have two pages loaded at a time, that's exactly how you view them — first one, then the other. To switch between the two pages, follow these steps:

1. **Choose <u>W</u>indow from the menu bar.**

   The Window menu appears (see Figure 2-3). In the lowest section of the menu are the two URLs that you have open.

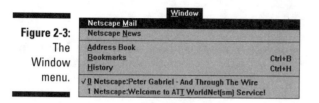

Figure 2-3:
The
Window
menu.

2. **Click on the URL you want to see.**

   A check mark appears in front of the URL you click on; then Netscape switches to that page. Of the home pages listed in Figure 2-3, the one with the check mark (✔) is the page currently displayed on the screen.

Viewing multiple pages as described above is not a good thing to try if:

   ✔ You're using anything slower than a Pentium-based PC.

   ✔ You have anything slower than a 28.8 modem.

   ✔ Your connection to your ISP is usually slow.

In such a situation, stick to viewing one page at a time, or else you risk being hypnotized by the hourglass cursor, staring at it for what might seem like forever and a day.

Back to viewing only one page

Ever wonder why people turn down the radio when they get lost while driving? It's as if a little peace and quiet will put them right back on track. Not! Like lost drivers, you may sometimes get lost as you navigate the Web, especially when you're viewing two pages. As you start browsing from each page, they each leave behind a trail of links that you may have a hard time following. It can soon become difficult to keep track of where you are on each of the pages. At such a time, you may just want to close the second copy of Netscape and return to running only one copy. To close a Netscape window, follow these steps:

1. **Choose Window from the menu bar — again.**

   The same old Window menu appears (refer to Figure 2-3). In the lowest section of the menu are the two URLs you have open — ho, hum.

2. **Click on the URL you want to close.**

   This URL now becomes the current page; Netscape displays it on your screen.

3. **Choose File⇨Close.**

   The page you didn't close is now displayed on the screen. Continue surfing normally.

Spread the Joy: Share a Hot URL

Sometimes you come across a Web page so good that you want to share it with a friend. But if you think that sending a friend a cool Web address means you have to painstakingly write down the entire URL of the page (which can be up to five miles long in your fancy handwriting, which everyone knows resembles Greek), then think again. I have an easy way to let your friend know about a hot new URL, but my way works only if you know your friend's e-mail address. Follow these steps:

1. **Choose File⇨Mail Document from the Netscape menu bar.**

   The Netscape e-mail window, shown in Figure 2-4, appears. Notice that Netscape has automatically inserted the URL of the page you were on — the URL you want to share with your friend — in the lower half of the screen. Isn't Netscape great?

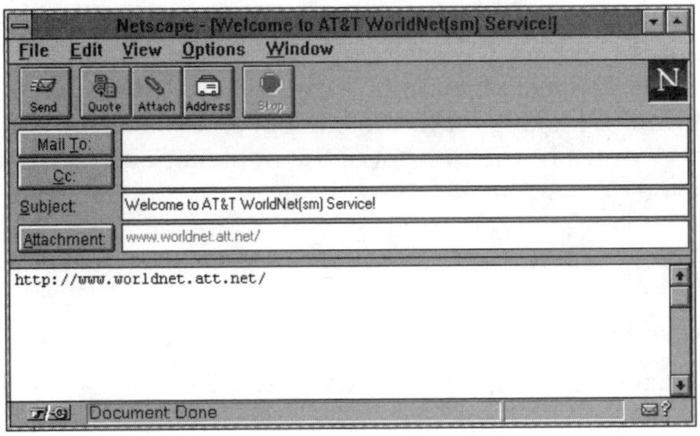

Figure 2-4:
The
Netscape
e-mail
window.

2. **Type your friend's e-mail address in the Mail To text box.**

   Notice that the Subject text box of the message also has a blurb in it. This blurb is actually the *title* of the URL you're sending. Title? Yeah. It's different from the heading you see on that Web page. The title of a Web page is usually hidden from you, but it usually appears automatically in the Subject text box. Usually? Yep. The title won't appear in the Subject text box if the author of the page doesn't specify a title for the page. If that's the case, you can fill in the Subject text box with anything you want to say there. Just move the cursor there and start typing.

3. **Click on the Send button.**

   The URL is on its way to your friend by e-mail. How tough was that?

Netscape's Nifty Bookmarks

Bookmarks of all kinds make it easy for you to go back to a favorite page you've seen, should you ever need to. After all, that's the sole purpose of bookmarks, right? To mark your place in something. (Check out Chapter 1 to find out how to make bookmarks in Netscape.) After you've created some URL bookmarks, Netscape lets you do a lot of cool stuff with them.

I'm sure I bookmarked it. If I could only find it now

Do you get upset when you can't find your favorite Sega Genesis game or your favorite CD even though you're sure you placed it where you'd never lose it? You're not alone. Happens to me, too. And it's no different with Netscape bookmarks. I lose 'em all the time. They get buried under newer bookmarks, and then I have to scroll down the entire list until I find the one I'm looking for. Very time-consuming. Wouldn't it be cool if you could find the bookmark you're looking for in the blink of an eye instead of having to scroll all the way down to the bottom of the bookmark list? Guess what? Netscape lets you do just that.

To find a bookmark, follow these steps:

1. **Click on Bookmarks.**

   The Bookmarks menu appears (see Figure 2-5).

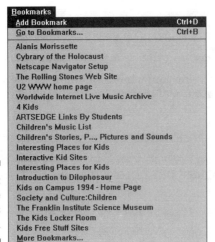

Figure 2-5:
The
Bookmarks
menu.

2. **If you find the bookmark you're looking for on the list in the menu, double-click on the bookmark.**

   Netscape connects you to the page. If you don't see the bookmark and the list extends to the bottom of the menu as shown in Figure 2-5, you're not finished. Continue on.

3. **Click on More Bookmarks at the bottom of the menu and then look for the bookmark in the additional list that appears. If you find your link, double-click on it, and you're on your way (see Figure 2-6).**

   If you still haven't found your bookmark, hang on a second.

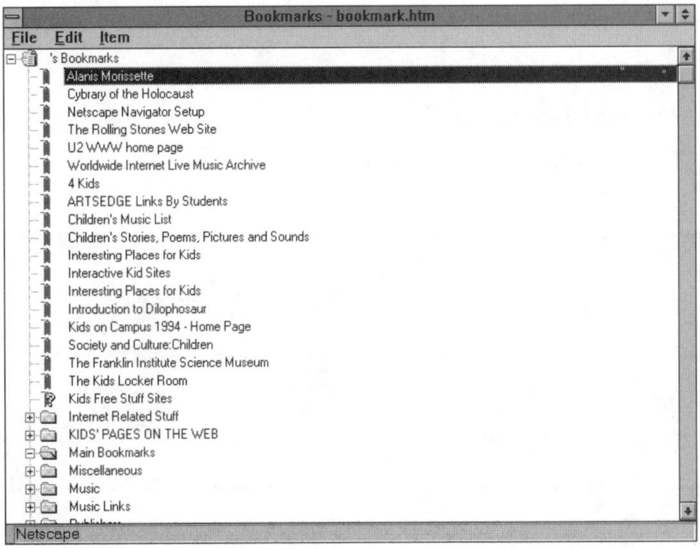

Figure 2-6:
The full-
screen
display of
bookmarks.

4. **Choose Edit⇨Find.**

   The Search Headers window appears on your screen.

5. **Type what you're looking for in the Find What dialog box.**

6. **Select Match Case if you want your search to be case-sensitive. See the sidebar for an explanation of that case-sensitive stuff.**

7. **Click on OK.**

   If Netscape finds a bookmark matching your request, Netscape highlights the bookmark.

8. **To connect to the highlighted URL, press Enter, or double-click on the link.**

   This action tells Netscape, "Please connect to this URL." Netscape says, "Sure friend. In a second," and attempts to make a connection. As soon as you click on the bookmark link, the bookmark window disappears from the screen, Netscape makes the connection, and the page you selected is displayed.

9. **If Netscape finds a bookmark but it's not what you're looking for, press F3 to repeat the search.**

   Netscape finds the next bookmark that matches what you're looking for.

Duplicate bookmarks? Zap one

I often find myself bookmarking a URL more than once. I do it because I like to make sure that I don't lose a good URL. Yes, I tag the Web page even though I think I may have done it once before. After all, I can always delete the extra bookmark if I don't need it. Deleting a bookmark is easy. Finding a site that you didn't bookmark is a waste of time.

1. **Highlight the bookmark you want to zap.**

2. **Press the Delete key.**

   The duplicate bookmark is gone. Outta there.

Case-sensitive searching

You know what UPPERCASE and lowercase letters are, right? Cool. A case-sensitive search means that Netscape will look up the word you search for exactly as you type it. In a case-sensitive search on *Country*, Netscape finds only *Country*, not *country* or *COUNTRY* or any other combination of uppercase and lowercase letters.

Zapped the wrong one? Oh, nooooo! Now what?

Fear not. If you accidentally delete the wrong bookmark, you need not sweat. Bringing the bookmark back is easy. Just choose Edit⇨Undo.

In Windows 3.1*x,* the Undo command undoes the last command you performed. If you delete a bookmark and then delete a second bookmark, for example, the Undo command brings back only the second bookmark you deleted because that was the last command you performed. The first one you deleted is gone forever.

What a mess. Let's get organized

If you're like me, as you surf around the Web and bookmark more and more cool pages, your bookmark collection may soon become so large that it'll take over your room. Like your room has any space to spare! Getting from one corner of it to another is like doing the 100-meter hurdles. Well, before things get any worse, you'd better get your bookmarks organized.

A folder for every type of bookmark

I have my bookmarks set up in *groups* or *folders.* I have folders for Sports, Music, Computers, and so on. When I get a new bookmark, I just store it in the right folder. That way, if I'm looking for, say, the URL for the Pearl Jam site, I know I need look only in the Music folder because that's where I save my music URLs.

To create a bookmark folder, follow these steps:

1. **Press Ctrl+B, or choose Bookmarks⇨Go to Bookmarks.**

2. **Highlight the very first line in your bookmark list — the one that has your name on it.**

3. **Choose Item⇨Insert Folder.**

   A Bookmark Properties dialog box like the one shown in Figure 2-7 appears.

4. **In the Name text box, replace the words** New Folder **with the name you want to give your new folder.**

   To replace the words, just start typing something like **Ultra Cool Music Sites**. The text New Folder disappears, and your new folder name appears in its place.

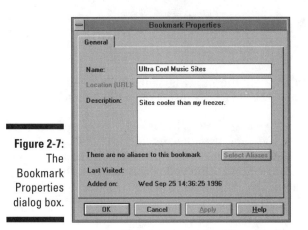

Figure 2-7:
The
Bookmark
Properties
dialog box.

5. **In the Description text box, type a description for your new folder and then click on OK to create the folder.**

   You should now see the newly created folder listed with the bookmarks.

6. **Create as many folders as you want.**

   Make sure that no two folders have the same name. Because Netscape lets you create two or more of anything — bookmarks or folders — with the same name, be careful that you don't create duplicates.

You can even create folders within folders within folders within folders within . . . I think you get the picture. If you don't, see Figure 2-8.

Figure 2-8:
Folders
within
folders.

Hey, you! Move 'em in — one at a time

Okay, so now you have a bunch of folders with nothing in them. That reminds me of what Grandma once told me when I was a little boy. She said, "Yo! Listen up! An empty folder is not a good folder." Now Grandma was tuff. I mean, tuff. She wore army boots and made grown men cry. Obviously, I listened to her. I didn't want a sore toosh when I went to bed. I think we should all live her words of wisdom, so hurry up and fill those empty folders. Pronto!

To move one bookmark to a folder, follow these steps:

1. **Select the bookmark you want to move to a new folder.**

   For example, suppose that you save a <u>Dallas Cowboys</u> link as a bookmark, and then move the bookmark to the Sports & Fitness folder (see Figure 2-9).

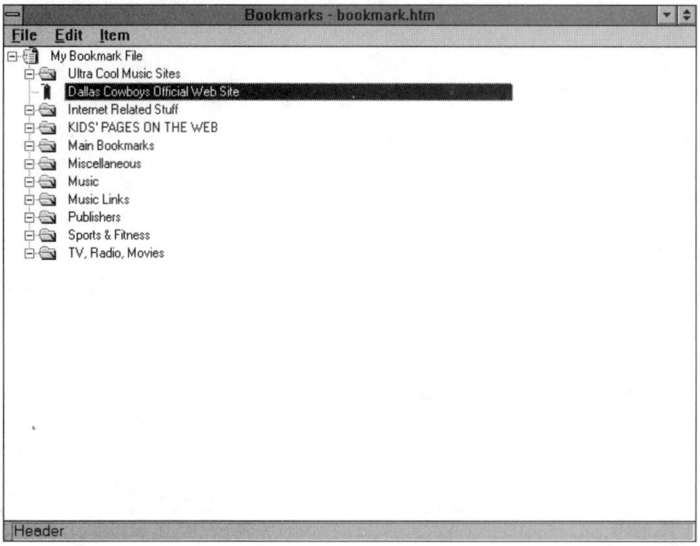

Figure 2-9:
A selected
bookmark.

2. **Hold down the left mouse button and drag the bookmark to the new folder.**

   In this example, drag the <u>Dallas Cowboys</u> link bookmark and drop it in its new folder.

3. **Release the mouse button.**

   The bookmark now appears in a different folder (see Figure 2-10).

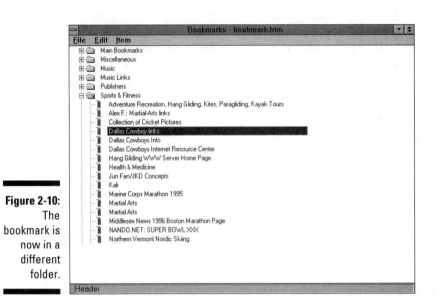

File   Edit   Item

⊞ 🗀 Main Bookmarks
⊞ 🗀 Miscellaneous
⊞ 🗀 Music
⊞ 🗀 Music Links
⊞ 🗀 Publishers
⊟ 🗁 Sports & Fitness
     🔖 Adventure Recreation, Hang Gliding, Kites, Paragliding, Kayak Tours
     🔖 Alex F.: Martial-Arts links
     🔖 Collection of Cricket Pictures
     🔖 Dallas Cowboy links
     🔖 Dallas Cowboys Info
     🔖 Dallas Cowboys Internet Resource Center
     🔖 Hang Gliding WWW Server Home Page
     🔖 Health & Medicine
     🔖 Jun Fan/JKD Concepts
     🔖 Kali
     🔖 Marine Corps Marathon 1995
     🔖 Martial Arts
     🔖 Martial Arts
     🔖 Middlesex News 1996 Boston Marathon Page
     🔖 NANDO.NET: SUPER BOWL XXX
     🔖 Northern Vermont Nordic Skiing

Header

Figure 2-10:
The
bookmark is
now in a
different
folder.

Get fancy and move a whole bunch of bookmarks at one time

You can move more than one bookmark to a folder all at one time, but you
need to know these clever ways to tell Netscape which bookmarks you want
to move:

- ✔ To move a group of bookmarks that are all next to each other (say, the
  first ten bookmarks), click on the first bookmark. Then hold down the
  Shift key and click on the last bookmark you want to move. You've
  selected all the bookmarks at one time.

- ✔ To move bookmarks that are all over the place, hold down the Ctrl key
  while you click on the bookmarks you want to select, one at a time.

If you're a klutz like me and you click on a bookmark by mistake, just click
on it again to deselect it. Netscape will understand that you really don't
want the bookmark — you're just having a bad clicking day.

So here's the scoop on moving those bookmarks to a folder:

1. **Select all the bookmarks you want to move.**

2. **Hold down the left mouse button, drag the selected bookmarks to the
   new folder, and then release the mouse button.**

   All the selected bookmarks move to the folder in one shot.

Two bookmarks, one name. Let's rename

Do you have two kids in your class with the same first name? What happens when the teacher calls that name? Do either of the kids know whom the teacher is calling? Nope. Wouldn't it be better if the teacher called them by their full names? That way, one would have to answer the math question, and the other would go, "Whew! That was close." In your bookmark list, you may find more than one listing for "Cool Links," or "Hot Links," or "Useful Links," and they'll make absolutely no sense to you. So, you can rename the links to something more meaningful by following these steps:

1. **Press Ctrl+B, or choose Bookmarks⇨Go to Bookmarks.**

   The Bookmarks window appears . . . again.

2. **Highlight the bookmark you want to rename.**

3. **Choose Item⇨Properties.**

   The Bookmark Properties dialog box that you saw in Figure 2-7 appears looking a little different but basically the same.

4. **Type the new bookmark name in the Name text box and click OK.**

Rename a folder

Renaming a folder is similar to renaming a bookmark. Follow these steps:

1. **Press Ctrl+B or choose Bookmarks⇨Go to Bookmarks.**

   There's that Bookmarks window again.

2. **Highlight the folder you want to rename.**

3. **Choose Item⇨Properties.**

   A slightly different-looking (but still the same old) Bookmark Properties dialog box appears.

4. **Type the new folder name in the Name text box and click on OK.**

Storing Web Pages on Your Computer

Suppose that you're viewing a totally jammin' Web page. You don't just want to mark it as a bookmark, do you? You can go one step further and store the Web page on your hard drive. It's really easy. Here's how you do it:

1. **Choose File⇨Save As.**

   The Save As dialog box shown in Figure 2-11 springs up. The File Name text box could already have a filename in it, but that filename may as well be written in Swahili. The file may have a name you'll never remember when you need it most — trust me. If you want to play a round of "Waste an Hour Guessing What's in That File," be my guest. But why not rename the file to something more descriptive?

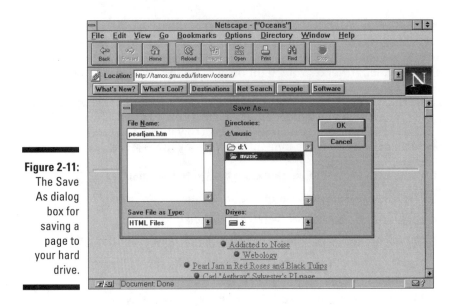

Figure 2-11:
The Save
As dialog
box for
saving a
page to
your hard
drive.

2. Type a new, more descriptive filename.

Make sure the file has an `.htm` extension — for example, type a filename like `Pearljam.htm`. Remember the folder to which you save the file. You can find the directory on the right half of the dialog box under Directories.

3. Click on OK.

Whoosh. Did ya hear that? The Web page just got copied to your hard drive.

If the page you're saving to your hard drive has images on it, the images are not saved with the page. To copy images to your hard drive, see the section "Images, too" later in the chapter.

Page saved. What's next?

Now, how do you display the page you just saved to your hard drive? Easy. Just follow these simple steps:

1. Choose File⇨Open File from the Netscape menu bar.

The Open dialog box appears, as shown in Figure 2-12.

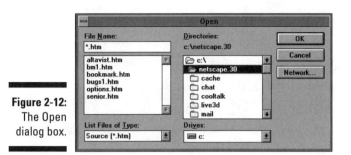

Figure 2-12:
The Open
dialog box.

2. **Type the filename in the File Name text box or select the file in the File Name list box and then click on OK.**

The page loads fifty thousand gazillion times faster from your hard drive than it does when you download it off the Web.

If you copy a Web page to your hard drive as explained here, you may want to copy the images, if any, that appear on the page. See the following section to find out how to copy images from a Web page.

Images, too

You'll often come across some really neato pictures on the Web. The pictures may be so realistic that they jump out at you from the screen. To copy an image to your hard drive, follow these steps:

1. **Move the mouse pointer to the image you want to copy, assuming that there's a picture on the screen, duh!**

2. **Press the right mouse button.**

A shortcut menu like the one shown in Figure 2-13 appears.

Figure 2-13:
The
shortcut
menu for
doing all
sorts of fun
stuff.

3. Select Save Image As.

A Save As dialog box like the one shown in Figure 2-14 appears.

4. Type a descriptive name in the File Name text box.

You *must* use the same three-letter extension for the new name as is in the current filename. For example, if the current name of the image is athome_a.gif (as shown in Figure 2-13), your new filename must include .gif in the new filename, as in newimage.gif. Sometimes the three-letter filename extension of the picture's filename may be jpg. In that case, the new image name should end with .jpg.

Make sure that you save the picture to the same folder on your hard drive that you saved the Web text to. Otherwise, when you load that page from the hard drive, it won't display the image — only the text.

5. Click on OK.

Buzzzz! The image just got copied to your hard drive.

If you need a printout of the page only, not a permanent copy, just print the page on your printer. You can print using the Print button on the toolbar. Mosey on over to Chapter 1 to find out more about printing, my friend.

Now you know enough to cruise the information superhighway without getting stuck in the slow lane. Warp speed ahead!

Figure 2-14:
The Save
As dialog
box that
you've seen
before.

	Save As...	
File Name:	Directories:	OK
athome_a.gif	d:\images	Cancel
	d:\	
	images	
Save File as Type:	Drives:	
GIF File [*.gif]	d:	

Chapter 3

Finding New Worlds with the Internet Explorer

- -

In This Chapter

▶ Meeting and installing Internet Explorer

▶ Setting sail on the Internet Explorer

▶ Getting familiar with the innards of Internet Explorer

▶ Using the toolbar to take control

▶ Jumping ship

- -

*W*hen you hear the word *Explorer,* what immediately comes to mind? The 4-wheel drive from Ford, right? And probably that guy named Chris? Yeah, Chris. You know him. The guy who set sail in like the 1400s or something, looking for India, missed a turn at the second light, and ended up in America. That's right, Christopher Columbus. Well, let me introduce you to yet another explorer. This one will help *you* discover new lands, meet people, and get to know new cultures. But that's where the similarity ends. Don't expect any favors from a Spanish queen.

Hello! I'm Internet Explorer. I'll Be Your Guide

The Explorer — Internet Explorer to be precise — that I'm talking about is software you can use to browse the Web. Browse? Huh? What's that mean? Well, let's say that the video store has a clearance table stacked full of games and movies. While your sister is trying to find that latest release, you check out every single game and movie on the table. This one's too old. This one's no good. This one's kinda cool, but you bought it for 30 bucks more than what it's on sale for now. You're browsin' through the games and movies.

Internet Explorer is software that lets you go from one spot on the Web to the next. The spots are called *Web sites* or *home pages*. Using Internet Explorer, you can look at one Web site and then hop on over to another Web site. *Cruising* and *surfing* mean the same thing as browsing.

Internet Explorer is a browser made by Microsoft, the same folks who make Windows. Internet Explorer 3.0 is a wonderful product and is easy to use, so don't be afraid. Sit back, relax, and you'll be sailing your way around the Web in no time. ✓

Question: Who's the head of Microsoft Corporation?

Answer: Billionaire Bill Gates. Often called "King of the Nerds," Bill's the richest man in America. Not bad for a guy who dropped out of Harvard University, right? Right. That doesn't mean you should drop out of school, too. Even though Bill did, his company Microsoft hires only the brightest college grads. And some of them have ended up making millions, too. At last count, up to 1600 millionaires work at Microsoft. So you wanna work there? Then hit your books hard.

Figuring out which version of Internet Explorer to use

Internet Explorer is a fairly new software. The version that this book uses is Internet Explorer 3.0 and is for a PC with Windows 95. An Internet Explorerr version for Windows 3.1*x* is being written. Currently, no Mac version is available.

Also, if you look carefully at the figures throughout the book, you will see Netscape Navigator in most of them. I didn't do that because I think Netscape is better than Internet Explorer; both are good products. I chose Netscape Navigator. Internet Explorer is excellent; it's becoming quite popular.

Getting a copy of Internet Explorer

You can get Internet Explorer from many places:

- ✔ Buy it at a store. No money? Read on.
- ✔ Copy it (called *downloading* by the Web geeks) from the Microsoft Web site. Too hard!

✔ Ask your Internet Service Provider (ISP) for it. (Don't know what an ISP is? Check out the Introduction to this book.)

✔ Get it from the CD enclosed with this book. Just right!

I recommend the last option. Internet Explorer is one of the many software packages I've put for you on the CD. You're welcome! Flip open the back cover of the book, and you'll find the CD there.

Installing Internet Explorer

Appendix B gives the details on how to use the CD to install Internet Explorer. You don't need to be concerned with that. You have better things to do, and I've reserved the pleasure of installing Internet Explorer for your parents. After all, they need to have something to do between driving you to piano practice, ballet lessons, football tryouts, baseball games, dentist appointments, choir recitals, soccer sessions, attending parent-teacher meetings, and the countless other things they just loooooooove to do for you. So why not add to their pleasure, right? Absolutely. Go on . . . hurry up and find a parent. And when you do, get that look on your face that could persuade a stranger to hand you a five-dollar bill. Then lead your parent by the hand, point to the paragraph below, and politely ask, "Will you install this for me?" Add that magic word to the end of your question. No, I'm not referring to *Now!* I'm referring to *Please. Now!* works better for parents than it'll ever work for kids. Put it in your back pocket and save it for when *you're* the parent.

Note: If you already have Internet Explorer 3.0 on your computer, leave your parent alone. He or she deserves a break! You just skip on ahead to the section "Sailing away on the Internet Explorer."

Okay, so your kid has that look which just melts you. . . . or makes you wonder, "What now?" Fear not, my friend; it's only a request for installing software. No biggie, right? You could do it in your sleep! What? Never installed software? No problem. There's always a first time for messing things up! Just kidding.

The instructions for installing Internet Explorer are in Appendix B. They're pretty simple and straightforward. Follow them, and I promise you won't find yourself in the shoes of that other explorer, Christopher Columbus, with angry sailors behind you and a bunch of men with feathers in their hair, brandishing tomahawks in front of you. So get on with it; and do tell your lovable kids when you're finished. Who knows, you may have the next Bill Gates or Sally Ride on your hands.

Sailing away on the Internet Explorer

Awright. Now that your parents have finished installing Internet Explorer, let's get started. One last thing, though . . . Don't forget to thank 'em for the installation.

To open Internet Explorer, follow these steps:

1. **Double-click on the Internet Explorer icon (or picture) shown in Figure 3-1.**

Figure 3-1:
The Internet
Explorer
icon.

Clicking on this icon starts your Internet connection. If Internet Explorer opens, you should be one happy sailor. You can skip the rest of the steps and go on to the next section. Just keep your eyes on the Internet Explorer, shown in Figure 3-2. It'll take good care of you.

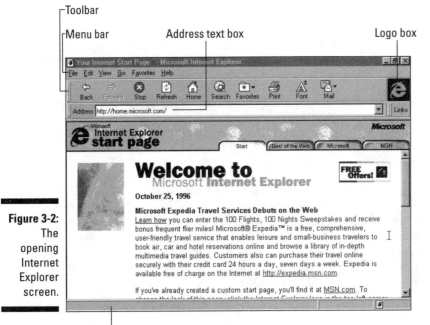

Figure 3-2:
The
opening
Internet
Explorer
screen.

Status bar

If you see the Connect To dialog box, shown in Figure 3-3, you have some more work to do.

2. **Enter your User name and Password information — if they're not already in the text boxes in the Connect To dialog box shown in Figure 3-3 — and click on Connect.**

As soon as you click on Connect, a message box like the one shown in Figure 3-4 appears, and you can hear the modem dial.

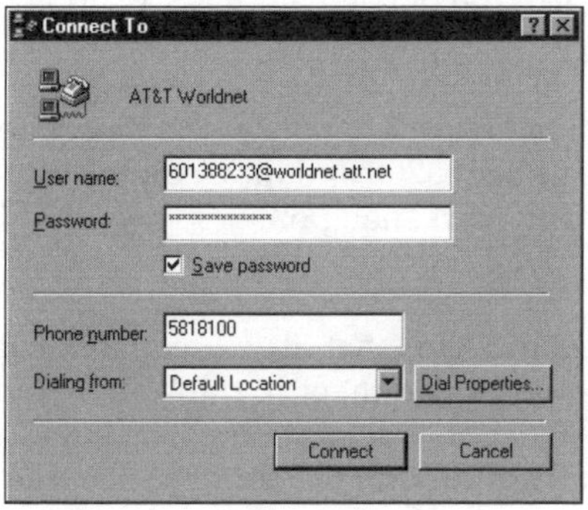

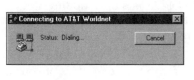

Figure 3-3:
The
Connect To
dialog box.

Figure 3-4:
Connecting
to AT&T
WorldNet
message
box.

Sometimes, for a variety of reasons, the system can't make a connection. Don't go spastic if you see one of two messages (see Figures 3-5 and 3-6).

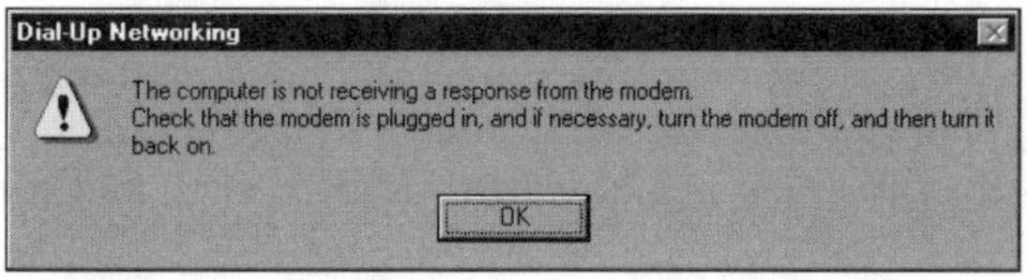

Figure 3-5:
Dial-Up
Networking
— Error 1.

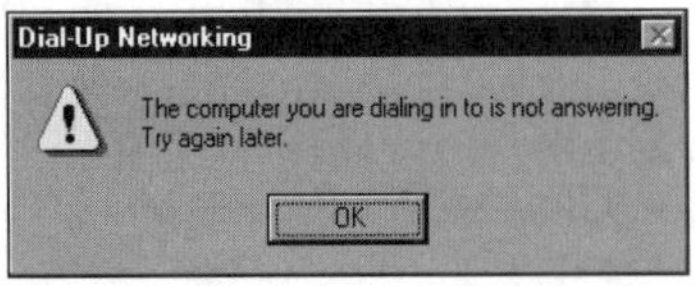

Figure 3-6:
Dial-Up
Networking
— Error 2.

Dial-Up Networking

⚠ The computer you are dialing in to is not answering.
Try again later.

`    OK    `

3. **Click on OK.**

   You then see a dialog box like the one in Figure 3-3 again.

4. **Click on Connect to try connecting again.**

   If Internet Explorer, shown in Figure 3-2, opens this time, congratulations! You just passed Go. Collect $200 and move on to the next section. If clicking on Connect doesn't work, hang on.

5. **Try these approaches:**

   • Turn off your external modem (that little box that sits around doin' nothin' until you try to connect to the Web or send a fax — then it grunts, groans, clicks, clacks, whines, or buzzes), turn on the modem again, and go through the process one more time.

   • If you can't see your modem, you have an internal modem. No duh! Get a chain saw, tear open the computer, rip the modem from its socket, bang it with a hammer a few times, reinstall it, and then try logging on again. STOP!!!! I was only kidding. Put down the chain saw. Instead, just exit properly from your computer, restart it, and try logging on again.

   If you keep getting the message shown in Figure 3-6 no matter what you try, the problem definitely lies with the computers of your ISP.

6. **Dial your ISP technical support phone number. If someone answers, "Hello, Toys R Us," it's time to change your ISP.**

   If your ISP is AT&T WorldNet Service, for example, phone 1-800-400-1447.

Getting to Know Internet Explorer

Welcome aboard the Internet Explorer. C'mon. I'll take you on a quick tour of the important parts of the browser. First, take a look again at Figure 3-2 — especially the toolbar, the menu bar, the Address text box, and the status bar.

Navigating with the Internet Explorer toolbar

The Internet Explorer toolbar makes it easy for you to tell Internet Explorer what to do — like having a remote control within arm's reach of your TV. Hey, have you ever noticed that if your remote is a little more than two feet away, it may as well be on the Moon because you're not going to go get it. Even if you have to torture yourself through an agonizing infomercial on chia pets, you'll sit through it — I mean, slouch through it — but you will not get your behind off the couch to zap the channel. I guess software programmers know how that feels all too well. That's why they design software to make things easy for the rest of us. God bless them.

See those icons on the Internet Explorer toolbar — the house, the printer, the letter *A,* and so on? Move the mouse pointer over an icon and see what happens. The icon changes from boring old black-and-white to somewhat awesome colors; the icon has become *active.* To use an active icon, you just click on it. Pretty nifty, huh?

A neat feature of Internet Explorer is that you can change the toolbar. Changing a toolbar is good if you're comfortable with using the computer; changing a toolbar can be scary if you're new to computers. Wanna know what I mean when I say, "Change the toolbar?" If you click on Links on the toolbar, hold down the mouse button too long, and move the mouse, for example, the Links section can get bigger or hop from where it is to another spot. If this happens, you haven't broken anything. Just put your mouse pointer on the changed thing, and drag it back to where it was.

Hanging out at the Internet Explorer menu bar

The menu bar is a larger version of the toolbar. The menu bar has all the commands the toolbar has and more — options for Help, organizing stuff about Web sites, opening a second browser, saving files and pictures to disk, and a ton of other options, just to name a few. Check out Chapter 4 if you're really interested in knowing more about Internet Explorer. You can read it to find out how to do nifty things in Internet Explorer — without becoming a closet computer geek!

Checking out addresses

To get anywhere on the Web, you need to know the address of the place you want to visit. It's like wanting to talk to someone on the phone. Unless you know the phone number of the person you want to talk to, you can't call him or her. Like, duh! But you don't need a map to use the Web. A Web address is what you need. Here's what one looks like:

```
www.disney.com/
```

The technical term for an address on the Web is *URL — Uniform Resource Locator.* (In this book, I use URL and address to mean the same thing.) Most URLs (or addresses) look like meaningless, jumbled mixtures of letters and sometimes numbers; they make absolutely no sense. Imagine a postal carrier trying to deliver a letter with nothing but `dfr.cc.com` written on it. To Internet Explorer, however, the strange mixture makes a lot of sense. Let's see how.

Figuring out what all those dots and `com`*s mean*

If you look carefully at the weird combination of letters, you probably can see the name of the company (or person) the address belongs to. You already know where you'd end up if you went to `www.disney.com/` address, don't you? I thought so — the Disney site. Try some more. You can probably tell from the following addresses what companies the addresses belong to:

Web Address	*Company*
`www.microsoft.com`	Microsoft Corporation
`www.ibm.com`	IBM Corporation
`www.nbc.com`	NBC Corporation

The dot and the three letters, `com`, tell you that the address belongs to a *com*mercial organization, meaning a company like Sony, Microsoft, AT&T, or Taco Bell. Every address has one of the three-letter codes in it, but the codes aren't all `com`. Some other three-letter codes and the types of organizations the letters stand for are

Code	*Type of Organization*	*Example*
`.edu`	Educational (colleges and universities)	`www.ucla.edu`
`.org`	Non-profit	`www.ets.org`
`.gov`	Government	`www.whitehouse.gov`
`.mil`	Military	`www.navy.mil`
`.net`	Internet Service Provider	`www.worldnet.att.net`

Sometimes a dot and a two-letter code, such as uk or in, follows the three-letter organization code. This abbreviation is the country code, telling you that you're looking at the address of an organization in a particular country. For example, www.ibmpcug.co.uk is the address of the PC User Group in the United Kingdom.

If you don't know the address of a company you want to visit, just add www. (including the dot) in front of the name of the company, followed by .com. That works in most cases. If you want a college or university, use .edu instead of .com.

Slashing your way through the Web

Pirates would have a ball on the Web. The Web has slashes all over the place. But why all these slashes? Aren't the dots and coms enough? Well, not really. The slashes make traveling the Web very specific. You see, Web sites usually have more than one page. The slashes make it easier to get to the page you want, like putting a very specific address on a letter. Isn't it easier for the postal carrier to deliver a letter if the name, street, town, state and ZIP code are mentioned in the address, as in Kathy Smith, 123 Alphabet Street, New York, NY 12345-1234 than if the address were just Kathy Smith, New York? Can you imagine how long it would take a postal carrier to find the right Kathy Smith in New York if the letter didn't have the street address? Following are the URLs for a typical Web site with several pages:

URL for the opening window or home page	www.disney.com
URL for Disney World	www.disney.com/DisneyWorld
URL for Disneyland	www.disney.com/Disneyland

Get the picture? If you know that the information you're looking for is on the Disneyland page of the Disney Web site, you don't have to go through page after page. All you do is type the address, a slash, and the word *Disneyland*.

Linking up with other spots

Hyperlinks (I call them *links* because I'm lazy *and* because that's what most people call them) are words or pictures that are linked to other spots on the same page or to an entirely different page. If you click on a linked word or picture, Internet Explorer takes you to the spot or page it is linked to. But how can you tell if a word or picture is linked? Well, how can you tell if you hit your thumb with a hammer? Eaaaaasy. It sticks out like a sore thumb. Well, so do linked words. They're of a different color than the rest of the words on a page. It's also easy to tell which images are linked, too. To find the links on a Web page, follow these steps:

1. **Move the mouse pointer over one of those different-colored words or over an image.**

   The pointer changes from an arrow to a little hand with a pointing index finger. This little hand shown in Figure 3-7 means that the word or image is linked.

2. **Look at the status bar at the bottom of the page.**

   Internet Explorer displays the URL for that link in the status bar. Cool, huh?

3. **Move the pointer to another link.**

   The URL in the status bar changes again (see Figure 3-8).

4. **Click on the word you're pointing to.**

   Your page goes blank within a few seconds, the Stop icon on the menu bar lights up again, and information from the new URL starts streaming to your computer. Internet Explorer is transporting you to the page that is linked to the word you clicked on.

5. **Watch the changes in the status bar and the Address text box as the new page loads.**

The cursor pointing to a link

Figure 3-7: The friendly little hand points out a link.

The URL for the link

The cursor pointing to an image link

Figure 3-8:
The status
bar
changes to
show the
URL for the
link.

Changed status bar

The secret behind links is something called *HTTP — HyperText Transfer Protocol,* a set of rules that allows information can move from one computer to another, as long as both computers use the same rules. On the Web, all computers use HTTP. Essentially, HTTP tells your browser, "Yo, Internet Explorer! If someone clicks on a linked word, go to the URL to which it is linked and get the info." Internet Explorer replies, "Your wish is my command," and hurries off to get the information.

Question: Who invented HTTP and where?

Answer: Tim Berners-Lee invented HTTP at CERN, the European Laboratory for Particle Physics, in Switzerland.

Putting Internet Explorer to work

Ooooooookay! I know you're itching to blast off into Cyberspace, so I'll keep you waiting no more. Let's go!

1. **Click on the Address text box on the Internet Explorer toolbar.**

2. **Type the URL in the Address text box.**

   For example, I typed `www.yahooligans.com/` (see Figure 3-9).

The URL

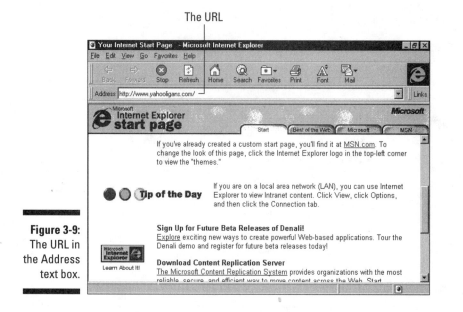

Figure 3-9:
The URL in
the Address
text box.

3. Press Enter or Return.

Internet Explorer starts downloading information from the Web page to
your screen. While the downloading is happening, pay close attention
to the status bar and to the logo box. In a few seconds, you'll find
yourself staring at an awesome site — Yahooligans Web site for kids
(see Figure 3-10).

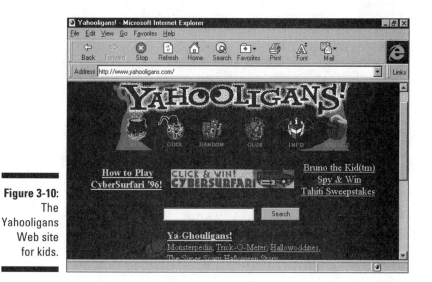

Figure 3-10:
The
Yahooligans
Web site
for kids.

Getting your bearings

The status bar at the bottom of the screen tells you what's happening as you're downloading information — how much information Internet Explorer has downloaded and how much remains. When Internet Explorer downloads the entire page, the status bar displays the message, Done. Sometimes even a fast modem just seems to crawl, and the plant in the corner of your room will grow six inches or more before Internet Explorer downloads all the information. That's when you take down the sails and tell Internet Explorer to *STOP* it.

Using the Toolbar to Take Control

When you want things to happen and you want them to happen fast, go directly for the Internet Explorer toolbar. The next few sections tell you how to use the toolbar for maximum speed as you browse through the Web.

Taking down the sails

The Stop icon automatically lights up as soon as you connect to a Web site. When you click on Stop, you drop the sails; you end the connection you just made to that address; you call it quits. Why would you want to do that? Here are some reasons:

- You have a sloooooow connection. You want to get on with your life, so you stop the downloading and try another address.

- You realize that the address you're connecting is not the address you really wanted.

- Sometimes an entire page has been downloaded with the exception of one measly little piece of information, but you won't know this because your screen will appear blank even after what seems like ages. This slowness usually happens when the URL you have connected to has a counter on it that counts the number of people who stop by there. (Chapter 17 tells you how to add a counter to your home page, but you have to read Chapter 16 first.) By clicking on the Stop icon, you tell Internet Explorer, "I don't care about that piece of information. Just give me what you've downloaded so far," and Internet Explorer obeys. Just like you obey your parents. Yeah, right.

Pressing the Esc key does the same thing as clicking on the Stop icon.

The screen is frozen — How can I thaw it?

When the image in the logo box freezes in space for a few seconds, the information is downloading slowly. On the other hand, if the image stays frozen for, say, five minutes, a problem has occurred. You should then exit Internet Explorer, start it again, come back to the opening window, and try the address one more time. Sometimes the entire screen freezes, preventing you from exiting Internet Explorer the normal way. Don't use a crowbar to get your computer to work. Instead, gently restart the computer. That works much better.

We know that you can type fast, but can you type correctly?

If you get the message shown in Figure 3-11, check whether you've typed the address correctly. As you see in the figure, I mistyped the address by leaving out one of the *w*'s in www portion of the address.

Figure 3-11:
The error message that means, "Excuse me please, but I think you typed the address wrong — you dingbat!"

Problems That Need A Hammer

The message shown in Figure 3-12 means that you could have any one of a number of problems:

Figure 3-12:
The error message that means, "Sorry, but this situation is a little more serious."

The most common reason for this problem is usually not yours at all: The computers of your Internet Service Provider are being weird. However, rather than begin by bugging your ISP, make sure that everything is okay on your end.

First, maybe you're using too much memory on your computer: You may have way too many software applications open right now. To take care of the problem, follow these steps:

1. **Check whether you have other programs open.**
2. **Close any programs that you don't need right now, such as PaintShop.**
3. **Return to Internet Explorer and try to connect to the address again.**

If the problem persists, follow these steps:

1. **Close all applications.**
2. **Shut down the computer.**
3. **Restart the computer.**
4. **Start Internet Explorer, and try to connect to the address again.**

If you *still* haven't solved the problem, throw yourself down on the floor, kick and scream, and then get up and calmly call your Internet Service Provider to see whether they're experiencing problems on their computers.

Using your two-way ticket — Back and Forward

When you use the toolbar to travel on the Web, any place in the world is only a click of the mouse away, and you quickly acquire frequent flier miles. One minute you're in the U.S., the next minute you're in Australia, then Norway, Egypt, Pakistan, Canada, Nigeria, Sweden, Sri Lanka, France, Peru, Ghana . . . all within a matter of minutes. Before you know it, you're lost in the jungles of Africa, the Andes, the Sahara desert, or in the Alps. So how do you back-track? Just click on the Back icon on the toolbar . . . again, and again, and again, until you're back to the page you want.

Sometimes you may click on the Back icon once too often, and, like Michael J. Fox, go back — way, way back. Too far back. When that happens, click on the Forward icon. You return to the previous page — one at a time.

Going Home

Sometimes *browsing* the Web seems more like *circling* the Web. You feel like you're going around in circles, lost and confused. When that happens, it's time to cash your travelers checks and go home. How? Just click on the Home icon on the toolbar. In one quick motion, you are right back where you started because, in Internet Explorer, *Home* is the first page that comes up automatically each time you start Internet Explorer, not the place where you eat, sleep, and hang out.

Finding refreshments on Internet Explorer

Sometimes you might accidentally stop a page from loading. When you do, don't panic. Just click on Refresh on the toolbar. Internet Explorer loads the page again. Refresh is also useful if you connect to a page on which the information changes frequently. I couldn't get enough of the Olympics Games in Atlanta. I was sure I'd win one of McDonald's prizes, so I fired up the old Internet Explorer and refreshed my CNN site ever so often. When you connect to such a site and you want to keep up with the changes in the site, click on Refresh; you'll get the latest information.

Searchin' for the gooood stuff

Looking for information on the Web is easy with Internet Explorer. Just click on Search on the toolbar. You'll see a ton of resources for all kinds of information (see Figure 3-13). You can either type in a word that describes what you want, or, if you're lazy like me, you can drag the scroll bar down and click on one of the many links listed on that page. Internet Explorer takes over from there. For a detailed discussion on searching the Web, refer to Chapter 6. *Nooo Problem.*

Printing a page

Printing a home page is really easy. Just click on Print in the toolbar. Like you actually needed me to tell you that. Okay, okay. I won't insult your intelligence, but I'll still show you what the Print window looks like after you click on Print. Take a look at Figure 3-14. I feel better now that I know you've seen it.

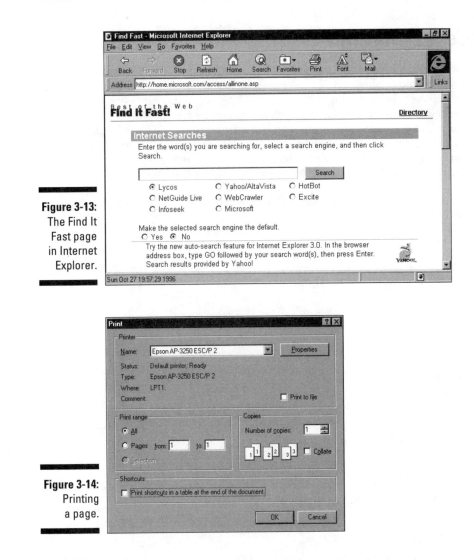

Figure 3-13:
The Find It
Fast page
in Internet
Explorer.

Figure 3-14:
Printing
a page.

What if you wanna share a really cool site with a couple of friends who don't
have computers, and the only way you can is to print out the pages of the
site? Well, watch out for this: The way the Print dialog box is set up, your
printer will print all the copies of page 1, all the copies of page 2, and so on.
If you don't want to have to sort the pages yourself, click on the Collate
check box in the Print dialog box until it has an X in it.

Collecting and visiting your Favorites

The Web has hundreds of thousands of sites that are truly awesome. And although you probably don't have time to see them all, you will run into hundreds of them on your explorations. The well-organized person that you are, I guess you already have a system of keeping track of all these sites, right? And your room also ought to be featured in *Good Housekeeping* magazine, right? Yeah, rrrright! Another cool feature of Internet Explorer that I'm sure you'll like is Favorites, and like the name suggests, it keeps track of your favorite sites. (Netscape calls these *bookmarks*.)

To add the site you're viewing to Favorites and then go to the site, follow these steps:

1. Click on Favorites on the toolbar.

The Favorite menu appears, as shown in Figure 3-15. Just like a menu at a restaurant. I'll have some . . .

Figure 3-15:
The
Favorites
menu.

2. Click on Add to Favorites.

Internet Explorer, understanding that it *is* your servant, immediately adds the URL to a list it's keeping just for you.

3. Click on Favorites in the toolbar.

The Favorite menu appears, but you knew it would. That's what happened in Step 1.

4. Click on the favorite site you want to go to.

Away you go — off to the site you wanted.

You now know enough to cruise the Web and tour the world. Like that Chris dude, you can cross the oceans. Go ahead; don't be afraid to explore. You can always return Home at the click of an icon — the Home icon.

Jumping Ship: Exiting from Internet Explorer

After you've had enough and are ready to say good-bye to Internet Explorer for the day, choose File⇨Exit.

To return to Internet Explorer, double-click on the Internet Explorer icon. Your favorite sites will be waiting for you.

Chapter 4

Exploring Internet Explorer a Little Further

In This Chapter

▶ Downloading multiple pages simultaneously

▶ Organizing your favorite URLs

▶ Sharing URLS

*I*n this chapter, you uncover the hidden areas of Internet Explorer, the ones beneath the deck. You get to look at some of the commands on the menu bar and really put Internet Explorer to work. Come on. You have a lot of exploring to do.

Doubling Your Internet Explorer Fun

Sometimes, watching a page come onto the screen of your computer is like waiting for Mom or Dad to get ready to go somewhere. Very exciting. Not! So instead of tapping your fingers or heading for the fridge, just fire up a second copy of Internet Explorer from within the browser. This way, while Internet Explorer downloads the first page, you get your computer busy downloading a second page. This double-downloading works great if you know that the first Web page you're connected to is usually slow and gets a lot of visitors. Follow these steps to download one page and open another in Internet Explorer:

1. **Click on the Internet Explorer icon.**

   Guess what? Internet Explorer opens, but you knew that it would, didn't you? Figure 4-1 shows my start page; yours won't look exactly like mine, but I included the figure so that you'd at least know you're in the right neighborhood.

Toolbar

Menu bar

Figure 4-1:
The
Internet
Explorer
start page.

Status bar

2. Click in the Address text box, type a URL, and press Enter.

Internet Explorer begins its search for the URL you want, the URL of your dreams, the URL upon which you pin all your hopes for completing that history assignment you left to the last minute.

3. Choose File⇨New Window.

The same old Internet Explorer opens. Wait! It's not the same old one; it just *looks* like the same old one. How can you tell?

4. Check your operating system for two Internet Explorer windows.

In Windows 95, you can see two minimized Internet Explorer icons on the Taskbar.

In Windows 3.1, press Ctrl+Esc, and you then see two listings of Internet Explorer.

On the Mac, your desktop shows two Internet Explorer windows.

5. Choose File⇨Close from the menu bar when you're ready to zap one of the Internet Explorer windows.

Keeping Track of Pages You Like

Internet Explorer has an easy way for you to go back to a page you like: You use the Favorites menu. The menu lets you do a lot of cool stuff with your list of Favorites. (Check out Chapter 3 if you forget how to use Internet Explorer to store your favorite sites.)

Finding a favorite site

Do you get upset when you can't find the homework you know you did? You're not alone. Happens to us all. And it's no different with URLs. I used to lose 'em all the time. They'd get buried under newer URLs, and then I'd have to scroll down an entire list until I found what I was looking for. Very time-consuming. Wouldn't it be cool if you could find the URL you're looking for in the blink of an eye instead of having to scroll all the way down to the bottom of some hairy list? Guess what? Internet Explorer lets you do just that.

To find a favorite URL in Internet Explorer, follow these steps:

1. **Click on F̲avorites in the menu bar.**

   The Favorites menu appears (see Figure 4-2).

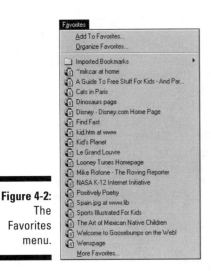

Figure 4-2:
The
Favorites
menu.

2. **If you find the URL you're looking for on the list in the menu, double-click on the address — and you connect to the page.**

   If you don't see the URL and the list extends to the bottom of the menu as shown in Figure 4-2, you're not finished. Continue to Step 3.

3. **Click on <u>M</u>ore Favorites at the bottom of the menu.**

   The Favorites dialog box appears (see Figure 4-3).

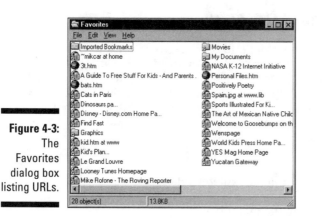

Figure 4-3: The Favorites dialog box listing URLs.

4. **Double-click on the URL you want in the Favorites dialog box.**

   Just like that! You've got the Web site you want on your screen.

If you don't like the way the URLs look in the dialog box, you can change them by clicking on View in the Favorites dialog box and then selecting Large Icons, Small Icons, List, or Detail. A Favorites dialog box with large icons looks like Figure 4-4.

Figure 4-4: The Favorites dialog box with large icons.

Zapping your unfavorites

Sometimes I save a URL and then I get tired of it or don't like the changes the creator makes to it. When that happens, I just zap the ol' thing. Yes, I zap it real good. Deleting an unfavorite URL from Internet Explorer is easy — and it makes you feel so powerful when you do it. Zap! You can just feel the energy pouring through your veins. To do a little zapping yourself, follow these steps:

1. Choose Favorites⇨Organize Favorites in the menu bar.

The Organize Favorites dialog box appears (see Figure 4-5).

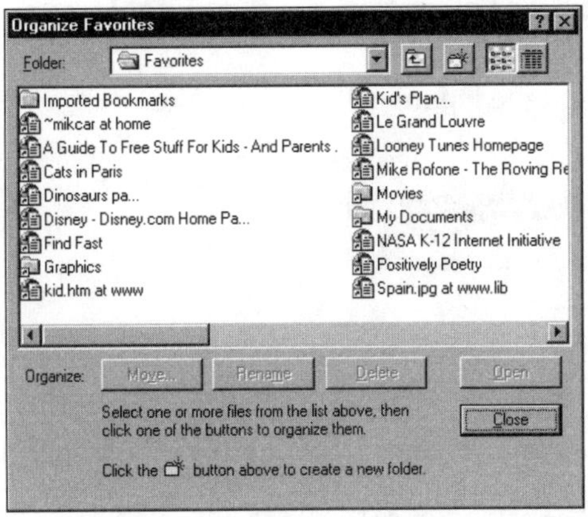

Figure 4-5:
The dialog box where you zap old faves that are faves no more.

Organize Favorites	? ☒
Folder: 🗀 Favorites	▼ 🔼 📂 ⊞ ⊞

🗀 Imported Bookmarks   🔖 Kid's Plan...
🔖 ~mikcar at home   🔖 Le Grand Louvre
🔖 A Guide To Free Stuff For Kids - And Parents .   🔖 Looney Tunes Homepage
🔖 Cats in Paris   🔖 Mike Rofone - The Roving Re
🔖 Dinosaurs pa...   🔖 Movies
🔖 Disney - Disney.com Home Pa...   🔖 My Documents
🔖 Find Fast   🔖 NASA K-12 Internet Initiative
🔖 Graphics   🔖 Positively Poetry
🔖 kid.htm at www   🔖 Spain.jpg at www.lib

Organize: [Move...]   [Rename]   [Delete]   [Open]

Select one or more files from the list above, then click one of the buttons to organize them.   [Close]

Click the 📂 button above to create a new folder.

2. Highlight the URL you want to zap.

3. Click on the Delete button.

It's gone. Outta there. You just zapped that poor little sucker!

Better double-check before you zap something in Internet Explorer. Unless you have Windows 95 or a Mac and can go pickin' through the Recycle Bin or the Trash Can, you can't undo your deletion.

Organizing your favorites

If you're like me, your Favorites collection will soon become so large that it'll take over your room. Like your room has anything to spare to begin with! Getting from one corner of your room to another is like slashing your way through the Amazon jungles. Well, before things get any worse, we'd better get your Favorites organized.

A folder for every type of URL

I have my URLs set up in groups or *folders*. I have folders for Movies, Music, Art, Pets, and so on. When I get a new URL, I just store it in the right folder. That way, if I'm looking for, say, the URL for the Pearl Jam site, I know I only need to look in the Music folder, because that's the only place it'll be.

To create a folder in Internet Explorer, follow these steps:

1. **Choose Favorites➪Organize Favorites.**

   The Organize Favorites dialog box is back again. You saw it in Figure 4-5 already.

2. **Click on the Create New Folder button. (It looks as if it has fireworks coming out of it.)**

   A new folder pops up (see Figure 4-6).

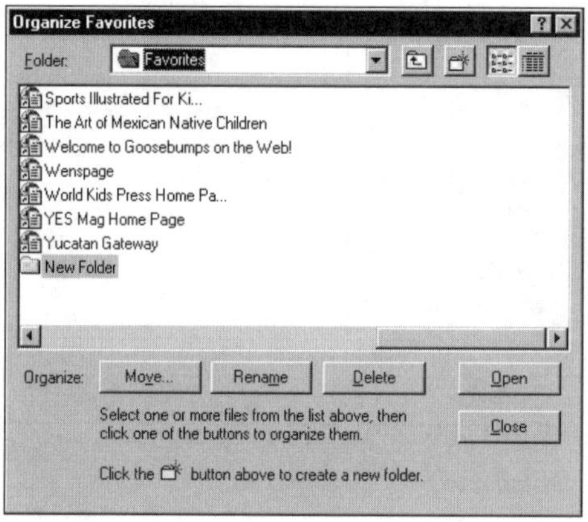

Figure 4-6:
A new
folder.

Organize Favorites	? X
Folder: ▣ Favorites ▼ 🗎 🗎 🗎 🗎	
📄 Sports Illustrated For Ki...	
📄 The Art of Mexican Native Children	
📄 Welcome to Goosebumps on the Web!	
📄 Wenspage	
📄 World Kids Press Home Pa...	
📄 YES Mag Home Page	
📄 Yucatan Gateway	
📄 New Folder	

Organize: [Move...] [Rename] [Delete] [Open]
Select one or more files from the list above, then
click one of the buttons to organize them.
[Close]
Click the 🗎 button above to create a new folder.

3. **Click on Rename, type the name you want to give the folder, and then press Enter or Return.**

   I named my new folder Music, and the new name now appears on the folder (see Figure 4-7).

If you got confused and clicked on Close, you're still "Okay." Just return to the Favorites menu, click on Organize Favorites, and go back to where you took the wrong turn. We'll wait for you.

Here's the new folder.

Figure 4-7:
The new
folder I
named
Music.

You can even create other folders and put them in the folder you just created, which I'm going to call the *main folder*. Here's how:

1. Create and name a new folder to put in the folder you created.

Don't tell anyone, but sometimes I like to energize my brain with a good rap, so I created a Rap folder to put inside my Music folder (see Figure 4-8).

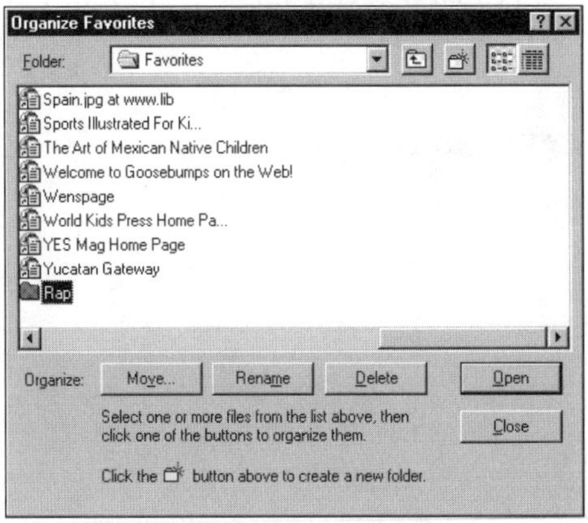

Figure 4-8:
The new
Rap folder.

2. Make sure that the folder you want to put inside the main folder is selected. Then click on the Move button in the Organize Favorites dialog box.

I clicked on Rap because . . . well, you already know why. The Browse for Folder dialog box appears (see Figure 4-9).

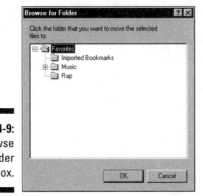

Figure 4-9:
The Browse
for Folder
dialog box.

3. **Click on the main folder, the folder in which you want to put the folder you're moving, and then click on OK.**

   That sounds confusing. Did you understand? Here's what I did: I clicked on Music because I wanted to put the Rap folder into the Music folder. Internet Explorer did what I told it to, and the Rap folder disappeared from the Organize Favorites dialog box. Where did it go? Did I destroy it? How could I? Hang on. I'm just kidding.

4. **In the Organize Favorites dialog box, double-click on the main folder, the one that should have a folder inside it.**

   Voilà! You have a new Organize Favorites dialog box that has the Music folder listed in the Folder text box and all the folders within the Music folder listed below (see Figure 4-10). Whew!

Figure 4-10:
The dialog
box now
shows a
folder
within a
folder.

A URL in every folder

Okay, so now you have at least two folders with nothing in them. What a waste. Time to fill those folders to the gills. To move one URL to a folder in Internet Explorer, follow these steps:

1. **Choose Favorites⇨Organize Favorites, and select the URL you want to move (see Figure 4-11).**

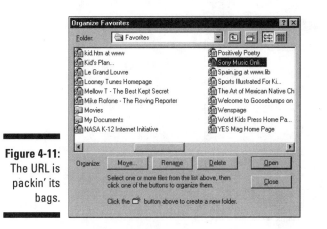

Figure 4-11: The URL is packin' its bags.

2. **Click on the Move button.**

   Hmmm. Doesn't this seem vaguely familiar to you? Yep. I thought so. You move URLs just like you move folders, using the Browse for Folders dialog box.

3. **Double-click on the main folder.**

   A list of the folders (in this case, just one folder) within the Music folder appears (see Figure 4-12).

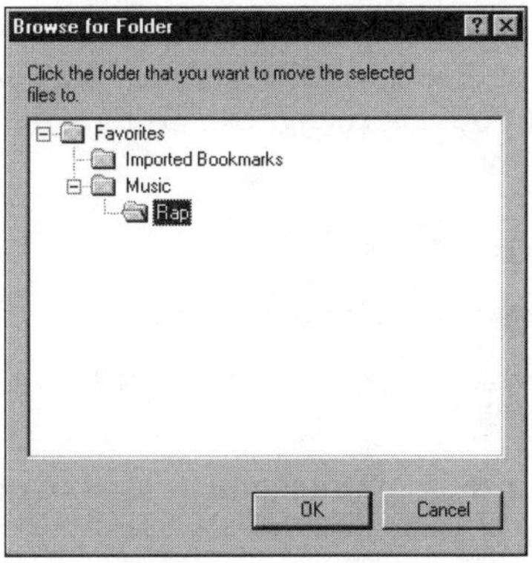

Figure 4-12: The folder within a folder.

4. Click on the folder where you want to put the URL, and then click on OK.

The URL picks itself up and walks with grace and dignity into its new home. You, however, can't see any of this happening. You have to either take my word for it or check it out in the Organize Favorites dialog box (see Figure 4-13).

Figure 4-13:
If you're
looking at
this figure,
you either
don't trust
me or
you're as
curious as
a cat.
Here's
living proof
that the
URL moved.

A name that really means something

When you save a URL in your Favorites folder, sometimes the name that shows up in your Favorites menu is that whole tangled-up Web address, something like `http://www2.hopper.com/mypage/look_here/index.html`.

Where some of these people get the names for their URLs, I'll never know. To try to figure out what some URLs mean is next to impossible. You have to actually open the site before you can remember why you saved the URL in the first place. You don't have time for that malarkey. You have places to go, people to see, things to do. You can give a Favorite a new name and change that confusing URL to a name that you can recognize. To rename Favorites in Internet Explorer, follow these steps:

1. Choose Favorites➪Organize Favorites.

The typical old Organize Favorites dialog box appears.

2. Select the Favorite that you want to rename and click on the Rename button.

3. Type the new name you want to give the Favorite and press Enter or click Close.

Sure enough. The new name replaces the old one, but you knew it would. You did the same steps when you named your new folder, didn't you?

Retracing your course

Did you know that because the moon has no atmosphere (and therefore no wind), footprints left on the moon's surface can stay there for years? And just like those natural footprints that you may leave behind when you get to walk the moon's surface, you leave behind footprints of your WebVentures, too. Yup, you sure do. Internet Explorer stores your footprints in its History folder. Wanna see 'em? Choose Go⇨Open History Folder.

But what can you use History for? Is there any purpose to it? Sure there is. You can use History to jump *directly* to any page or site you've been to — without using the Back button. And here's another cool thing about History. You can use it to jump to any page or site you've been to in the last 20 days. Although Internet Explorer comes with 20 days as its original setting (the *default* setting), you can increase the number of days to a maximum of 99 days by using the menu bar.

To change the number of days Internet Explorer tracks your history, follow these steps:

1. **Choose View⇨Options.**

   The Options dialog box opens.

2. **Click on the Navigation tab.**

   The Navigation page moves to the front of the dialog box (see Figure 4-14).

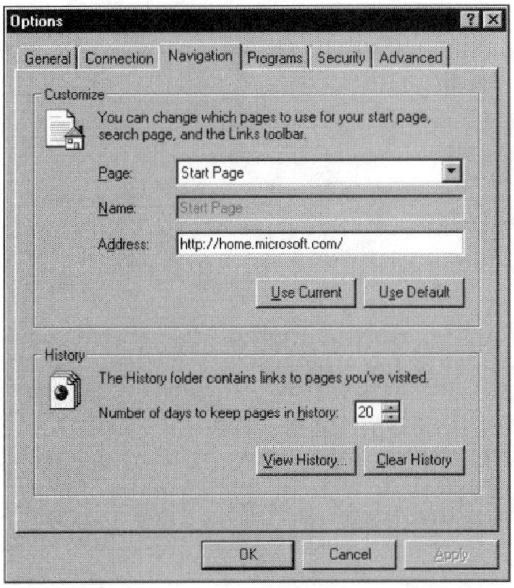

Figure 4-14:
The
Navigation
page.

3. Change the number of days in the History section.

To increase the number of days, click on the up arrow beside the number. To decrease the number, click on the down arrow.

4. Click on OK.

Internet Explorer says, "Ahoy, matey. I've recorded the change, and, from this day forward, I will trace your steps for that number of days."

Question: How many men have walked on the moon?

Answer: Twelve. Would you like to be the 13th person? No woman has ever walked on the moon, but, with NASA taking renewed interest in our solar system neighbor, the probability of that happening shouldn't be ruled out.

Sharing a Shortcut with a Friend

Sometimes you come across a page so good that you want to share it with a friend. But if you think that means you have to painstakingly write down the entire URL of the page, which can be up to five miles long, in your fancy handwriting (which we all know resembles Greek), then think again. I have an easy way to let your friend know about this cool Web page, but my way works only if you know your friend's e-mail address. Follow these steps:

1. Choose File⇨Send To from the menu bar.

A little cascade menu folds out from the Send To option (see Figure 4-15).

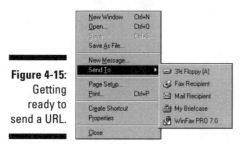

Figure 4-15: Getting ready to send a URL.

2. Click on Mail Recipient, the option with a little envelope beside it.

Internet Explorer opens up the window for new messages (see Figure 4-16). Notice that the Subject text box already has the URL of the page you were on — the URL you want to share with your friend. Yes! One less thing to type!

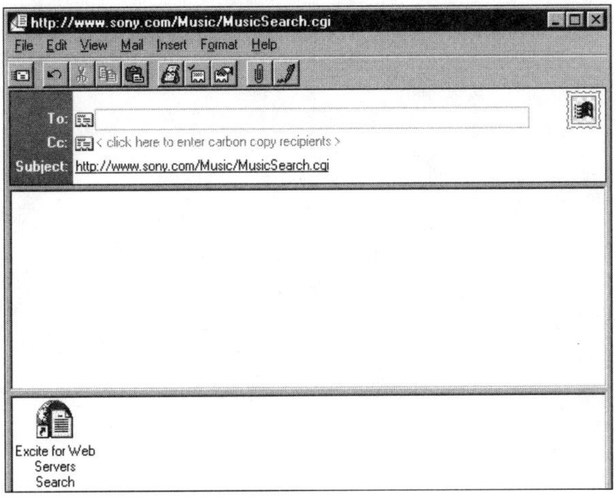

Figure 4-16:
The
message
window.

3. **Type your friend's e-mail address in the To text box.**

4. **Click on the Send button (the one with the envelope on it) in the toolbar.**

The URL is on its way. How difficult was that?

Now you're totally prepared to browse the Web using Internet Explorer. Have fun!

PART II
Browse Around the Web

The 5th Wave   By Rich Tennant

"Well heck, all the boy did was launch a search on the Web and up comes Tracy's retainer, your car keys and my bowling trophy here on a site in Seattle!"

In this part . . .

After you get the hang of browsers and how they behave, it's time to fly away to some cool destinations. In this part, that's what you do. I take you to some of the hippest sites on the Web; not just educational, but fun, and funny, too. Then in Chapter 6, I show you how you can find such sites and information on your own. Free as a bird, you can go out and explore the skies.

Chapter 5

Web Sites — Wild, Wacky, and Wonderful

....

In This Chapter

▶ Exhibit your art on the Web

▶ Sports

▶ Kids with disabilities

▶ Movies, TV, and celebrities

▶ Bands, music, and lyrics

▶ Cops, spies, and other cool stuff

▶ Teens sound off

▶ Games, games, and still more games

▶ UFOs and other alien things

▶ Other cool Web sites

....

The Web has about eight million sites, not all of which are cool. Some are lame, and others are yucky enough to make you barf. No kidding. One site is called the Yuckiest Site on the Internet. Now, I know you're dying to go there, but wait just a New York second. Before we cruise on over for a group hurl, I wanna tell you about the other stuff in this chapter. I've put together a collection of really neat sites — sites that help you find the lyrics to that song playing in your head since you woke up this morning and sites that give you movie reviews and fashion trends. You can find sites that help you with your math homework and sites that answer science questions. Sorry, no Web sites can change your grades, though.

Make no mistakes in typing the URLs for the sites you want to visit. In some URLs, you *must* type uppercase letters in uppercase or you get an error stating that the URL or web-site doesn't exist.

Awright, everyone. Ready for a group hurl? Here we go! Take a peek at Figure 5-1.

Figure 5-1:
The
Yuckiest
Site on the
Internet.

Does this figure look a little different from most of the figures in the book? That's because all the screen shots in this chapter are taken using a Mac.

Picasso in the Making: Exhibit Your Art on the Web

The Web has plenty of sites that accept your artwork and display it for the world to see. Kids' Korner, shown in Figure 5-2, is one such site. Sending your artwork to this Web site is no biggie. If you have a scanner, you can scan your drawing, save it as a file, and then send it to Kids' Korner via e-mail at Dee@finalfront.com. If you don't have a scanner, no problem. Send your drawing via snail-mail, I mean via the U.S. Postal Service to Diane Barnett, Route 7 Box 2300, Elizabethton, TN 36743. Remember to include your name, age, and address with your drawing and a SASE — a self-addressed stamped envelope — so that the Kids' Korner folks can return your drawing after they've put it up on the site.

Other art-displaying and interactive art sites:

✔ The Peace in Pictures Project at www.macom.co.il/peace/index.html

✔ The Refrigerator at users.aimnet.com/%7Ejennings/refrigerator/index.html

✔ Etch-a-Sketch at www.etch-a-sketch.com

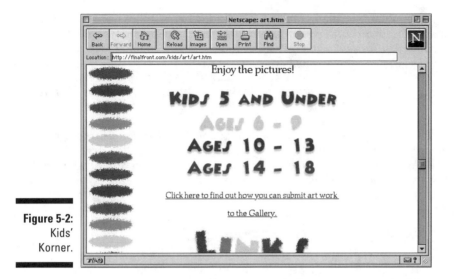

Figure 5-2:
Kids'
Korner.

✔ Mr. Showbiz Plastic Surgery Lab at `www.mrshowbiz.com/features/games/surgery/`

✔ Carlos' Coloring Book at `www.ravenna.com/coloring/`

✔ The Children's Art Gallery at `redfrog.norconnect.no/~cag/`

✔ Global Show-n-Tell at `www.telenaut.com/gst/`

Armchair Quarterback: Sports

The Web has enough sports-related info to make you break out in a sweat — without shooting a single basket or scoring a bone-jarring touchdown. And whether you're a regular sports fan or one of those crazies who jumps outta airplanes on skateboards, you're sure to find what you're looking for on the Web. One thing you oughta remember — the sports that we Americans play are *not* always the sports the rest of the world plays. This section gives you links not only for baseball, basketball, and football (no surprise there), but also for Australian Rules Football (no body protection — Ouch!), badminton, and Ultimate Frisbee. You can find Web links for hacky sack, disc golf, Jeet Kune Do, Muay Thai, and of course, archery (now that we won a gold at the Atlanta Olympics). So go ahead and gear up; you won't be benched this time. I promise.

If you could ask Shannon Miller a question, what would it be? Would you like to ask Sheryl Swoopes what it was like to play one-on-one with Michael Jordan? At the Sports Illustrated For Kids site, you can now talk to the pros (see Figure 5-3). Unlike most sports sites where you're no more than a couch potato (er . . . mouse potato), this site lets you be part of the action. You can send in your questions, which might, just might, appear in an issue of the *Sports Illustrated For Kids* magazine.

At this site, in addition to finding regular sports news, you can also get answers to questions you probably can't get answered elsewhere. Questions like, "What's the oldest sport that people still play?" Answer: Bowling. A bowling ball and bowling pins were found in a 7000-year-old Egyptian tomb. Check out the Sports Illustrated For Kids site at www.sikids.com.

Figure 5-3:
Sports
Illustrated
For Kids.

Most sports-related Web pages in the U.S. carry information only for those sports that are popular in the U.S. So, what if you want info on, say, broomball . . . uh huh, broomball. Whatsamatter? Sounds funny? Awright, awright, it is funny, I agree. Who plays broomball, anyway? Stop laughing. There's milk coming out your nose. Listen to what I have to say; go to MegaResource, located Down Under, in the land of kangaroos and wombats. There's a lot of action at that site (see Figure 5-4). Yes, yes, there's basket-ball and hockey and baseball, too. Although you won't see a listing for football, you can find football links under the listing Gridiron. And while you're checking out Gridiron, also check out Australian Rules Football at www.toyota.com.au/mega/sports.html.

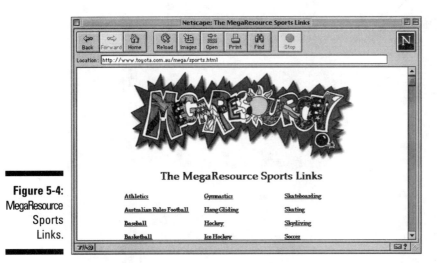

Figure 5-4:
MegaResource
Sports
Links.

Other sports nuts' sites:

✔ ESPN SportsZone at `www.espn.com/`

✔ Nando Sports at `www.nando.net/nt/sports/`

✔ Do-It at `gnn522.gnnhost.com/disinfo.html`

Triumph of the Spirit: Kids with Disabilities

One of the things I do in my spare time is volunteer for things I care about. The Special Olympics is an organization I love to work with (see Figure 5-5). Because I'm an athlete myself, I know exactly what it's like to feel tired and exhausted during a workout. For kids with disabilities, getting tired is only a minor obstacle compared to those challenges that they overcome every day. If you want to get an insight into the life of a kid with a disability, sign up as a volunteer and you'll know what I'm talking about. It's a great cause, one that requires very little time and one that'll make you thankful for all the things you may take for granted. Check out the Special Olympics site at `www.specialolympics.org`.

Other courageous sites:

✔ Webable at `www.webable.com`

✔ Special Education Resources on the Internet at `www.hood.edu/seri/serihome.htm`

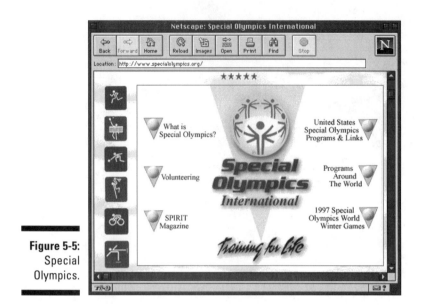

Figure 5-5:
Special
Olympics.

Hollywood Dirt: Movies, TV, and Celebrities

After I saw Twister and Independence Day, I just had to know how the crews filmed those tornadoes without getting sucked up into one of them. And, how did they blast the slimy aliens back to where they came from? Wouldn't you like to know, too? If so, go straight to Hollywood Online, shown in Figure 5-6. You can find trailers, audio clips, movie reviews, pictures, scripts, casting info, and lots of behind-the-scenes stuff about your favorite movies at `www.hollywood.com`.

Other movie and TV sites:

- Teen Movie Critic at `www.dreamagic.com/roger/teencritic.html`
- TV Guide Online at `www.tvguide.com`
- *People Magazine* at `www.people.com`
- Entertainment Weekly at `pathfinder.com/ew/`
- Hollywood Autographs at `http://www.alfies.com/`
- The Internet Movie Data Base at `www.imdb.com`
- David Letterman, *The Nanny,* and Other CBS Shows at `www.cbs.com`
- *Friends, The Tonight Show with Jay Leno,* Other NBC Shows at `www.nbc.com`

Figure 5-6:
Hollywood
Online.

✔ The Discovery Channel at www.discovery.com

✔ Personalized TV Listings at www.theGIST.com

✔ Movies.Com at www.movies.com

✔ Independence Day at www.id4.com/

✔ Film.Com at www.film.com

It's Just Rock & Roll to Me: Bands, Music, and Lyrics

The largest category of home pages on the Web is probably music pages. Loyal fans have set up totally jammin' sites for their favorite bands. It's not at all uncommon to find twenty, maybe thirty Web sites for some bands, complete with pictures, sound clips, and lyrics. Figure 5-7 shows one of my favorite sites, The Ultimate Band List. This site rocks! It has info on of tons of bands, most even *I* haven't heard of. You can find album reviews, fan clubs, lyrics, guitar tabs, audio and video clips, pictures, info on band numbers, and links to other Web sites. The site also has information on concerts, record stores, and other mega-music sites. This Web site is a groupie's dream; you'll love it at www.ubl.com.

Figure 5-7:
Ultimate
Band List.

Other rockin' sites:

- ✔ The Lyrics Data Base at `music.wit.com/uwp/music/lyrics/`
- ✔ Sony Music at `www.music.sony.com/Music/`
- ✔ Internet Underground Music Archive at `www.iuma.com/`
- ✔ Rock 'N' Roll Hall of Fame at `www.rockhall.com/`
- ✔ FireFly at `www.ffly.com`

Bad Boys, Bad Boys, Watchugonnado: Cops, Spies, and Other Cool Stuff

Watchugonnado when they come for you? The FBI is the country's number one crime-fighting organization. We've seen the agents in movies, and on TV's *America's Most Wanted* and *Unsolved Mysteries*. Now they're on the Web. At the FBI Web site shown in Figure 5-8, you can see the "Ten Most Wanted Fugitives." Hey, you never know; you just may bump into one of them at the mall. If you do, try to control the urge to practice your tae kwon do on them, okay? At the FBI Web site, you can also find out what it takes to be a Special Agent and how you can tell a real Special Agent from an impostor. Meet the bad boys at `www.FBI.gov`.

Figure 5-8:
FBI Home
Page.

Other criminally interesting sites:

- ✔ CIA at `www.odci.gov`
- ✔ Unofficial CIA Home Page at `www.3rdplanet.com/~evan/gov/cia.html`
- ✔ Danny Goodwin's Intelligence Museum at `www.inch.com/~dna/`
- ✔ Intelligence and CounterIntelligence Page at `www.kimsoft.com/kim-spy.htm`
- ✔ The Funniest Police Logs at `www.star.net/people/~masterds/funny/police.htm`

We Interrupt This Program For . . . The News

These days, you can get the latest news from around the world on the Web. Some of the world's finest newspapers are online (see Figure 5-9). You can find American, German, British, Canadian, Australian, Polish, and Russian newspapers on the Web. Here's something interesting you can do: Go through some of the newspapers and see whether they give the same amount of coverage and importance to today's leading news events. You'll see that some news stories are important only to a newspaper's native country and are covered only in one country's newspaper, while other stories affect people all over the world and are covered in all newspapers. Find out why a story has international importance as opposed to one that has national importance only on The Ultimate Collection of News Links Page at `pppp.net/links/news/`.

Figure 5-9:
Online
newspapers.

Other newsworthy sites:

- ✔ The Nando Times at `www2.nando.net/`
- ✔ MEDIAPOLIS at `www.partal.com/mediapolis/ANG/index.html`
- ✔ CNN at `CNN.com/index.html`
- ✔ Good News Every Day at `www.positivepress.com`

Get Some Fresh Air: The Great Outdoors

If you love bees and fleas, ticks and sticks, boats and goats, you don't complain in the rain, or when ants crawl up your pants, you're a true adventurer. So what're you doing indoors on your computer? Get out there! But wait — before you head outside, hit one last Web site. You'll be thankful you did. GORP — Great Outdoor Recreation Pages — is an award-winning site that'll satisfy even Indiana Jones (see Figure 5-10). Perhaps someone should ask Indy to check it out. Seems like he's always getting himself into a jam. Plus, this Web site doesn't serve unexpected delicacies like monkey brains! You can find the site at `www.GORP.com`.

Other adventurous sites:

- ✔ National Geographic at `www.nationalgeographic.com`
- ✔ Super Outdoors at `www.ool.com/kids/`

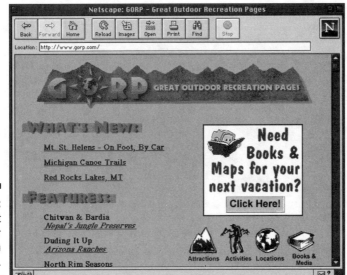

Figure 5-10:
Great
Outdoor
Recreation
Pages.

✔ Outdoors OnLine at `family.values.net/`

✔ Environmental News Network at `www.enn.com`

✔ America Outdoors Association at `www.americaoutdoors.org/`

✔ Outdoor and MORE Online at `www.outdoornet.com/`

✔ Terraquest at `www.terraquest.com/`

✔ OutDoorNet at `www.Dks.com/outdoornet`

✔ BackPacker's Guide at `www.hostels.com/guides/`

I've Fallen and I Can't Get Up: Health Stuff

I'll bet you've never seen a virus, let alone seen one attack a cell in your body and make you sick. Wanna see a video of a virus in action? How about watching an antibiotic defend your body and kill a virus? Wanna see a 3D image of a brain or some other organs? Jonathan Tward's Multimedia Medical Reference Library, shown in Figure 5-11, is a cure for all that ails you in your search for medical information. Everything from allergies and backaches to sports medicine and virology (uh . . . that's the study of viruses) is at `www.med-library.com/`.

Figure 5-11:
Jonathan
Tward's
Multimedia
Medical
Reference
Library.

Other sickly sites:

- ACHOO at www.achoo.com/achoo/human/index.htm
- Cells Alive at www.comet.chv.va.us/QUILL/
- Medicinenet at www.medicinenet.com
- National Center for Sports Medicine at www.maf.mobile.al.us/business/b_dir/ncsm/
- The New York Times Syndicate at nytsyn.com/medic/
- Center for Disease Control at www.cdc.gov

The Mad Scientist: Science and Other Crazy Things

I'm sure you've had times when you've sat down in your favorite chair and pondered the mysteries of life. You've wondered why things are the way they are and what makes them so. Serious questions like "Why is poop brown?", or "Where do farts come from, and why do they smell?", or "Why do feet smell?" (Have you spewed yet?) The Why Files has the answers to such life-and-death questions (see Figure 5-12). This Web site is set up by the same folks who make the *Beakman's World* TV show. You can also watch interactive demos of science experiments at whyfiles.news.wisc.edu/.

Figure 5-12:
The Why
Files.

Other mind-boggling sites:

- ✔ The MAD Scientist Network at `128.252.223.239/~ysp/MSN/`
- ✔ Newton's Apple at `www.mnonline.org/ktca/newtons/index.html`
- ✔ Yahoo Science Listing at `www.yahoo.com/Science/Indices/`
- ✔ Science Daily at `www.sciencedaily.com/`
- ✔ The Exploratorium at `www.exploratorium.edu/`
- ✔ The Interactive Frog Dissection at `curry.edschool.Virginia.EDU:80/~insttech/frog/`
- ✔ NPR Science Friday Kids Connection at `www.npr.org/sfkids/`
- ✔ Ask Dr. Science at `www.drscience.com`
- ✔ The "Kids and Computers" Web site at `www2.magmacom.com/~dsleeth/sitetoc.htm`

Teens Sound Off: I Have an Opinion, Too!

Just because you don't have a real job yet doesn't mean you don't have an opinion. No reason for adults to treat you like a child. Like everybody, you have a say in matters of importance, too. Hear what cyberteens like you are sounding off about. Someday, this world will be yours, so start making a difference. Get the word out about Teens Sound Off at `www.uvol.com/family/sndoff.html` (see Figure 5-13).

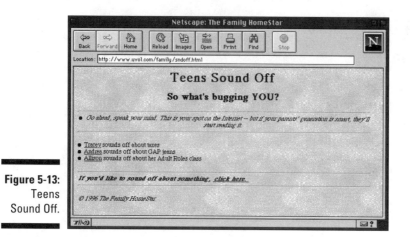

Figure 5-13:
Teens
Sound Off.

Other say-what-cha-really-think sites:

✔ CyberTeens at `www.mtlake.com/cyberteens/`

✔ KidsCom at `www.kidscom.com`

This is What I Do in My Spare Time: Collecting Stuff

Do you like to collect stuff? Have a hobby? Have I got a site for you (see Figure 5-14). Oh, but talking on the phone doesn't count. And neither does hanging out with your friends. With a few exceptions like these, you can find most hobbies listed at Yahoo! at `www.yahoo.com/Recreation/Hobbies_and_Crafts/Collecting`.

Other top hobnobbin' sites:

✔ Collector's SuperMall at `www.csmonline.com/home.html`

✔ Yahoo - Recreation at `www.yahoo.com/Recreation/Hobbies_and_Crafts/`

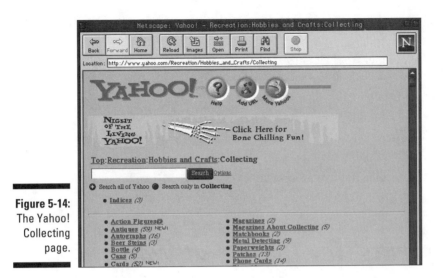

Figure 5-14:
The Yahoo!
Collecting
page.

Games, Games, and Still More Games: Wanna Play?

The largest collection of games and gaming resources on the Web is at GamesDomain, shown in Figure 5-15. Not only can you download more games than you can ever play, you can also find hints, tips, and tricks from other users, read game reviews, and follow links to other game sites. This site has games for all kinds of systems — DOS, Windows 3.1, Windows 95, OS/2, Apple Macintosh, and Amiga. The site at `www.gamesdomain.com` is rad.

Figure 5-15:
GamesDomain.

Other fun-filled sites:

- ✔ PC Gamer Hot List at `www.futurenet.co.uk/computing/pcgamer.html`

- ✔ Entertainment Online at `www.e-on.com`

- ✔ Tim's Clubhouse at `www.heatersworld.com/timspage.html`

- ✔ BrainTainment Center at `world.brain.com` (Play this game and increase your brain power!)

- ✔ PC Gamer Hot List at `www.futurenet.co.uk/computing/pcgamer.html`

Your Parents' Tax Dollars at Work: The U.S. Government

The United States Government is the world's largest user of paper, and now it probably is the largest provider of electronic information, as well. FedWorld is a one-stop site for all kinds of Government information (see Figure 5-16). Not only can you look up official government documents, you can also get a copy of documents like the President's Christmas greeting to the nation at `www.fedworld.gov/index.html`.

Figure 5-16:
FedWorld.

Other Fed sites:

> ✔ The United States Senate at `www.senate.gov`
>
> ✔ The House of Representatives at `www.house.gov`
>
> ✔ Government Information Xchange at `www.info.gov`

Geography — Where in the World Is It?

Excite City.Net (`www.city.net/`), shown in Figure 5-17, is an electronic version of the world's major cities, with their weather, restaurants, theaters, hotels, and everything else you'd find in a real city. If you want to know what it's like in a different part of the world, hop on to Excite City.Net, and with a few clicks of the mouse, you are transported there. I wanted to see how accurate the information on Excite City.Net was, so I picked a city I'm very familiar with — Bombay, India. When I got to `City.Net/Bombay`, I must say I was impressed with all the information they had on my hometown.

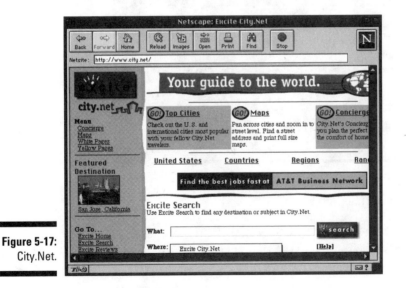

Figure 5-17:
City.Net.

Other world-cruisin' sites:

> ✔ How Far Is It? at `www.indo.com/distance/` (Find the distance between two cities.)
>
> ✔ The GeoNet Game at `www.hmco.com/hmco/school/geo/`
>
> ✔ Mapmaker, Mapmaker, Make Me a Map at `loki.ur.utk.edu/ut2Kids/maps/map.html`

Nothing but the Facts: History

If Excite City.Net (discussed in the preceding section), takes you to a city as it exists today, the Gateway to World History site, shown in Figure 5-18, can take you back in time. This site is a rare collection of historical information from every corner of the world. And, of course, I had to check to see if the information was really good. So I followed the links to the country I was born in — India — and looked up some stuff. Sure enough, the collection was awesome. What surprised me was that the Web site even had links to audio clips of that most famous Indian — Mahatma Gandhi. Check the facts about world history at `library.ccsu.ctstateu.edu/~history/world_history/`.

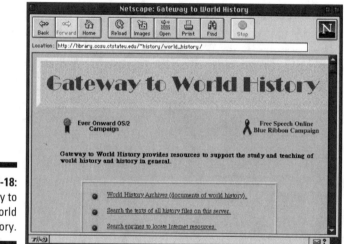

Figure 5-18:
Gateway to
World
History.

Other past-times sites:

- ✔ The History Channel at `www.historychannel.com/`
- ✔ The Constitution of the United States at `www.cs.cmu.edu/~karl/general/constitution.html`
- ✔ Historical documents at `gopher://vax.queens.lib.ny.us/11[gopher._ss._histdocs]`
- ✔ Social Science Information Gateway at `sosig.ac.uk`
- ✔ United States Civil War at `www.uscivilwar.com`

I Hate Math

That's what most kids say. But math *can* be fun. And who says mathematicians are nerdy? Did you know that rock star Sting was a high school teacher in England before he became famous, and one of the things he taught was math? Now, there's a nerdy professor for you — NOT! Math can be a lot of fun. And you can even use math to do magic. Math Magic Activities has a few really easy math tricks to impress your pals (see Figure 5-19). Make your appearance at `www.scri.fsu.edu/~dennis/topics/math_magic.html`

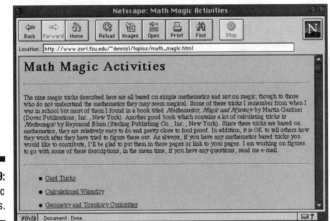

Figure 5-19: Math Magic Activities.

Other numerical sites:

- Fun with Math at `www.uni.uiuc.edu/departments/math/glazer/fun_math.html`
- MathMagic at `forum.swarthmore.edu/mathmagic/`
- Ask Dr. Math at `forum.swarthmore.edu/dr.math/`
- The Internet Pizza Server at `www.ecst.csuchico.edu/~pizza/`

It's Out of This World: UFOs and Other Alien Things

Did you know that the United States actually has a law that prevents people from making contact with aliens? I'm serious. It's in Title 14, Section 1211 of the Code of Federal Regulations. If you break the law, you can be fined

$5,000 and jailed for up to a year. Not cool. So, you still wanna meet aliens? If you do, you'd better use the UFO Guide to brush up on UFO terminology (see Figure 5-20). Then if someone mentions Area 51, or the Cash/Landrum Case, or the Valee Classification System, or Foo Fighters (nope, not the band), you won't have to say, "Huh?" Check out this totally alien site at `www.ipacific.net.au/~pavig/theufoguide_494.shtml`.

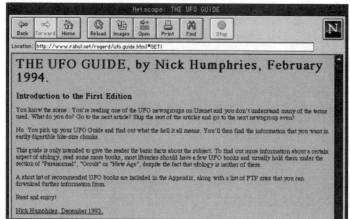

Figure 5-20:
The UFO
Guide.

Other outta-this-world sites:

- UFO's at `ernie.bgsu.edu/~jzawodn/ufo/`
- The National UFO Reporting Center at `www.nwlink.com/~ufocntr/`
- UFOmind: Area 51 at `www.UFOmind.com/area51/`

Four-Legged Friends: Pets and Other Loyal Pals

Pets give unconditional love — unless your pet is a piranha. I know a guy who had one. Suffice it to say that piranas don't make very good pets. Besides, they have funny eating habits. They like fingers, especially those attached to your hand. Anyway, if you'd like to see one of the coolest pet sites on the Web, go to PetStation, shown in Figure 5-21. At this Web site, you can talk to a vet, discuss pet stuff with other pet owners, and enter your pet in "Pet Photo of the Month." Visit PetStation at `www.petstation.com`.

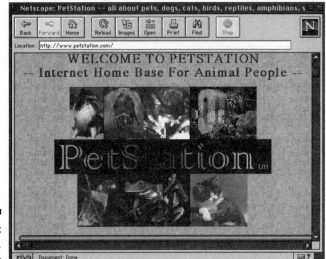

Figure 5-21:
PetStation.

Other animalistic sites:

- ✔ The Virtual Dog Show at www.dogshow.com
- ✔ CyberPet at www.cyberpet.com
- ✔ Pet Source at www.petsource.com
- ✔ Your Guide to Pets on the Internet at www.acmepet.com/
- ✔ Cat Fanciers at www.fanciers.com
- ✔ ZooNet at www.mindspring.com/~zoonet/

Them Folks in Funny Costumes: The Performing Arts

The Kennedy Center has a unique program that encourages kids to pursue the performing arts — it's called "Young Performing Artists Showcase," and it presents the wonderful achievements in the performing arts by kids all across America (see Figure 5-22). This site has audio and video clips of the plays that have been showcased. The Web Spotlight area provides access to arts-related information worldwide. Other areas include arts-related "By Students" and "For Students" pages. Follow your dreams to town.hall.org/places/Kennedy/ArtsEdge/YoungArtist/ or to artsedge.kennedy-center.org/artsedge.html.

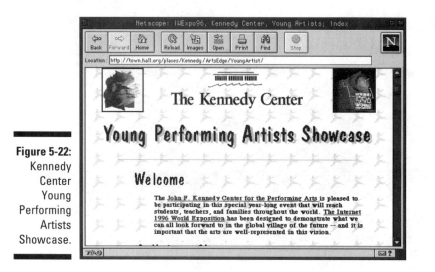

Figure 5-22:
Kennedy
Center
Young
Performing
Artists
Showcase.

Other on-stage sites:

- Joe Giegel's Favorite Theatre Related Sources at `pscinfo.psc.edu/~geigel/menus/Theatre.html`
- The Complete Works of Shakespeare at `the-tech.mit.edu/Shakespeare/works.html`
- Playbill On-Line at `www.playbill.com`
- OnBroadway at `artsnet.heinz.cmu.edu/OnBroadway/`

My Personal Favorites: Bookstores and Libraries

If I go to the mall, my shopping experience can be summed up with "Me want shoes; me buy shoes; me leave mall." My sister, on the other hand, has a different opinion of shopping. Hers is "Me want shoes; me buy shoes, dresses, makeup, perfume, more shoes, more dresses; me want to live in mall." My sister can spend days in there. It's a shame the malls close at night. As you can tell, shopping with her is not an easy task. But when we *do* go shopping together, I make sure that the mall has a bookstore. Then, when she's in the midst of trying her sixteenth outfit, I make a break for it and head for the nearest bookstore. What was the purpose of this story? The purpose was . . . I forget. Oh, yeah. Bookstores! That's right, bookstores. The Web has an extensive collection of bookstores and libraries. Although I have more fun in real bookstores, the ones on the Web are nothing to sneer at. Amazon.com Books, for example, has a catalog of over a million books (see Figure 5-23). You can look up a book even if you don't know the exact title of the book or the exact name of the author. This cool site is at www.amazon.com.

Figure 5-23:
Amazon.com
Books.

The Library of Congress is also on the Web (see Figure 5-24). The Library of Congress probably has the largest catalog of books in the world. But that's not all it has — it also has a learning section with information about people, places, and events. This great source for research on school projects is at lcweb.loc.gov/.

Other bookish sites:

✔ The Ingram Book Kahoona at www.ingrambook.com/TITLEWAVE/ titlewave.html (Parents, check out the titles of good books at this site.)

✔ The Children's Literature Web Guide at www.ucalgary.ca/~dkbrown/

✔ The On-line Books Page at www.cs.cmu.edu/web/books

Figure 5-24:
The Library
of
Congress.

Artsy-Fartsy Stuff: Museums

The world's greatest museums are on the Web. Although nothing can compare to actually visiting the Sistine Chapel in Vatican City, seeing it on the Web is the next best thing. The International Council of Museums has a site on the Web, titled "Museums Around the World," at which you can find links to hundreds of museums, including the famous Louvre and Smithsonian museums (see Figures 5-25 and 5-26). Enjoy meandering through the museums at `www.icom.org`.

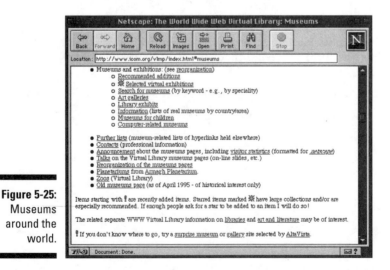

Figure 5-25:
Museums
around the
world.

Figure 5-26:
The Louvre.

Other fascinating sites:

- ✔ The New York University listing of children's museums at www.nyu.edu/gsas/nyunyc/science.html
- ✔ Eureka! The Children's Museum at www.demon.co.uk/eureka/
- ✔ The Leonardo da Vinci Museum at cellini.leonardo.net/museum/main.html
- ✔ World Wide Arts Resources at wwar.com

Family Fun: Amusement Parks

Don't you just love going to places like Disney World or Universal Studios? For one day, you can let yourself go. Run from ride to ride, eat totally obnoxious and unhealthy food, spend scads of money — all guilt-free. No reading boring books, no writing too-short papers, no homework assignments, no cleaning up your room. The fun parks, such as Disney World and Universal Studios, now have home pages, too. And are they beautiful! Check out the Disney World site at www.disney.com/DisneyWorld/ (see Figure 5-27).

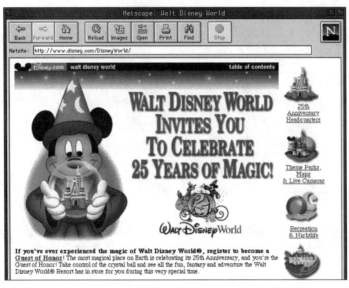

Figure 5-27:
The Disney-
World Web
site.

Other fun-filled sites:

- Disneyland at `www.disney.com/Disneyland/`
- Universal Studios at `www.mca.com/`
- Six Flags at `www.SixFlags.com/`

Chapter 6

Research: Needle in a Webstack? Nooo Problem

. . . .

. . . .

*I*f the Web was an organization or a company, it would be the largest single storehouse of information in the world. The Web has more information than any single library anywhere. And people are adding more and more information to the Web every day — 24 hours a day, seven days a week. Even when you're sound asleep and snoring away (and boy do you snore loud! I can hear it all the way in New Jersey) someone in another part of the world (where it's still daylight) is working on the Web and adding stuff to it. And because of that, whatever you're looking for is probably somewhere on the Web. Your information may be buried somewhere in a college or a laboratory, in a country far, far away, or in a library just around the block.

So how do you dig up this stuff? How can you get your hands on it? How do you find the stuff you're looking for? Simple — *ask and you shall receive*. You do need to know *who* to ask and *how* to receive, though.

Who Put All This Information on the Web?

Doctors, adventurers, engineers, news reporters, scientists, poets, high school kids, college students, and people like you and me can put info on the Web. Yeah, really! Even *you* can add stuff to the Web. Everybody and his brother does it, so why not you? Refer to Chapter 16, and you'll see how easy it is to add your two cents to the Web. Not only is it easy, it's free. Doesn't cost a penny. None. Zip. Nada. No strings attached.

Okay, So How Do I Find What I Want?

In this chapter, I show you two main ways to find information on the Web:

- ✔ Look for information in a *cyber-library* — a place where information has already been stored subject-wise for you. One such cyber-library, and probably the best one of them all, is *Yahoo!* The fine folks at Yahoo! spend every minute of the day on the Web. They search the Web so that you don't have to. When they find something that looks good, they add the Web site to their list, a list that is very extensive, covers a wide variety of subjects, and is very well-organized.

- ✔ Search the Web yourself. Although Yahoo! is a great place to look for stuff, you may not find what you want in its list, especially if you're looking for something very, very specific. The reason? Yahoo! can't possibly keep track of all the stuff people put out on the Web. Its staff does a very good job of finding and organizing information, but sometimes even Yahoo! can fall short.

Are you ready to begin searching? A ton of treasure is just waiting to be discovered. By the way, the figures in this chapter are Windows 3.1- and Netscape-based.

Yahoo!

Yahoo! has many categories — and many subcategories within each of the categories. Most of what you're looking for will fall into those categories. To search Yahoo! follow these steps:

1. **Open your browser, type** www.yahoo.com **in the Location text box, and press Enter or Return to get to the Yahoo! site (see Figure 6-1).**

2. **Click on the topic you want to search.**

   Let's see if Yahoo! has anything about one of the greatest athletes of our times; the man who defies gravity, the greatest basketball player ever, Mr. Basketball himself, Mr. I-can-run-circles-around-you-even-though-I-was-away-for-a-year . . . Mr. You Know Who I Mean. You don't? Quick! Somebody alert the UFO patrol. We've finally found an alien. Of course, you know who I'm talking about. Michael Jordan. . . . That's MISTER Jordan to you. To get to information about Michael Jordan, you select the topic <u>Recreation and Sports</u>. A window like the one in Figure 6-2 appears.

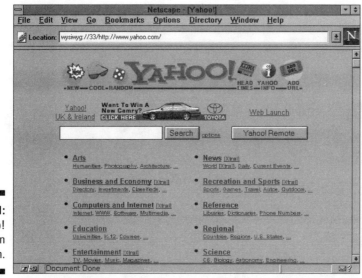

Figure 6-1:
The Yahoo!
main
screen.

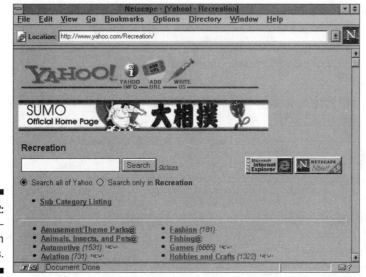

Figure 6-2:
Yahoo! —
Recreation
and Sports.

Whaddaya mean you don't see no <u>Sports</u> in Figure 6-2? Did your mother teach you to talk like that? I think not! And, No. I don't want you to click on <u>Fashion</u>.

3. Click on the scroll bar on the right side of the screen to scroll down until you see the topic you want to search.

If you're searching for big MJ like I am, when you *do* see <u>Sports</u>, click on it. Another Yahoo! window appears with another list (see Figure 6-3).

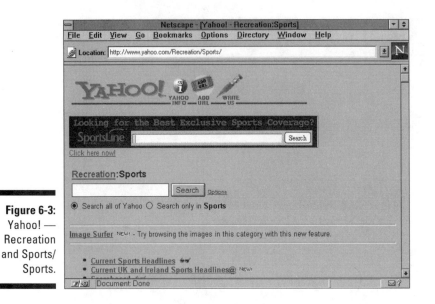

Figure 6-3:
Yahoo! —
Recreation
and Sports/
Sports.

4. Scroll down and click on the topic you want to search.

Yes, you click on <u>Basketball</u> if you're doing the same search I'm doing. Do you need me to show you the figure that appears? I thought not. Here it is anyway (see Figure 6-4).

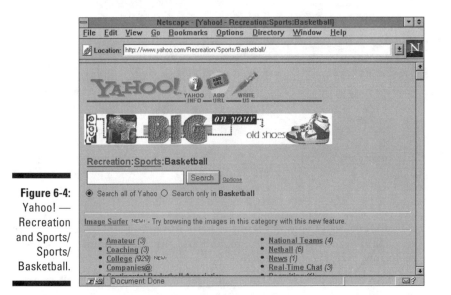

Figure 6-4:
Yahoo! —
Recreation
and Sports/
Sports/
Basketball.

5. Click on the subtopic you want to search.

Don't know 'bout you, but I'm clicking on <u>National Basketball Association (NBA)</u>@. And guess what? You have to put up with yet another figure — Figure 6-5. Now you know why what we're doing is called browsin' around the Web; we're certainly not zipping through any galaxy. I suspect that one of these days, when you're moving through a Web site at a snail's pace, a big, old spider's gonna come up behind you and say, "Whatcha doin' in *my* Web?"

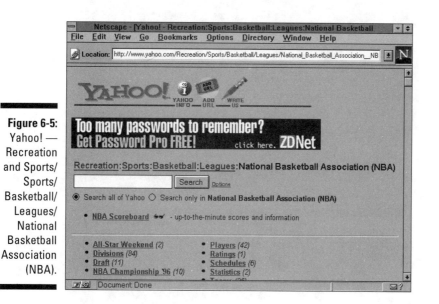

Figure 6-5:
Yahoo! —
Recreation
and Sports/
Sports/
Basketball/
Leagues/
National
Basketball
Association
(NBA).

6. Click on the appropriate topic.

(My editor wants me to sound more dignified.) The topic on which I prefer to click is <u>Players.</u> (There. Is that dignified enough?)

I was hoping we were finished, but no. You have to take a look at Figure 6-6. Well, at least we're getting close, real close.

7. Scroll down the list of players and click on the topic.

Tada! There's his name: M-i-c-h-a-e-l. Right there in Figure 6-7. Click on <u>Michael</u>@.

Yahoo! has several sites listed for Mr. Chicago Bulls. Click on any of them to pay homage — and remember to do the "We're not worthy" salute once you get there (see Figure 6-8). Remember, too, that you've seen only the tip of the iceberg. These sites lead to many more resources on the $50-million man.

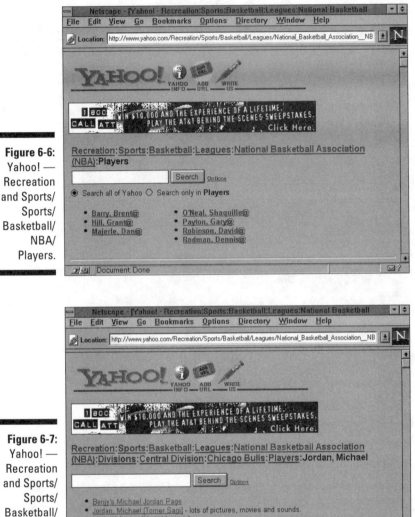

Figure 6-6: Yahoo! — Recreation and Sports/ Sports/ Basketball/ NBA/ Players.

Figure 6-7: Yahoo! — Recreation and Sports/ Sports/ Basketball/ NBA/ Players/ Jordan.

Now the Web is yours. You can use Yahoo! to explore the Web until your fingers can't click, your eyeballs pop out, and cobwebs hang from your elbows.

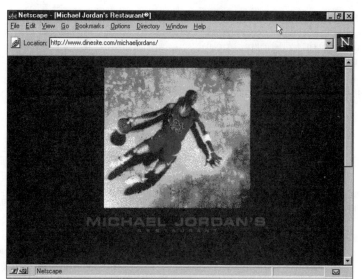

Figure 6-8:
Benjy's
Michael
Jordan
home page.

AltaVista — Mother of all searches

Let's leave Yahoo! and search the entire Web for what you want. Remember this URL — www.altavista.digital.com — 'cause you're gonna use it often; and you're gonna hand it out often, too. To whom? To your friends who'll come complaining to you, "How come you find all that neat stuff, and we don't?" That's when you say, "Dude, did you try AltaVista?" (Substitute "Girrrrl" for "Dude" whenever necessary.) Obviously, your friends haven't used AltaVista, so you hand them the address faster than Urkel puts on a pair of uuuuuugly plaid pants.

Quite simply, AltaVista is the best search tool on the Web. And boy, is it fast! In case you're wondering just how fast AltaVista is in finding the information you request, consider this. In the time you take to press the Enter or Return key on your keyboard, AltaVista goes through 30 million home pages, trying to match your request. When AltaVista finds matches, called *hits*, it puts all of them together in one neat package and sends it to you. Yup. All that in less than a second. And AltaVista does that second after second, minute after minute, hour after hour, all day long. AltaVista answers 21 million requests each day from people all over the world. AV kicks!

Question: What company makes AltaVista?

Answer: Digital Corporation. And if you're one of techies who's just dying to know — AltaVista runs on an AlphaServer 8400 5/300 machine, the most powerful computer made by Digital.

As scientists grow old, they lose their ability to talk in easily understood language. It's as if they're told, "Now that you're a scientist, you're forbidden to use words that normal people can understand. You are expected to make up ten new words every year." So every night the Mad Scientists Club meets for a game of Scrabble, and the scientist who ends up with the highest number of weird new words wins. Why am I telling you this? The next few paragraphs answer that question.

AltaVista's powerful search engine is a lot stronger than the little engine who thought he could. A *search engine* is nothing more than a software program that takes your request for information and tries to match it with a gigantic collection of information it has. When the search engine finds a match, it tells you, "Listen up! Here's what I found," and then throws the matches on your screen.

The AltaVista search engine gives you the choice of performing either a simple query or an advanced query. Huh? A *query* is a search request that you make to the computer. That's it. A *simple query* is a search request that is simple. No duh! Okay, here's what I mean. A question like "How many flavors of ice cream does Baskin Robbins have today?" is a simple query because the person behind the counter with the funky ice cream scoop doesn't have to think much to answer that question. An *advanced query* is something like "How many flavors of ice cream does Baskin Robbins have today that are neither brown nor white in color, have nuts in them, don't have *chocolate* in their name, and have marshmallows?" Then you duck to avoid the funky ice cream scoop coming at you at warp speed.

AltaVista can handle simple and advanced queries. You don't have to take my word for how well AltaVista answers your queries. Come along. Test it yourself.

Giving AltaVista a simple query

Ease into using this AltaVista thing the simple way. To make a simple query, follow these steps:

1. **Open your browser, if it's not already open, and go to the address** www.altavista.digital.com.

   You don't get a choice here. If you want to use AltaVista, you gotta do things her way. Figure 6-9 shows the main AltaVista screen, which always automatically gives you the Simple Query option. Don't ask me why. Maybe AltaVista wants to make things simple or something.

Query text box

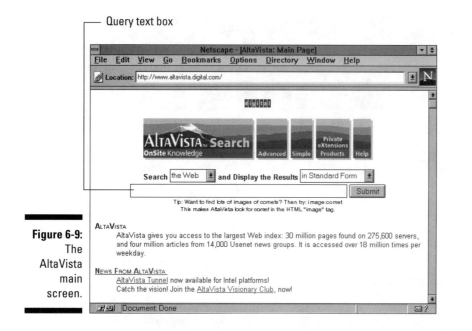

Figure 6-9:
The
AltaVista
main
screen.

2. **Type the subject you want to find in the query text box and click on Submit.**

To do a search for the TV show *Friends,* for example, type **friends**. AltaVista's reply to your query is shown in Figures 6-10 and 6-11. Remember that these results may be a little different from what you see, because . . . yup, you guessed it. . . . While you were snoring, somebody was adding new Web sites. A round of applause! Khrrrrrrrrrrrr!

When you take a closer look at the results, you probably notice a bunch of links you don't really care about, like listings for somebody's high school friends and childhood buddies. All you care about is Chandler, Phoebe, Ross, and the gang. So be a little more specific in your query, by using a plus sign (with spaces on either side of it) and another word.

3. **Click once in the query text box, type the topic you want, a space, a plus sign (+), a space, and more specific information to narrow your search.**

For example, you can type **+Friends + "TV show"** (with no punctuation at the end) to tell AltaVista to find Web sites that contain the word Friends (with a capital *F,* which is different from friends with a small *f)* and also includes the exact phrase *TV show* in it. Notice also that I used quotation marks. That's just a little habit I picked up in English class. Just kidding. The quotation marks tell AltaVista that I want it to look up two words, *TV* and *show,* when they appear together. Without quotation marks, AltaVista finds *TV* and *show,* but not necessarily together.

Figure 6-10:
AltaVista
lists the
results of a
search on
the word
friends.

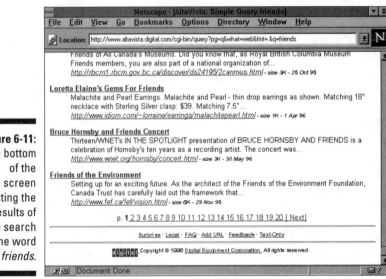

Figure 6-11:
The bottom
of the
screen
listing the
results of
the search
on the word
friends.

4. Click on Submit.

Figure 6-12 shows the search results. You can see that AltaVista got rid of 99.5 percent of the previous search results, narrowing them from 700,000 to just 2,000. But you still have too many sites to go through unless you have absolutely nothing to do between now and the time you graduate.

You can perform an even more specific search. This time, look for sites that contain the lyrics to *Smelly Cat* and other gems from Phoebe that didn't quite make it to the top of the Billboard charts.

5. Click once in the query text box and type the topic you want to find, a plus sign, another topic, another plus sign, and a third topic.

For example, you can type **+Friends + "TV show" + "phoebe's song*"** (again with no period at the end). The asterisk (*) after *song* means that I want AltaVista to find *song* and *songs*.

6. Click on Submit.

Figure 6-13 shows the result of this search. AltaVista narrowed its results to just 9 sites. Now, is that awesome or what; from 700,000 to just 9. Ready for a sing-along? Er, make sure that you put some feeling into *Smelly Cat.* Phoebe's kinda sensitive about it.

Figure 6-12:
AltaVista
search
results for
the words
Friends and
TV show.

Figure 6-13:
Search
results for
the words
Friends with
TV show
and
*phoebe's
song*.*

Giving AltaVista an advanced query

Whew! That simple query got really complicated, didn't it? Do you think you can take on an advanced one? Sure. Come on. You can handle it. I'll make it easy. An advanced query is different from a simple query in two ways:

✔ You have to use *operators,* words that give added meaning to a query. The following words are operators: AND, NEAR, OR, NOT. You get to practice using operators before you finish this chapter. Whoa! Get back here. It's not that tough.

✔ You can tell AltaVista to *rank* or display the results in order of their importance to you. For once, you get to say what's most important.

Let's say your science class has a trip planned for next week. Cool! A whole day outside the classroom. You're going to hang out in the woods, look for bugs and beetles, and become one with Mother Nature. Aaaah, this is life! But before you go, you want to get some information on this disease that the bully from seventh grade caught on his science trip last year. You remember that it had something to do with ticks and — maybe Lyme Disease, too. You can use AltaVista to dig up some info on those two topics — ticks and Lyme Disease. A search on *ticks* would result in thousands of hits, but you can use some fancy footwork to narrow down the results. Call in the operators.

AND *and* AND NOT *operators*

Our first operators AND and AND NOT are really cool — and easy to use, too. If you haven't given up on me and started a MUD game, you should have AltaVista on your screen and be ready to follow these steps:

1. **Click on the Advanced Query icon at the top of the page.**

   You then see Figure 6-14. Hmm. Looks as if AltaVista's waiting on you to type a bunch, right?

2. **Click in the Selection Criteria text box, type the first topic you want to find, the word and, and then the next topic you want to find.**

   In the example, you type **ticks and "Lyme Disease"** in the Selection Criteria text box. The operator AND in the text box tells AltaVista to find pages with the words *ticks* and *Lyme Disease* in them. The quotes around *Lyme Disease* are the way to tell AltaVista, "Yo! AV Dude! I want you to find the words *Lyme* and *Disease* together." If you don't use the quotes, AV finds pages with *Lyme* and *Disease* in them, but they may or may not be together. The words may be in separate paragraphs, something you're not particularly looking for. For example, the page could talk about the beautiful town of Lyme in Connecticut and then further down discuss diseases in the town of Lyme.

3. **Click in the Results Ranking Criteria text box and type the subject that is most important to you.**

   Not pizza, you turkey! You're working on your investigation into *ticks* and *Lyme Disease*, remember? When you type **"Lyme Disease"**, you tell AltaVista, "When you find matches for my advanced query, arrange them so that pages containing *Lyme Disease* in the title or header appear at the top of the list, followed by the pages that mention *Lyme Disease* the most (see Figure 6-15).

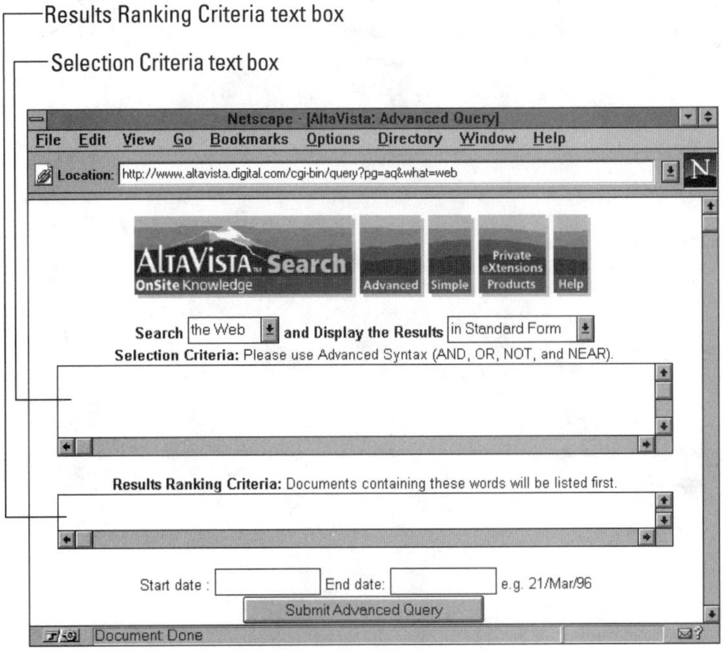

Results Ranking Criteria text box

Selection Criteria text box

Figure 6-14: The AltaVista Advanced Query page.

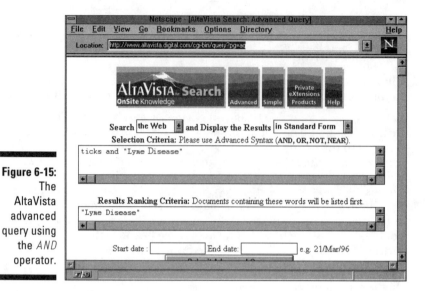

Figure 6-15:
The
AltaVista
advanced
query using
the *AND*
operator.

4. Click on Submit Advanced Query.

Figure 6-16 shows that AltaVista found about 800 matches for the query. Mega results!

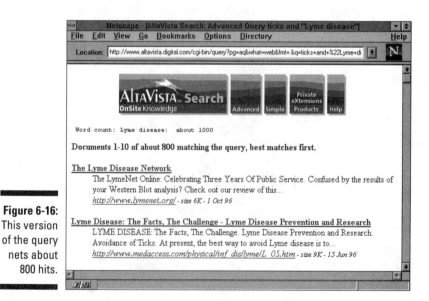

Figure 6-16:
This version
of the query
nets about
800 hits.

The AND operator and the AND NOT operator are cousins who behave the same way. Suppose that you want AltaVista to look for information on *ticks* but don't want any information on *Lyme Disease*. In that case, type your advanced search query like the one in Figure 6-17. Not very difficult, right? Hey, hey, hey! We're not done yet. Get back here.

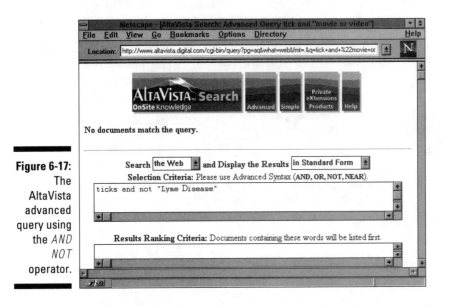

Figure 6-17:
The
AltaVista
advanced
query using
the *AND*
NOT
operator.

NEAR *operator*

The operator NEAR in the Selection Criteria text box tells AltaVista to find pages with words that are within ten words of each other. Why would this be helpful in an advanced query? Suppose that you're looking for information about someone's experience with *Lyme Disease*. Well, you can always go ask the bully, but that isn't in your best interests. Better stick with your pal AV and see if it can find a personal account by someone out there on the Web. In a case like this, the NEAR operator works wonders: by using NEAR, you're telling AV, "Yo! Alta Baby! Find me every page in which these two words are no more than 10 words apart from each other." Follow these steps to use the NEAR operator:

1. Click on the Advanced Query icon at the top of the page.

You then see Figure 6-14 again. Okay. You can handle that.

2. Click in the Selection Criteria text box, type the first topic you want to find, type the word near, and then type the next topic you want to find.

In your never-ending search for *tick* and *Lyme Disease* stuff, you type **"Lyme Disease" near "personal experience"**, as shown in Figure 6-18. Now if you use the operator AND instead of NEAR, AltaVista finds every page with *Lyme Disease* and *personal experience* in it, *but* the personal experience may very well relate to the author's wonderful experience on his recent trip to Disneyland. Although you're concerned with bugs on your class trip, I don't think Bugs Bunny is what you're looking for, right? The NEAR operator in your query keeps Bugs away.

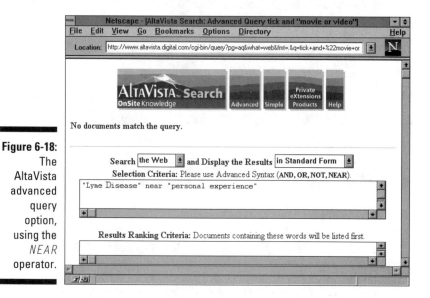

Figure 6-18:
The AltaVista advanced query option, using the *NEAR* operator.

3. Click on Submit Advanced Query.

AltaVista finds more matches for the query than you can even imagine!

OR *operator*

The operator OR says to AltaVista, "Give me information on at least one of the things I ask for." Okay, so you found a whole bunch of info on *ticks* and *Lyme Disease*, and you also read someone's sorry tale of what those nasty ticks did to him. But you want more. You want pictures of yucky skin sores. You want to see movies of yucky tick larvae. You are greedy. Well, if that's what you want, that's what you get. All you do is — yup, you guessed it —

ask AV. Pictures on the Web usually have .gif or .jpg attached to their filenames (.Gif and .jpeg are the two common graphics formats on the Web. Video clips on the Web usually have .avi, .mov, or .mpg attached to their names.) So follow these steps to get what you want — ugly pictures:

1. **Click on the Advanced Query icon at the top of the page.**

   There's that old Figure 6-14 again. Ho-hum.

2. **Click in the Selection Criteria text box, and type only one of the following:**

   ```
   tick* and (gif or jpg) and "Lyme Disease"
   ```

   or

   ```
   tick* and (avi or mov or mpg) and "Lyme Disease"
   ```

Whoa! Figure 6-19 shows the terribly complicated, overwhelming depressing query. With this query, you tell AltaVista to find pages with *ticks* and either .gif or .jpg picture files in them, or *ticks* and either avi, .mov, or .mpg files in them. Also, you ask AV to make sure that the pages are relevant to *Lyme Disease* and not to something like the *tick-tock* of a grandfather clock. Notice how I used the asterisk (*) after the word *tick* because I wanted AV to find information on *tick and ticks.* Also notice how I used the AND operator before and after the OR operator.

Figure 6-19:
The AltaVista advanced query option, using the *OR* operator.

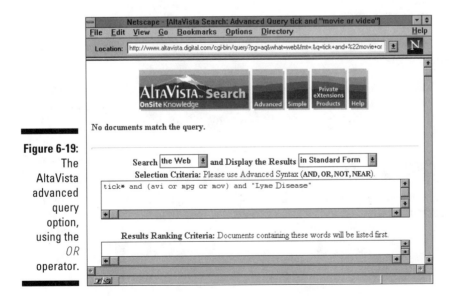

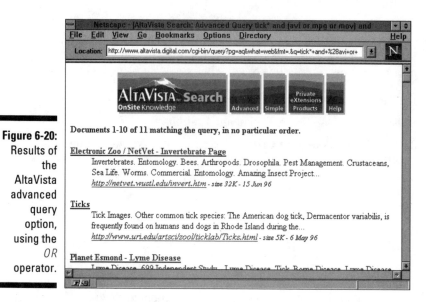

Figure 6-20:
Results of
the
AltaVista
advanced
query
option,
using the
OR
operator.

Figure 6-20 shows that AltaVista found 11 pages with videos or movies of ticks. Cooool!

In the preceding examples, you pushed AltaVista (and your brains!) to the limit when you used more than one operator together. Queries that use only the OR operator, for example, look something like this:

jordan or rodman

Now is that a pair or what? Frankly, I'd take either one of them on my team, wouldn't you?

If you want more information about using the computer in your school work, check out the book *TakeCharge Computing For Teens & Parents* by Pam Dixon (IDG Books Worldwide) or visit the Dummies Web site at www.dummies.com.

Keyword searches

What causes a home page to have its links highlighted in a different color and its title show up at the top of the page? Is it magic? Is it a secret code? Well, you're half right. A code creates the home page, a code that you can't see when you view the page, but it's not really a secret. It's just hidden away. Hidden away from our eyes, but not from mighty AltaVista.

Example of a keyword search

Suppose that you want to look for a picture of Jim Carrey on the Web. If we do a search on Jim, we'll end up with matches — thousands of 'em — of pages containing news and pictures of that totally crazy Jim. If we want a picture, we have to wade through all of the sites. Wouldn't it be great if we could simply home in on a picture? Absolutely! Here's where a keyword search comes in. (See Table 6-1 for some examples of keywords.) To create a search based on a keyword, follow these steps:

1. **Click on Simple to let AltaVista know that you're going with a simple query this time.**

2. **Click in the Selection Criteria text box and then type your keyword.**

   If you want a picture of Jim, for example, type **image:jcarrey.jpg**. When you do, you're telling AltaVista, "Find all pages that have *jcarrey.jpg* in the code."

   I know, I know, you're wondering what the .jpg is. Well, most pictures on the Web are one of two types: JPEG (.jpg) or GIF (.gif). When you see .jpg or .gif, you know you've got a picture on your hands. You don't want to know much more than that.

3. **Click on Submit.**

   AltaVista searches for the images.

4. **If you don't find any images you like, repeat Steps 1 through 3, but type this:**

   image:jcarrey.gif

Isn't AltaVista fantastica? Table 6-1 lists a few more neat keywords you can use in your searches:

Table 6-1	Keywords You Can Use in Searches	
To Find	*Use the Keyword*	*Example*
A picture of your favorite star	*image*	`image:claire.jpg` or `image:claire.gif`
A friend's home page	*url*	`url:bob.html`
A page with specific words in its title	*title*	`title:"NASA Home Page"`
A page with a link in it	*link*	`link:Oasis`

Just remember these important points as you type your keyword search:

- ✔ Type the keyword in small letters (*a, b, c*, not *A, B, C*).
- ✔ Put a colon (:) immediately after the keyword.
- ✔ Don't put any spaces between the colon and the next letter.

You now know enough about searching the Web to keep you busy for a long, long time. Go ahead. Search away.

PART III
Travel the Net

The 5th Wave   By Rich Tennant

"I don't care what your e-mail friends in Europe say, you're not having a virtual sleep-over here tonight."

In this part . . .

In this part, I introduce you to the most common use of the Internet — electronic mail, or e-mail. I show you how to send and receive messages. I also introduce you to the world of newsgroups in which you can talk to people, ask questions, and get answers you might not get elsewhere. A newsgroup is a great place for getting people's opinions and views on matters ranging from serious issues to cars to pets.

Chapter 7

E-Mail — A Way to Keep in Touch

In This Chapter

▶ Getting aquainted with e-mail

▶ Getting a message

▶ Answering a message

▶ Making a message

▶ Sending a message

▶ Snatching a message you shouldn't have sent out of the mailbox

▶ Printing a message

▶ Attaching files to a message

▶ Getting rid of files you don't want

▶ Using e-mail to receive news

E-mail, or *electronic-mail,* the most widely used part of the Internet, is also very easy to use. *E-mail* is software that lets you send messages over your computer. In the blink of an eye, you can send a message halfway around the world. You don't need to attach a stamp to it, you don't have to drop it off at the post office, and you don't need to wait for the postman to deliver a reply. Your message gets delivered at night, on weekends, on holidays, on birthdays, on bad hair days, on rainy days, on every days . . . I mean every day, 365 days a year. You type your message, you click on a button, and WHOOOOOSH! The mail's gone. It flies through the air at the speed of light and lands in your friend's mailbox . . . um, electronic mailbox, that is. If your friend is out somewhere, at a picnic, at the shore, at a sleep-over, gone camping, shopping, wherever, your message stays put in the mailbox until your friend comes home, opens the computer mailbox, and reads your message.

What Do You Need to Get E-Mail?

To use e-mail, you need the following:

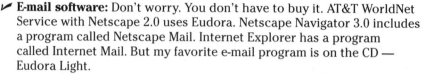

- ✔ **A modem:** You obviously have one by now.

- ✔ **E-mail software:** Don't worry. You don't have to buy it. AT&T WorldNet Service with Netscape 2.0 uses Eudora. Netscape Navigator 3.0 includes a program called Netscape Mail. Internet Explorer has a program called Internet Mail. But my favorite e-mail program is on the CD — Eudora Light.

- ✔ **An e-mail address:** Just as the post office needs to know your home address to deliver mail to you, the Internet also needs to know your electronic address to deliver e-mail to you. You already have an e-mail address. Don't know what your e-mail address is? No problem. Easy to find out: Just ask your parents. If they followed my instructions in Appendix B, they wrote it down on the Cheat Sheet in the front of this book. If they didn't, bug 'em to death until they do — politely, of course — or read the sidebar "What's my e-mail address?"

What Do You Do to Send an E-Mail Message?

How hard is it for you to write a note to your friend or, better yet, write a list of what you want for Christmas — or your birthday? Not too hard, huh? Well, using e-mail is just as easy. In fact, after you get the hang of using e-mail, you may never again scrounge around for a piece of paper or look for a pen that still has ink. Using e-mail is so much better.

So just how do you use e-mail? Well, regardless of which e-mail program you have, and you can find a bunch (check out the "So Many E-Mail Programs" profile if you don't believe me), the programs all work about the same.

To send someone an e-mail message, follow these steps:

1. **Open the window for creating a message.**

   Usually the programs don't leave you in the dark; they have a button with a picture that reminds you of writing a letter, or they have a Mail menu. Double-click on the button or the Mail menu option for sending or composing messages. The window for composing a new message appears. In Netscape, for example, choose Window⇨Netscape Mail. In Internet Explorer, click on the Mail icon on the toolbar and then choose New Message.

NERD ALERT

What's my e-mail address?

So you want to know your e-mail address? You want to be able to find it on your own? Well, here's how. Don't be afraid. It's really not that techie. You just have to do a little looking and thinking. Follow these steps to find your e-mail address in any browser or e-mail program:

1. Start the program.

2. Look closely at the menu bar.

   Do you see a menu titled Options or Special or Settings?

3. Click on the menu.

   Do you see any option in the menu that mentions mail?

4. Click on the mail-related option.

   A dialog box probably appears, listing all kinds of technical information. If you look closely at the information, you'll find something that has an *at* sign (@). That's your e-mail address.

   Do not change any information in this dialog box, or your e-mail won't work right.

5. Click on Cancel to close the dialog box.

   Aren't you good? You found your e-mail address without becoming a technogeek.

Those e-mail programs that don't have a button or a Mail menu just want to make you work, but don't let them trip you up. Try the File menu. Do you see a New Message option? If so, click on it. If not, keep opening and closing menus until you see one that has an option that mentions sending or composing new messages. Then click on the option. The window for composing a new message appears. Now was that a lot of work or what? Next time, maybe the programmers will wise up and just put the button out there in plain sight!

2. **Tell the program the e-mail address of the person you want to send the message to.**

   You don't know your friend's e-mail address? Don't look at me! I don't know it either. For this first time, you're going to have to call your friend to find out the address.

3. **Fill in the Subject text box.**

   The Subject text box is kind of like Caller ID. What you type in the text box lets the person receiving your message know whether he or she should read the message — or just blow it off. Don't be cute, here, unless you're in a wild and crazy mood or your friend needs a good laugh.

4. **Type your message.**

   Okay, I must admit — hunting around for the keys *is* a little frustrating, but not nearly as frustrating as reading your handwriting! So type your message and check it fro errors. (I'll bet you noticed that I misspelled *for!* Typos are annoying, aren't they?)

5. Send your message.

Most e-mail programs have a button that either says Send or has an envelope or postage stamp on it. Click on that button and away your message goes.

You clicked on Send, but your message didn't go anywhere — it just plopped to the ground, stuck in your computer. Know what the problem is? Make sure that you're connected to your Internet Service Provider — AT&T WorldNet Service, America Online, or CompuServe, for example.

Okay, now you have the basics of sending an e-mail message. If you can follow these steps, you can probably figure out how to use the rest of the program. In case you can't, read on. In the last half of the chapter, I explain step-by-step how to use Eudora Light, the e-mail software included on the CD. If you don't want to use Eudora Light but don't know how to do something in your e-mail program, read through the section that explains how you do it in Eudora Light and then try it out on your e-mail program. I'm certain you'll be able to figure it out.

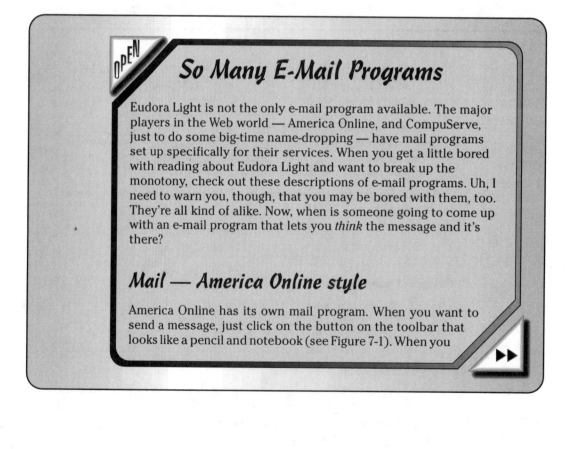

So Many E-Mail Programs

Eudora Light is not the only e-mail program available. The major players in the Web world — America Online, and CompuServe, just to do some big-time name-dropping — have mail programs set up specifically for their services. When you get a little bored with reading about Eudora Light and want to break up the monotony, check out these descriptions of e-mail programs. Uh, I need to warn you, though, that you may be bored with them, too. They're all kind of alike. Now, when is someone going to come up with an e-mail program that lets you *think* the message and it's there?

Mail — America Online style

America Online has its own mail program. When you want to send a message, just click on the button on the toolbar that looks like a pencil and notebook (see Figure 7-1). When you want to check for messages coming to you, click on the mailbox. To do fancier mail-type things, you have to use the Mail menu. What do I mean by fancier? Oh, you can look through lists of the mail that you've received or sent, and, if you're in a hurry, you can tell AOL to start up, go get your mail, send out messages you've written, and then close again, all in a matter of seconds. A cool thing about AOL is that you can make up your own e-mail name, something that shows your personality, such as KoolKid or 2Good2BTrue. Figure 7-2 shows the window for composing mail.

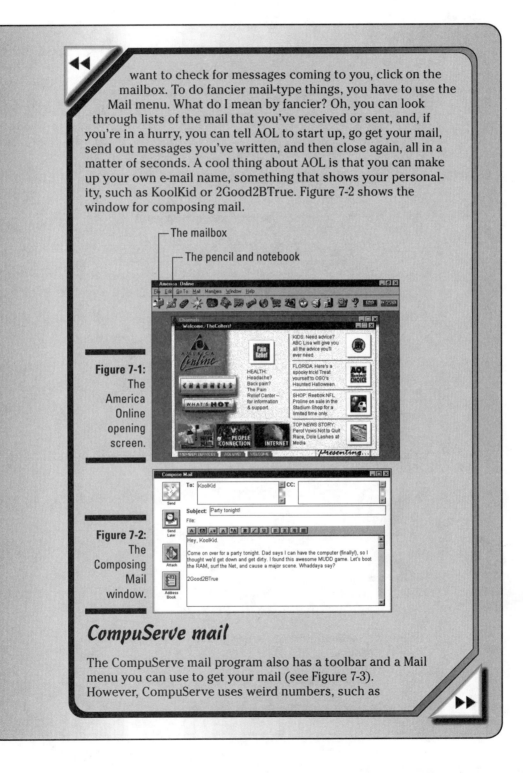

— The mailbox

— The pencil and notebook

Figure 7-1: The America Online opening screen.

Figure 7-2: The Composing Mail window.

CompuServe mail

The CompuServe mail program also has a toolbar and a Mail menu you can use to get your mail (see Figure 7-3). However, CompuServe uses weird numbers, such as

012345,6779, for their members' addresses. Boy, are those numbers hard to remember! Also, the way you address CompuServe messages and add names to the address book is pretty complicated (see Figure 7-4). Pretty strange-looking, isn't it? To make up for the inconveniences, CompuServe has a Member Directory that's easy to use. Just choose Mail➪Member Directory and type in whatever you know about the person you want to send a message to: first name, last name, city, state, ZIP code . . . then click on Search.

Figure 7-3:
The CompuServe opening screen.

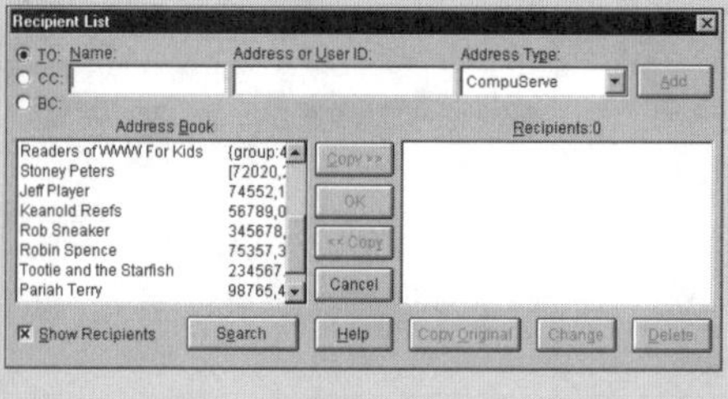

Figure 7-4:
The Recipient List you have to complete before you can begin a new message.

Internet Explorer Mail service

Guess what you do in Internet Explorer to create a new message? I'll give you a hint. Figure 7-5 shows the opening screen. Do you see any mail buttons? Do you see a Mail menu? Yup! In Internet Explorer, you choose File➪New

Message or click on the Mail button and choose New
Message. Then a New Message window appears, looking
like a memo pad with To, Cc, and Subject lines, plus these
little Rolodex-like buttons you click on to get to the address
book (see Figure 7-6). I especially like the Internet Mail toolbar at
the top. What do I like? The Undo button for undoing my mistakes,
the Paper Clip button for attaching files, and the Pen button so
that I don't have to type my name at the end of every message.

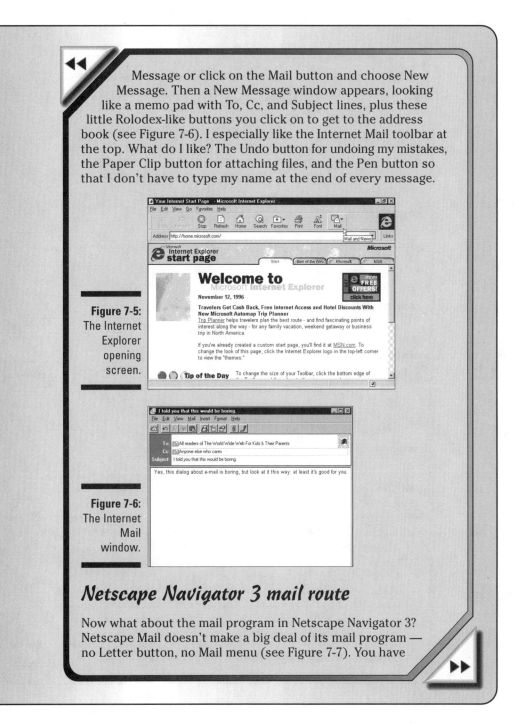

Figure 7-5:
The Internet
Explorer
opening
screen.

Figure 7-6:
The Internet
Mail
window.

Netscape Navigator 3 mail route

Now what about the mail program in Netscape Navigator 3?
Netscape Mail doesn't make a big deal of its mail program —
no Letter button, no Mail menu (see Figure 7-7). You have

◀◀

to click on the Window menu to get to Netscape Mail, a special window for conducting all your mailing business (see Figure 7-8).

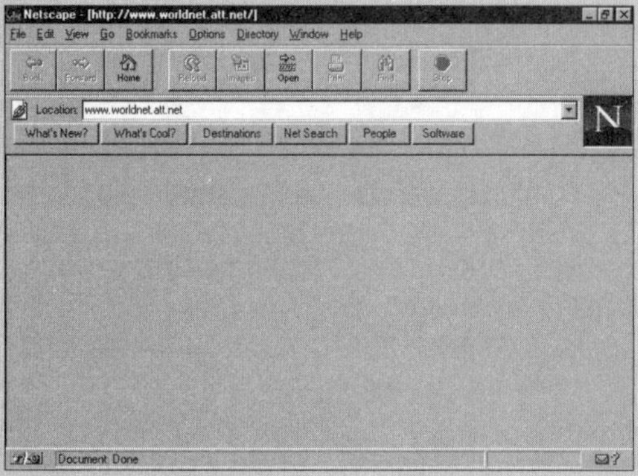

Figure 7-7:
The Netscape opening screen.

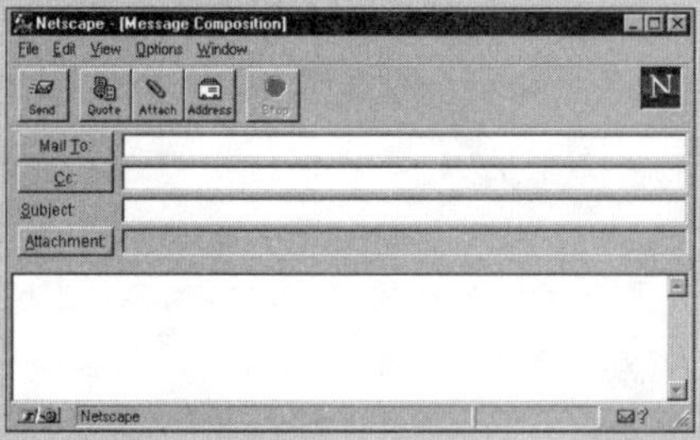

Figure 7-8:
The Netscape Mail window.

By the way, do you know what *Cc* in all the mail programs stands for? Neither did I, so I tracked down the oldest person I know and asked her. Back in the days before copiers, faxes, and e-mail, when people wanted a copy of a letter, they made a *carbon copy,* kind of like a sandwich. They put one piece of paper on the top, another piece of paper on the bottom, and, in the middle, a piece of carbon paper; it was regular paper (but light purple) on the side facing up, and coated with this black powder-like stuff (carbon) on the side facing down. Then, when the person typed or wrote a letter, the carbon copied everything to the paper on the bottom. (The things I write to get out of describing yet another e-mail program!)

Using Eudora Light

Eudora Light is the e-mail software of my dreams — no guessing here, and it's on the CD. See Appendix B for installation instructions. When you click the Eudora Light e-mail icon, you see a screen similar to the one shown in Figure 7-9. The menu bar has buttons for seven things you'll do all the time with Eudora Light. When you move your mouse pointer to any button and leave it there for about a second, a message describing the button appears.

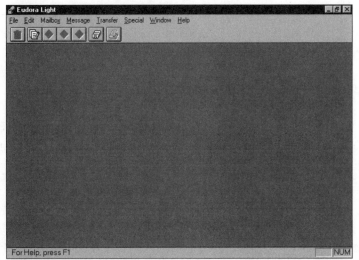

Figure 7-9:
The Eudora
Light
opening
screen.

Composing and sending an e-mail message

The section "What Do You Do To Send an E-Mail Message?" gives you the general steps for sending a message. Now let's get specific — Eudora Light-specific. *Composing a message* means creating or typing a message. After all, you do need to type something in your message before you send it. Sending a typed message — good! Sending a blank message — not good — unless, of course, you have supernatural powers and can communicate like Spock using mental vibrations in which case you wouldn't need e-mail to begin with. So while you're perfecting your telepathic skills, let me show you how to use Eudora Light to compose and send an e-mail message. (If you totally understood this the first time around, you'll breeze through this section in nothing flat.)

1. **Click on the New Message button (the one with the paper and pencil on it).**

   The window for composing a new message, shown in Figure 7-10, appears. The cursor is on the To line.

Figure 7-10:
The window
for
composing
a new
message.

2. **Type the e-mail address of the person you want to send the message to.**

   Be very careful when you type the address. To show you how easily you can make an error in typing an address, see if you can find the difference between the three addresses below.

Address 1:	bobsmith@worldnet.att.net
Address 2:	b0bsmith@worldnet.att.net
Address 3:	bobsmith@worldnet.attnet

   Address 1 is the correct one, while addresses 2 and 3 have errors. If you look closely, Address 2 has a zero, not an *oh,* in bob. Address 3 is missing a dot between att and net. Either of these mistakes prevents your message from being delivered to Bob Smith. So always make sure you type the address correctly, or else you'll keep wondering why Alan in Allentown or Tim in Timbuktu never replied to your messages when they never even got your messages!

3. **Click once on the Subject line and type a few words describing the purpose of the message, something like "A cool Web site!"**

   You don't have to type anything on the Subject line if you don't want to, but doing so tells the person who receives your message what the message is about. Not doing so is like calling someone on the phone and then refusing to tell them why you called.

4. **Click once in the body of the message (under the line beneath the word Attachments) and start typing your message.**

5. **Read through the entire message after you finish typing it.**

   Always remember to read your message before you send it. After you click on the Send button, it's difficult to stop a message from being sent — not impossible, but difficult.

6. Click on Send after you correct any mistakes.

As soon as you click on Send, Eudora Light turns on your modem, connects to the POP server, and sends your message. Eudora Light then stores the message in the Out mailbox.

If you want to check whether Eudora Light actually did store the message, choose Mailbox⇨Out. The Out mailbox appears and the message you just sent is listed last. Good going, Eudora Light.

Question: Is Timbuktu a real city?

Answer: Yup, it's a city in the African country Mail . . . ooops, my mistake. That should be Mali.

Ooops! I shouldn't have sent that. Can I fix it?

If you click on Send and then wish you hadn't, it may not be too late to stop your message from being sent. You can still stop the message from leaving your computer if you follow these steps:

1. Click on the Cancel button in the dialog box that appears as the modem begins dialing, shown in Figure 7-11.

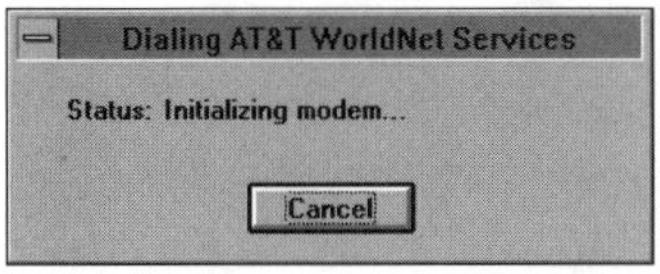

Figure 7-11:
This dialog box says that the e-mail is about to be sent.

> Dialing AT&T WorldNet Services
>
> Status: Initializing modem...
>
> [Cancel]

Eudora Light stops that message from being sent, but not before sending you a slightly hostile message similar to the one in Figure 7-12. No cause for concern. She's not really mad, just checking to see whether you know what you're doing.

2. Click on OK.

Eudora Light drops the stopped message into the Out mailbox and puts a Q in the left margin beside the message. Now. Are you ready to correct your mistake?

3. Choose Mailbox⇨Out to open the Out mailbox.

Q does not mean "You Quazy Kid." Q shows that the message has been *queued* — put into storage to be sent at a later date. The next time you send messages, all the queued messages are sent together.

4. Double-click on a queued message to change it.

Abracadabra! The message opens.

5. Make the necessary changes to the message and click on Send to send the new and improved message.

Eudora Light does the usual modem routine and sends your message on its way.

6. If you're still not ready to send the message, choose File⇨Close.

You see the message shown in Figure 7-13.

7. Click on Yes.

The message closes and hangs out in the Out mailbox until you're ready to send it.

Checking for Mail — Any Messages for Me?

You know how when you come home and find messages on your answering machine, you hit the Play button, and then wait while your machine rewinds to the first message, which takes forever, but you have to stand right there next to the machine, because if you step away to hang up your coat, your messages start playing, and you have to rush back to the machine, sometimes stepping on your cat, and you still end up missing a portion of the message, so you have to hit the Rewind button to listen to the portion you missed? (Wow! Was that question looong enough for you?)

When checking e-mail messages with Eudora Light, you're spared this hassle. You don't have to sit looking at your computer while it checks for messages. Consider this — every morning, the first thing I do is check my e-mail for new messages. I tumble out of bed, eyes half open, stagger over to my computer in a daze, sometimes stubbing my toe on my way there — ouch, dat hoyts — turn on my computer, and walk away. Yup, I roll right back into bed. Meanwhile, my trusty little computer boots up and automatically checks for mail. If the computer finds any, it downloads the mail, after which it yells (I'm serious about this) "You have mail!" When I hear that, I roll out of bed again and go read the mail. If my computer doesn't yell about new mail, I know that I don't have any — which means a few more minutes of sleep! Yeah!!!

To check for mail, all you do is double-click on the Eudora Light e-mail icon and start Eudora Light. Every time you start the program, the first thing it does is check for messages. Then you'll hear your modem start up and begin dialing.

Eudora Light automatically connects to another computer, which you can call *Mail Headquarters* for now, and asks, "Yo! Any mail for me?" If messages are waiting for you, Mail Headquarters replies, "Yup!" and starts downloading the mail from Mail Headquarters to your computer. After Eudora Light downloads all the messages, you see the message "You have new mail!" If you don't have any new mail, you see the message "Sorry, you don't have any new mail."

After Eudora Light copies (called *downloading*) all messages to your computer, your modem automatically disconnects from Mail Headquarters. All you had to do was double-click on one little icon. Is that service, or what?

No doubt by now you've seen the words *POP Server* on your screen. A POP server isn't what some dads think their kids are — their own personal servants — it's the Mail Headquarters computer from which your mail is downloaded. Your mail stays on the POP server until you ask for it.

Getting the mail

Eudora Light stores all the new messages that come for you in an In mailbox. Your job is to make Eudora Light hand over your messages. You do that by following these steps:

1. **Choose Mailbox⇨In or press Ctrl+I if you can't see the In mailbox.**

   Figure 7-14 shows the In mailbox and the messages in it. The messages with a black dot next to them in the left margin haven't been read yet.

	Admin	09:47 AM 10/7/96	11	IQuest Newsletter	
●	Viraf Mohta	12:30 PM 10/7/96	2	Chapter 11, callouts ar
	Viraf Mohta	04:47 PM 10/7/96	2	Chapter 17, callouts, e
	Linda Ericksen	09:23 PM 10/7/96	2	Re: Two chapters from n
	viraf mohta	08:39 AM 10/8/96	3	re: Book Cover material
R	Emily B. Kim	08:55 AM 10/8/96	4	chapter #1
●	Viraf Mohta	08:13 PM 10/8/96	2	Chapter 10 images
R	Viraf Mohta	11:43 PM 10/8/96	1	Cover
	viraf mohta	10:41 AM 10/9/96	2	re: Book Cover material
F	viraf mohta	03:31 PM 10/9/96	1	Add-on: Book Cover mate
	Viraf Mohta	10:33 PM 10/9/96	2	Chapter 18
R	Seta Frantz	03:06 PM 10/9/96	2	RE: TE for CDs
	Seta Frantz	09:15 AM 10/10/9	2	RE: TE for CDs
●	viraf mohta	12:05 PM 10/10/9	1	Chapter 19

Figure 7-14: The In Mailbox with unread messages — just a list. Ho hum.

2. **Double-click on a message to read it.**

   Without making a fuss, Eudora Light hands over your message.

3. **Choose File⇨Close or press Ctrl+W when you're finished with the message.**

   Eudora Light puts the message back in the mailbox and waits for you to tell her what to do.

PARENT TIP

Are you worried that your kid will be constantly checking the mail? How about scheduling a certain time or a couple of times a day to check the mail? You can set 4:00 p.m. as Mail Time at your house. If you establish this routine immediately, you'll have fewer hassles.

Replying to a message

Your friend Mikita sends you a message saying, "Listen, dude. I got two free passes to WaterWorld. Wanna go?" So? Are you going to wait forty days and forty nights before you tell Mikita you can go?" No way. You're gonna jump up from your seat, get your basic Parental Permission, run back to the computer, and zap your answer back ASAP! Here's how:

1. **Click on the Reply button (the one that looks like a U-Turn traffic sign).**

   Eudora Light pulls out the old reply window, which looks similar to the window for new messages (see Figure 7-15). Notice that the message you're replying to has been automatically copied into the text area of your reply message. The reason for this is simple. If you're writing to a hundred people everyday — I know people who get up to 300 messages a day — you may forget what you wrote and to whom. But when the person you wrote to quotes a piece of your original message in the reply, you can see what you wrote.

   The greater-than sign (>) in the left margin of each line tells you that the line belongs to the original message. You can delete the entire original message if you don't want to include it in your message. Or you can delete only certain parts of it and keep those parts which you're referring to in your message.

The greater-than signs

Figure 7-15:
The greater-than signs (>) show that this message is "quoting" from the original message.

```
vmohta@worldnet.att, Re: And the survey says.....
                                        Send
             To: "vmohta@worldnet.att.net"@worldnet.att.net
           From: "Barbara M. Terry" <barb_terry@iquest.net>
        Subject: Re: And the survey says.....
             Cc:
            Bcc:
    Attachments:
At 09:12 AM 10/4/96 -0400, you wrote:
>Hey there,
>
>I ran into this survey re: kids and the Internet. Thought you might like
>to see it. Go to:
>
>
>http://plaza.interport.net/kids_space/mail/FBdata/100396.html
>
>
>Viraf
>Content-Type: text/html; charset=us-ascii; name="100396.html"
>Content-Transfer-Encoding: 7bit
```

2. **Put the mouse pointer in the message area and press Ctrl+A to delete the entire message.**

   It's gone. But wait! I told you to leave the parts of the message that you're referring to in your message! Oh, another one of those "I didn't hear you" comments? Yeah, right. I was a kid once, too, ya know.

3. **Press Ctrl+Z.**

   You're cool. The message is back. All is right with the world. And you just used Undo, a handy little tool for anyone who messes up as much as you and I do.

4. Highlight the lines that you don't need and press Delete.

They're gone, but the really important stuff, Mikita's offer to take you to WaterWorld for free, is still there, waiting for you to type your response.

5. Type your message.

But you knew that was coming next, didn't you? Yeah, just put your mouse pointer under the line that you're answering, press Enter, and starting banging away at those keys, wherever they are.

6. Click on Send.

The message is on its way, and you're on your way to another day of sunburn, sand, water, and fun.

If you want to reply to a message without having to open it first, just select the message from the message summary by highlighting it, and then click on the Reply button.

Printing Messages

Sometimes you just have to get that message in writing — like the time that your dad phones from work and says, "I have to work late again tonight. But I promise you that tomorrow you and I will . . ." (fill in the blank with the thing you like to do most). Now you've got him, but you've got to get it in writing because tomorrow he'll forget what he promised. It's time to print that message. Just follow these steps:

1. With the message onscreen, click on the Print button — the one with the picture of the printer on it. Duh!

The Print dialog box shown in Figure 7-16 appears.

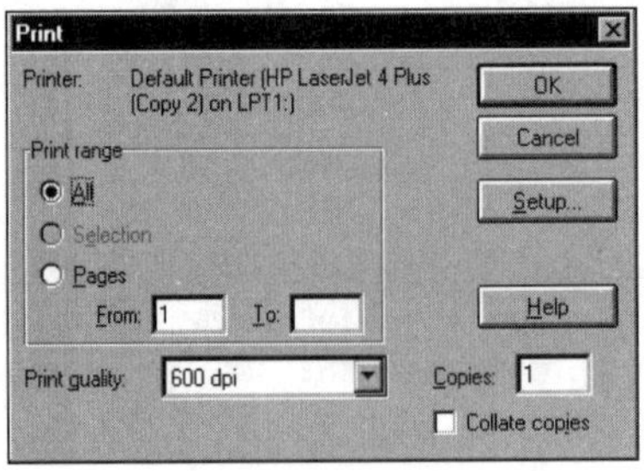

Figure 7-16: The Print dialog box — pretty boring.

2. Click on OK.

Now he's yours. Dad's got to follow through on his promise. You've got evidence that can and will be used against him.

What's that? You closed the message before you clicked on the Print button? No problem. Just open the In mailbox, highlight that valuable piece of incriminating evidence, and click on Print. There! You nailed him.

Sending Extra Stuff

I know you. You're not satisfied with just sending, receiving, and replying to messages. That stuff is too tame for you. You want something that will really prove how smart, how cool, how totally rad you are. Knock it off! Everyone knows that you're the best. Now show them by handling the tough stuff — attachments. (In case you don't know, *attachments* are files stuck to the message and sent along with it.)

Forming attachments — Sending a picture with your message

With Eudora Light, you can attach picture files — and nonpicture files too — to your message when you send it. Say that you want to send a picture of yourself to Grandma, who, by the way, is as hip as you are and can strap on her Rollerblades to cruise her way through the Web. None of this feeble browsing for her! To attach your picture to your message, follow these steps:

1. **Click on the New Message button to start a new message.**

   Yes, you already know how to do this. I'm just really scared that you haven't been reading every word I write, and you may skip over something important, so I repeat myself, repeat myself, repeat . . . .

2. **Insert the e-mail address.**

   I'm sure that you know your grandma's address. Don't look at me! I sure don't. Better call her if you don't.

3. **Type your message.**

   Don't make it so long that Grandma falls asleep waiting for it to download to her computer!

4. **Choose Mail⇨Attach File.**

   The Attach File dialog box shown in Figure 7-17 appears.

   You can't manually type a filename to add it to the Attachments line. You must follow Steps 4 and 5.

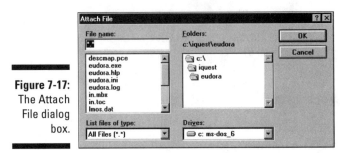

Figure 7-17:
The Attach
File dialog
box.

5. **Select the file you want to attach to the message.**

   Now, here you're going to have to show your stuff. You have to find
   the right folder or directory, find the right file, and then click on the file
   to attach it to your e-mail message. But I'm sure that you can handle it.
   No sweat.

6. **Click on OK.**

   Grandma's getting her file with the attached picture. My friend, you
   have done your good deed for the day. You have brought sunshine
   into someone's life. You have brightened someone's day. You are a
   true hero.

Detaching attachments

What if the picture you attached to Grandma's e-mail was actually a picture
of you in your school play costume when you were six? The one in which
you were a bee? Ugh. I can hear the laughing now. You've got to get that file
off Grandma's message immediately. To remove a file from the Attachments
line, follow these steps:

1. **If the message is still on the screen, highlight the file on the Attachments line.**

   Keep your cool. This will work. Trust me.

2. **Press the Delete key.**

   See? What did I tell you? The attached file is attached no more.

3. **Now get the right file and attach it.**

   Hurry up. Grandma's not going to sit around all day waiting for you to
   send her that picture, you know. She's got better things to do — like
   white-water rafting and backpacking through the Grand Canyon.

Finding out where Eudora Light stores attachments

When Eudora Light finds that a message sent to you has a file attached to it, she automatically takes that file and copies it to your hard drive. To use the file, you need to know where Eudora Light put the file. To find out, don't call Sherlock Holmes. Just follow these steps:

1. **Choose Special⇨Settings from the Eudora Light toolbar and scroll down to Attachments.**

   The Settings dialog box appears (see Figure 7-18). Pretty cool, huh? Don't bother anything in it. Just look at the bar under the words *Attachment Directory.* The bar tells you where Eudora Light keeps files she downloads.

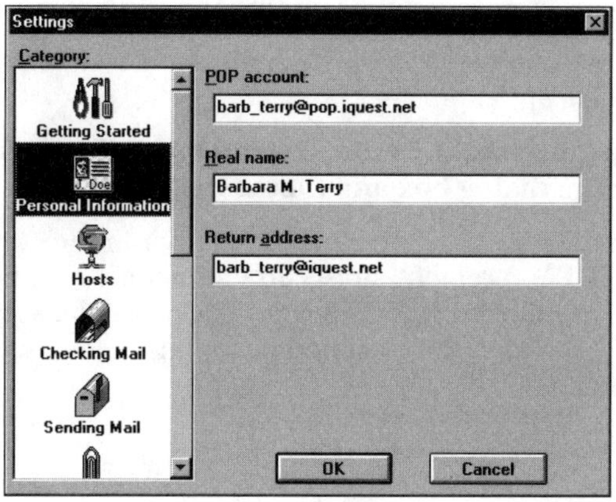

Figure 7-18:
The
Settings
dialog
box —
don't touch
a thing!

Figure 7-18:
The Settings dialog box — don't touch a thing!

2. **Write down everything on the bar, making sure that you get it right.**

   If you don't, you may never find your way to the file. Then you'll have to explain to whomever sent it to you, "Well, you see, I just couldn't find it. I'm sorry. I must have made a mistake when I wrote down the path." Yes, dude. Those letters on the bar are the *path* to your file.

3. **Click on OK.**

   I'll shut up about writing stuff down correctly so that you can go on your merry way toward taking a look at whatever file someone sent you for whatever reason.

Seeing attachments other people send to you

To view an attachment, you need to know which software was used to create the attached file. The easiest way to find out that is to ask the person who sent you the file. If he or she won't or can't tell you, check the letters at the end of the filename. If the file ends in .txt, you can view it by using any word processing program, such as Word or WordPerfect. On the other hand, if the file ends in something like .doc (a Word file) or .123 (a spreadsheet file), you usually need to have the software used to create the file before you can view the file. To view the file, follow these steps:

1. **Start the software used to create the file.**

   If your message has a letter created in Word attached, for example, start Word.

2. **Choose the software command for opening the file.**

   In Word (and most other programs), you choose File⇨Open. A dialog box for opening files appears.

3. **Open the file that you want by either typing the path and filename or selecting it from the dialog box and then double-clicking.**

   See? This is where the path — the name on the bar in the section "Finding out where Eudora Light stores attachments" — comes in handy. I told you you'd need it. Because you followed the steps, you get the Good Citizen's reward: The attached file opens, and you can use it however you want.

Zapping Made Easy

It's time to do a little housework. Get back here. Don't you run away the minute I mention housework. Your In mailbox is stuffed full, and your Out mailbox is not much better. Fortunately, you won't have to give up your Saturday morning snooze to get this job done. Zapping is a breeze in Eudora Light.

Zapping 101: message deleted

To delete one message, two messages, or a whole bunch of messages, follow these steps:

1. **Choose Mailbox⇨In.**

   The In mailbox list appears (see Figure 7-19). Boy, that sucker is crammed full. It has so many messages you can't even see them all. You can do this cleanup job the slow way, one message at a time, or you can do it the fast way, as many messages as you possibly can. The choice is yours. One at a time? Okay, but it's your life you're wasting.

2. **Click on the one message you want to delete in the In mailbox window.**

3. **Click on the Delete button (the trash can).**

   There! Are you happy? Your one measly message is gone. Now you have to repeat that action 200 more times. What? You're ready to do more than one at a time? Good.

4. **Click on the first message you want to delete in the In mailbox window, hold down the mouse button, and drag down until you have all the messages you want to delete.**

5. **Click on the Delete button.**

   One major zapping just took place. You are the Terminator of unwanted messages.

Hey, not so fast. You still have to clean out the Out mailbox. I'm waiting. Follow the same steps you used to empty the In mailbox. That's better.

Figure 7-19:
The In mailbox stuffed full.

	viraf mohta	11:55 AM 11/7/96	1	re: E-Mail changes
	viraf mohta	01:30 PM 11/7/96	1	Chapter 6 and revised images.
	Viraf Mohta	03:55 PM 11/7/96	2	Appendix B - 2 images
	Viraf Mohta	06:45 AM 11/8/96	2	(no subject)
	viraf mohta	07:41 AM 11/8/96	2	re: Appendix figure 2
	viraf mohta	12:11 PM 11/8/96	2	...no subject...
	viraf mohta	04:05 PM 11/8/96	2	Text for "See You See Me" Chapter
	Viraf Mohta	09:35 AM 11/11/9	11	Microsoft FrontPage 97 Beta for free.
	Viraf Mohta	10:40 AM 11/11/9	5	Online Kids: A Young Surfer's Guide to Cybe
	Viraf Mohta	10:50 AM 11/11/9	2	QuickCam picture
F	Winston M. Hogga	05:13 PM 9/26/96	3	Internet Explorer tech editing
	WWW Admin	04:26 PM 10/29/9	5	
R	LINDA E ERICKSEN	08:00 PM 11/11/9	1	Project 1
	Viraf Mohta	05:02 PM 11/11/9	2	Revised Websites URLs
	Viraf Mohta	05:13 PM 11/11/9	3	Permission for Using FreeZone
R	Viraf Mohta	06:03 PM 11/11/9	2	Message from FreeZone
	Emily B. Kim	04:29 PM 11/11/9	1	overview
	Robin Drake and	01:57 AM 11/12/9	1	Project 7 files attached

399/893K/57K

In

For Help, press F1 — NUM

Zapping 201: Oh no! I want my deleted message back

Sometimes you delete a message and then yell, "Oh, NOOOOOOOOO!" Not to worry. Deleting a message doesn't wipe it out of existence. The message just moves to the Trash mailbox. To recover a deleted message, follow these steps:

1. **Choose Mailbox⇨Trash.**

   A list of messages you've deleted appears. I'm not going to show you a figure because it looks just like an In mailbox, except that the word *Trash* is in the title bar.

2. **Click on the message you want to rescue from the dump.**

3. **Choose Transfer⇨In.**

   The selected message hops back into the In mailbox, happy to postpone its meeting with the Grim Reaper.

A deleted message can be recovered from the Trash mailbox only if the Trash mailbox hasn't been emptied since the message was deleted. Emptying the Trash mailbox gets rid of all messages within it.

You can now flood your friends' mailboxes with messages. Go ahead. It's free. But hold it. Have you done your homework and taken out the trash? You know your priorities.

Getting Personalized News — *Right in Your Mailbox*

Would you love to get your very own version of a news report delivered just the way you want it every single day? The latest sports scores and the hottest gossip can be yours if you go to www.merc.com and fill out a short form. I promise filling out the form won't take you more than five minutes. Tell Mercury Mail exactly what you want. Your customized news is then delivered hot off the press — straight to your mailbox every day.

Chapter 8

Newsgroups — A Whole New World

In This Chapter

▶ Discovering newsgroups

▶ Reading messages

▶ Replying to messages

▶ Adding new messages

*I*f you thought that the information on the gazillion home pages was more than you could handle, you ain't seen nothing yet. By the way, have you ever wondered about that phrase — you ain't seen nothing yet? Whoever invented it probably did so with only one purpose in mind — to confuse the people learning to speak English! Anyway, have I got a doozy for you — newsgroups!

What Are Newsgroups?

You know what a bulletin board is, right? When you have something to announce, you write it down on a piece of paper and stick it on the board. It's there for the world to see. You can consider a *newsgroup* to be a bulletin board — an *electronic* bulletin board. You don't need thumb tacks, paper, or glue to *post* (or send) messages on a newsgroup. All you need is a connection to the Internet. You type your message and send it to the newsgroup. After you send your message to a newsgroup, anyone on the Internet can read your message.

The Internet has about 18,000 newsgroups, collectively referred to as Usenet. Each newsgroup is devoted to messages on a specific subject. What kind of subjects, you ask? All kinds of subjects and all kinds of stuff. Everything under the sun: sports, science, computers, TV shows, music, hobbies, politics, games, jobs, religion, and astrology. Cool. You can find newsgroups for all these subjects and more. Some newsgroups obviously are set up by people with too much time on their hands. No, let me rephrase that . . . by people with waaaaaaay too much time on their hands.

But what's so special about newsgroups? After all, aren't there home pages for these things, too? Possibly, but home pages don't make for interaction like newsgroups do. When you see a home page, you go ooooooh, you go aaaaaaah; the graphics make you ga-ga. You go to the next page and do the same thing — that's usually the extent of your participation. On the other hand, think of a newsgroup as a place where you can exchange notes with people. You ask a question, and visitors to the newsgroup read those questions and offer help, if they can. With thousands of visitors to a newsgroup and potentially thousands of opinions, the discussions get pretty lively. Also, the chances of your question being answered are very high.

Here's an example of how you can use newsgroups: When my car was puking and flatulating and I couldn't make it stop, I asked for help from the auto newsgroups. Within two hours, people from various parts of the country sent in advice on what I ought to do. Their cars had gone through the same mood swings as mine, and they knew exactly what to do. Result: advice taken, car stopped puking, me happy man. What I'd been trying for over a month to figure out got solved in two hours on the Internet. Now is that cool or what? So, in short, if you don't know where to go with your questions, hit the newsgroups.

The world of newsgroups is no exception when it comes to the issue of adult content. Some adult Web sites have disclaimers, however ineffective they may be; newsgroups have none. Accessing adult newsgroups is no more difficult than accessing a nonadult one. I highly recommend that you install an Internet filter prior to using newsgroups. Refer to Appendix A for more information.

How Does a Newsgroup Get Its Name?

Newsgroups follow a very specific naming pattern. A newsgroup name looks like

```
alt.archery
```

Newsgroups are divided in large *categories* and that's how they get the first part of their names. In the case of alt.archery, the category name is alternative (shortened to the alt in the name). Examples of other newsgroups in the alt category are alt.culture.hawaii and alt.collecting.autographs and alt.books.anne-rice and alt.fashion and alt.fan.u2.

Some other categories and examples are the following:

Category	Example
Computer	comp.virus
Information	info.wisenet
K-12	k12.chat.senior
Miscellaneous	misc.fitness
News	news.groups
Recreation	rec.arts.comics.info
Sociology	soc.culture.jewish

Using Newsgroups

So are you ready to post a sign on the world's largest bulletin board, heh? Wanna see what kids like you from around the world have to say about issues that concern them? You're ready? Cool. Let's get going.

Reading a newsgroup

A newsgroup can have hundreds of messages within it. Sometimes you can get lost among all those messages. But because messages usually have subject titles, you can tell what a message is about — before clicking on it to read it. Get to a newsgroup, and I'll explain what I mean.

1. **Start your browser.**

   I'm using Netscape Navigator as you can tell from the figures, but Internet Explorer has access to newsgroups, too.

2. **Choose the commands for opening the newsreader.**

   When you choose Window⇨Netscape News in Netscape, a News Window similar to the one shown in Figure 8-1 appears. In Internet Explorer, you choose Go⇨Read News. Note that the figures in this chapter are shot in Windows 3.1.

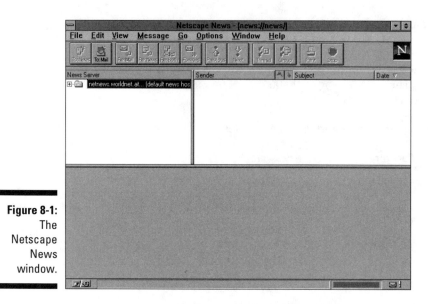

Figure 8-1:
The
Netscape
News
window.

3. **Double-click on the default news host folder icon.**

   If you have AT&T WorldNet Service, for example, click on
   `netnews.worldnet.att`. If you have Internet Explorer, you choose
   News⇨Options, click on the Server tab, and then select your Internet
   Service Provider (ISP).

4. **Choose the command to add the newsgroup to your list.**

   In Netscape, you choose File⇨Add Newsgroup, and the Netscape User
   Prompt window appears (see Figure 8-2). In Internet Explorer, you type
   the name of the newsgroup directly in the Newsgroups window, which
   is under the toolbar (and then skip Step 5).

Figure 8-2:
Netscape
User
Prompt
window.

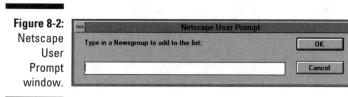

5. **Type the name of the newsgroup you want to read and press Enter or Return.**

If you type `alt.kids-talk.penpals`, you're telling your browser, "Dude, please connect to the `alt.kids-talk.penpals` newsgroup and download all the messages you see within it." Your browser wastes no time in fulfilling your command. After all, you're Aladdin and your browser's the Genie. The Genie gathers all the messages it can find within the `alt.kids-talk.penpals` newsgroup, displays them on your screen, and says, "Here you are, Master!" When this happens, your screen looks like the one shown in Figure 8-3.

6. **Click on a post to read it.**

Notice, in Netscape, that the window is divided into a section called News Server (on the left half of the window) and one with Sender, Subject, Date (on the right half of the window). Also notice that `alt.kids-talk.penpals` is listed in the News Server section and is also in the Netscape title bar. The things you see in the right half of the window are messages, called *posts*, within `alt.kids-talk.penpals`. Click on any post to read it. Figure 8-4 shows a displayed message. (The Intenet Explorer News window looks different but acts the same way.)

7. **To read the next post (the message listed directly under the current message in the message summary screen), click on Next. Within Internet Explorer, click on the next message in the list.**

The new post replaces the previous one.

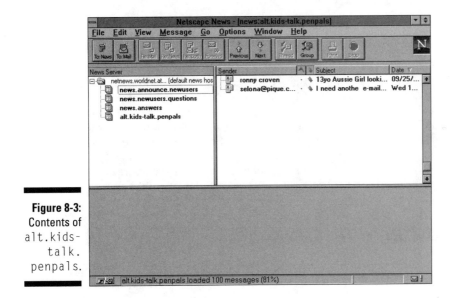

Figure 8-3: Contents of `alt.kids-talk.penpals`.

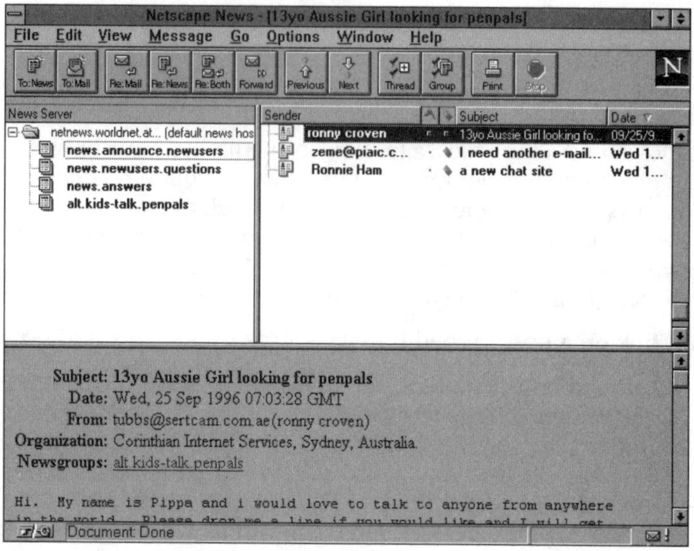

Figure 8-4:
Displaying a
message.

The message window shows:

Netscape News - [13yo Aussie Girl looking for penpals]

File Edit View Message Go Options Window Help

To:News To:Mail Re:Mail Re:News Re:Both Forward Previous Next Thread Group Print Stop

News Server

netnews.worldnet.at... (default news hos
news.announce.newusers
news.newusers.questions
news.answers
alt.kids-talk.penpals

Sender | Subject | Date
ronny croven | 13yo Aussie Girl looking fo... | 09/25/9...
zeme@piaic.c... | I need another e-mail... | Wed 1...
Ronnie Ham | a new chat site | Wed 1...

Subject: 13yo Aussie Girl looking for penpals
Date: Wed, 25 Sep 1996 07:03:28 GMT
From: tubbs@sertcam.com.ae (ronny croven)
Organization: Corinthian Internet Services, Sydney, Australia.
Newsgroups: alt.kids-talk.penpals

Hi. My name is Pippa and i would love to talk to anyone from anywhere
in the world. Please drop me a line if you would like and I will get

Document: Done

8. **To return to the previous post, the message listed directly above the current message in the message summary screen, click on Previous. Within Internet Explorer, click on the message listed above the current one.**

The message you clicked on is now displayed. I know, I know . . . like, duh! I'm only trying to help, okay?

9. **To read any another post, just click on it once.**

Sometimes, even though the message you selected is downloaded to your screen, you still can't see it. Huh? Does that make sense? Nope, but then neither do a lot of things. Have you wondered why people drive on the parkway but park on the driveway? See what I mean? So if your message is downloaded but you can't see it, your screen will probably look like the one shown in Figure 8-5. If it does, position your mouse pointer on the bottom edge of the message summary window. The pointer changes to a small double-line cursor, also shown in Figure 8-5. Hold down the left mouse button and drag the bottom edge of the window up to decrease the size of the window. Ta Da! There's your message. It was just hiding.

Posting a message

So far all you've done is read messages posted by others. How about posting a message of your own, too? Wanna do that? It's very easy.

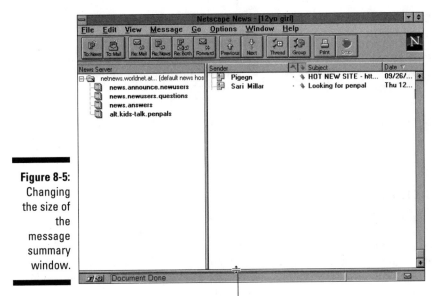

Figure 8-5:
Changing
the size of
the
message
summary
window.

Drag the bottom edge up

1. Click on the button or command to start a new message.

In Netscape, you click on the To: News button on the Netscape toolbar.
On the Internet Explorer bar, you click on New Message. A message
window like the one shown in Figure 8-6 appears. The cursor is automatically positioned in the Subject text box. Within Internet Explorer,
move the mouse pointer to the Subject text box, and click once.

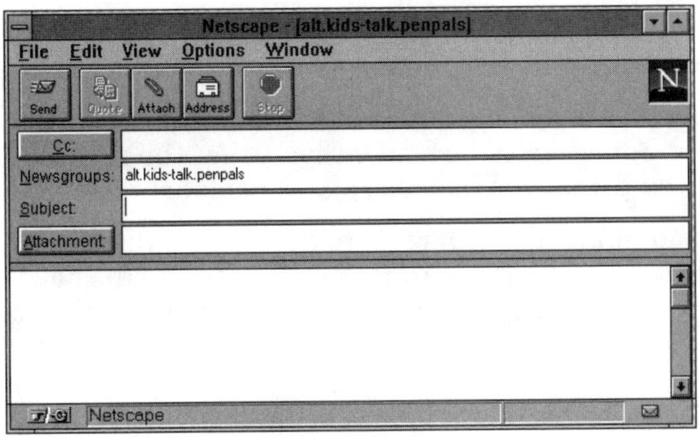

Figure 8-6:
The
Netscape
News
message
window.

2. **Type a subject in the text box.**

   Yes, you *have* to type a subject; I said so. It's the polite thing to do. Otherwise, people will have to open up your message and read it to know what it's about. What a waste of time that would be if you had 50 messages posted, none of them had a subject, and you had to open every single one to find out whether it interested you.

3. **Move the cursor to the message area of the window, and type your message there.**

   Don't try to be Shakespeare. Say what you wanna say and stop. The people reading your post will love you for it.

4. **Click on Send.**

   You're done! Easy enough for you?

Your message won't be displayed in the message summary window immediately. Sometimes it takes an hour or two for the message to show up. The length of time depends on many things, one of which is the frequency with which your Internet Service Provider sends the message to the Newsgroup. Some providers send messages immediately; others once every hour; and some once a day.

Replying to a post

Sometimes you want to add your two-cents worth to an ongoing discussion. Ever wonder how that phrase "add your two-cents worth" got started. Hmm? That'd be a good question to post in a newsgroup related to the English language. In the meantime, let me show you how to reply to a post. You can reply to a post in one of three ways:

- ✔ **Private reply:** A reply only to the person who posted the message.

- ✔ **Public reply:** A reply only to the newsgroup. Your reply is visible on the newsgroup and can also be read by everyone. The person who created the post you're replying to doesn't get a personal e-mail message.

- ✔ **Private and public reply:** A reply to the person who posted the message *and* to the newsgroup. Your reply is added to the newsgroup, and the person who created the post you're replying to gets your reply via e-mail.

Private reply

A reply only to the person who posted the message does not appear in the newsgroup message summary. Only the creator of the post gets your message via e-mail. To do this one-on-one type of replying, follow these steps:

1. Click on the button for replying to the person who created the post.

In Netscape, you click on the Re: Mail button in the toolbar. Within Internet Explorer, click on the Reply to Author in the toolbar. Figure 8-7 shows the window that appears. Notice that the original post, the message you're replying to, and the e-mail address appear automatically in the window. Finally, notice that the window doesn't have a text box titled Newsgroups: Your reply is being sent only to the person who posted the original message and not to the entire newsgroup. The cursor is positioned at the bottom of the window.

Address automatically entered

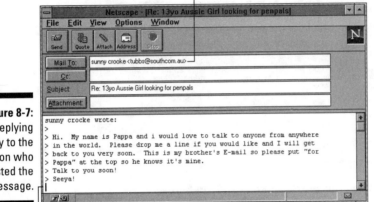

Figure 8-7:
Replying
only to the
person who
posted the
message.

Cursor

2. Type your message and click on Send.

Whooosh! The message is on its way.

Public reply

Before you post a public reply to a newsgroup, ask yourself whether you want everybody to read your message or just the person whose message you're replying to. Newsgroups often are flooded with posts that could very well have been sent directly to the person they were meant for, thereby reducing the number of posts on the newsgroup itself. To reply only to the newsgroup (also called *posting a public reply*) about a message you're reading, follow these steps:

1. Click on the button for replying to the group.

In Netscape, you click on the Re: News button in the toolbar. Within Internet Explorer, click on Reply to Group. Figure 8-7 shows the window that appears. Notice that the original message, the one you're replying to, is automatically typed in the body of the text. Also notice that, unlike the window shown in Figure 8-7, the one below doesn't have a text box titled Mail To, but it does have one titled Newsgroups. Netscape is telling you that the message is being posted to the newsgroup only. Notice that the original post (the message you're replying to), is automatically typed in the body of the text. The cursor is positioned at the bottom of the window.

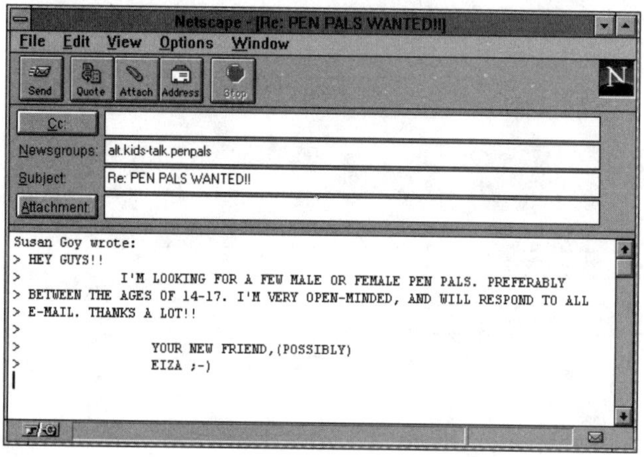

Figure 8-8:
Replying
only to a
Newsgroup.

2. Type your message and click on Send.

Away your message goes — available for the whole world to see. By the way, was that *tac* I saw instead of *cat?* You did check your spelling, didn't you?

Private and public reply

To send a reply to the person who posted the message you're reading and at the same time post the message on the newsgroup, follow these steps:

1. Click on the button for replying to the person who created the post *and* the newsgroup.

In Netscape, you click on the Re: Both button. Within Internet Explorer, click on Reply to Group, and then type the e-mail address of the person whose post you're replying to. A message window similar to the one shown in Figure 8-9 appears. Notice that on this screen, unlike the ones shown in Figures 8-7 and 8-8, both the Mail To text box and the Newsgroups text box are displayed: The message is being sent to the person who posted the original message and to the newsgroup.

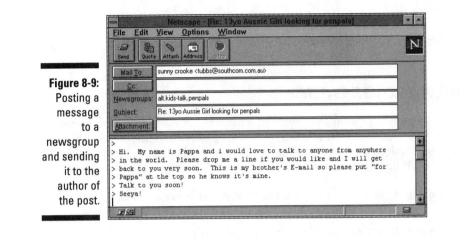

Figure 8-9:
Posting a
message
to a
newsgroup
and sending
it to the
author of
the post.

2. **Type your message and click on Send.**

Yes, I checked. You did spell *cat* correctly. Just kidding.

Printing a message

Since we all know how easily your handwriting can pass for Greek, don't you think you'd rather just print a message than write it down — especially if it's l-o-n-g. I thought so, too. Great minds think alike. Here's how you print a message:

1. **Highlight the message you want to print (or leave it open if you're reading it).**

2. **Click on the Print button. Within Internet Explorer, choose File⇨Print.**

The Print dialog box appears (see Figure 8-10).

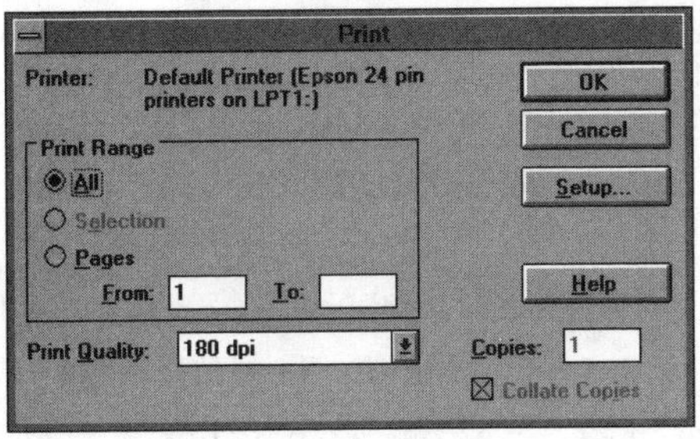

Figure 8-10:
The Print
dialog box.

3. Click on OK.

Buzzzzzzz — your message is coming out of your printer.

Saving a message

Sometimes you may want to download a message and keep it for reference. Finding a message on your hard drive is a lot easier than finding something in that bottomless pit you call your desk drawer. To save a message to your hard drive, follow these steps:

1. Highlight the message you want to save (or leave it open if you're reading it).

2. Choose the command for saving the message.

In both Netscape and Internet Explorer, this command is on the File menu. A Save Message As dialog box like the one shown in Figure 8-11 appears.

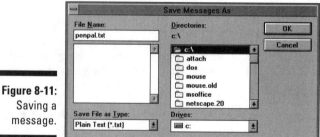

Figure 8-11:
Saving a
message.

3. Make sure that the folder or directory to which you want to save the message is selected.

I always save my messages from newsgroups to a special folder I created and named NEWS. Notice that the filename in the File Name text box is something really weird like untitled.htm. Whoa! How about changing it to something we all understand?

4. Type a different filename — something like penpal1.txt, **in the File Name text box.**

Now that's a little better, don't you think?

5. Select the Plain Text or .txt format in the Save File as Type text box.

The HTML Files format in Netscape has a whole bunch of code, making the message harder to read. You don't want that format.

6. Click on OK if you're using Netscape. Click on Save if you're using Internet Explorer.

Your message is saved.

Newsgroups for Kids

Now that you know how to move around a newsgroup, check out the following newsgroups:

- ✔ k12.chat.elementary
- ✔ k12.chat.junior
- ✔ k12.chat.senior
- ✔ rec.animals.wildlife
- ✔ rec.music
- ✔ rec.collecting.stamps
- ✔ rec.juggling
- ✔ rec.martial-arts
- ✔ rec.music.video
- ✔ rec.pets
- ✔ rec.puzzles
- ✔ alt.books
- ✔ alt.brain.teasers
- ✔ misc.fitness
- ✔ alt.chess.bdg
- ✔ alt.chess.ics
- ✔ alt.comics.batman
- ✔ alt.comics.superman
- ✔ alt.comics.peanuts

With 18,000 newsgroups in existence, newsgroups provide an ideal medium for kids to exchange ideas and get an insight into what people in other parts of the world have to say about issues of importance to them. As a class project, you can have your students connect to a newsgroup related to a topic you're studying and find out more about that subject by communicating with users of that newsgroup.

PART IV
Welcome to Funtasia

The 5th Wave   By Rich Tennant

"Hello, 911? A giant has my Mom and Dad trapped in a maze, and my sister's being chased by flying toasters. Can you tell me how to rescue them?"

In this part . . .

This part is my absolute favorite of the book. After you've had enough of home pages and e-mail messages, this part is where you'll hang out. It'll become your favorite part of the book, too. I guarantee it, because this is where I show you how to turn your computer into a radio, a telephone, a VCR for watching video, or a TV for watching others live on the Web. That's not enough, you say? Okay, you asked for it. I also show you how to chat with others in different parts of the world and play live games on the Web. How 'bout that, huh?

Chapter 9

So Much Software, So Little Time

. . . .

In This Chapter

▶ Games R Us — games on the Web

▶ Viruses and creepy things

▶ Freebies for the taking

. . . .

*B*efore I tell you anything in this chapter, I want you to drop whatever you're doing, copy the following note and post it on your refrigerator.

I_____ hereby request that all Aunts, Uncles,
   (sign your name here)
Grandparents, and well-meaning friends to refrain from giving me software for my birthday, Christmas/Hanukkah, Bar Mitzvah, confirmation, graduation, and all those wonderful times of the year when you show you love me. Feel free to substitute gifts with cold hard cash. Your cooperation will be truly appreciated. Thank you.

Signed_____
                    (sign your name here)

You're wondering why I'm asking you to shoot yourself in the foot, right? Why am I asking you to kill the goose that lays the golden egg? Fear not, my friend. Remember, I'm on your side. I'm lookin' out for you. I have only your best interest at heart. You see, most of the time when you get computer games as birthday gifts or whatever, the folks who give 'em to you have never played a game in their lives. They go to a computer store, pick up whatever's closest to the cashier, wrap it in fancy paper, and hand it to you with a big slurpy kiss — eeewww — hoping that you'll unwrap the paper and go "Keeeeeeeewwl. That's just what I wanted." And sometimes that's exactly what you do.

Being the nice person that you are, you hate to hurt their feelings. But who are you kiddin'? We all know that you'd rather get the latest and greatest computer game that money can buy, or even just the money itself so you can buy that latest version of *Quake* yourself. You've been dying to get your hands on it, even to try it once — *just once*. But it's too late now. You have your lame software, and you're stuck with it. But I feel sorry for you. So sorry, in fact, that I'll share a secret with you.

I'm going to show you a place where you can download the latest versions of the games you love to play. What's even better is that you can download them for *free*. Yeah, free! You download 'em, then take 'em out for a test drive, see if they get your adrenaline pumping just like you thought they would, and then drop hints on Grandma to pick 'em up for your birthday. Sometimes dropping hints is not enough. You have to write her a note.

Downloading software off the Web is easy and tempting, because there's software out there for almost any application you can think of. But a word of caution here. Over 8,000 viruses are mutating in downloadable files on the Web, waiting to go off like time bombs on unsuspecting users' computers. You can never be too careful. All it takes is one little virus to ruin your day — and your data. If you don't know what a virus is, you will know by the time you finish this chapter.

Shareware, Freeware — Whatware?

Shareware is software that the manufacturer shares with you — before you pay for it. The purpose of shareware is to let you try it, see if you like it, and then have you pay for it. *Freeware* is software that is . . . um . . . free. Doesn't take a rocket scientist to figure that one, huh? It's a gift from the manufacturer to you.

The Web has tons and tons of shareware and freeware. A lot of manufacturers make their software available on their Web sites for people to download freely. But I don't think you have enough time to go hunt down these manufacturers, hit their sites, look for the software, and then download it. Heck, you have other fun things to do like math homework. And because we all love math and wouldn't want you to lose a second working on it, I've decided to direct you to some Web sites that gather such software and put it all in one place for people to download. So, are you ready to get some software?

Games galore

Or should I say *Games Domain* galore. That's the site we're flying to. Games Domain is one of the most popular game sites on the Web. Not only does it have a bunch of games to download, but get this — it also has a section that gives you hints, tips, and tricks to kick some alien toosh on your favorite space invaders game so *you* don't get blown to bits every time they attack. Now is that cool or what? The site also has a Review section in which you can read game reviews. This section is particularly helpful in giving advice so that you don't buy a game, fire it up, and then go, "Ugh . . . this is lame. Why did I even bother?" Because if you take it back to the store where you bought it and demand a refund, the manager's polite reply usually goes something like, "Where's the security guy when you need him? SOMEBODY CALL SECURITY! We have a minor problem with this customer here, now *don't we?*" All you're asking for is your money back, and for the store to shelve games in proper categories — *"Awesome Games," "Games That Are Okay," "Bad Games" "Games That Should Be Burned."* Now is that asking too much?

Some Windows-based games that you can download are really large files and can take about half an hour to download on a 28.8 modem. Some files take even longer — as long as an hour. If you have a 14.4 modem, prepare to wait longer still. In Netscape, you can continue surfing by choosing File⇨New Web Browser even while the file is downloading. If you're using Internet Explorer, you can do the same thing by choosing File⇨New Window. But note that if you have a slow computer with a slow modem, opening another window isn't such a good idea because it slows down the download itself. In which case, I have a better suggestion. Go do your homework, and check back in an hour.

On that note, let's go to Games Domain and download some stuff, shall we?

1. **Open your Web browser and go to** www.gamesdomain.com.

   When you connect to the Games Domain site, you should see the screen shown in Figure 9-1.

2. **Click on the <u>Direct Download</u> icon.**

   You should see the screen shown in Figure 9-2.

3. **Click on the words <u>No plug-in</u> on the left side of the screen (look at Figure 9-2 to see what I mean).**

   You click on <u>No plug-in</u> because you don't want to waste time downloading and installing a plug-in when the main purpose of your visit here is to get your slimy hands on some gnarly games. Plug-ins can wait. Games can't. Don't get me wrong. The plug-in is pretty cool, but you want games, and you want them now!

Figure 9-1:
The Games
Domain
Web site.

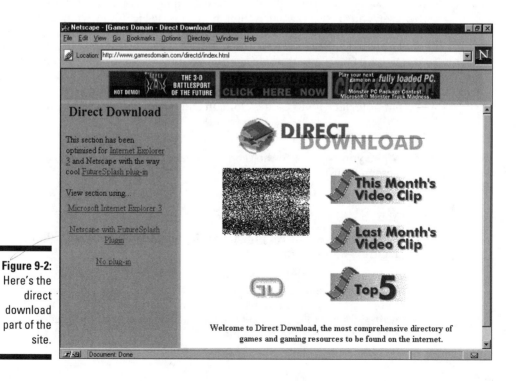

Figure 9-2:
Here's the
direct
download
part of the
site.

So what's the *plug-in* all about anyway? It's some cool animation to view while you're downloading games. It's a waste of time, however, if all you want to do is download games.

4. **Next, you get a screen listing a variety of computer systems. Click on the type of system you use from the choices in the left margin.**

   For example, if you run Windows 95, click once on <u>Windows 95</u>. The screen shown in Figure 9-3 then appears. The Contents section in the left margin lists the categories of games. I should think that you can find something to your liking in one of them.

5. **Choose the section that you want.**

   Suppose that you want to download DOOM95, for example. I guess that falls in the Arcade/Action section. So click on <u>Arcade/Action</u>. You should now see a window something like the one in Figure 9-4, listing all games within the Arcade/Action category.

6. **Click on the game you want to download.**

   In our example, you're after <u>DOOM95</u>, so click on it. The screen you get (shown in Figure 9-5) provides some information about the game and the file you're about to download.

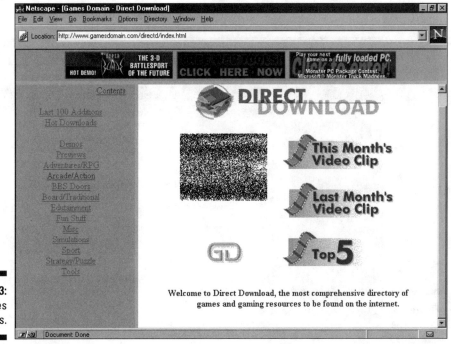

Figure 9-3:
Games
categories.

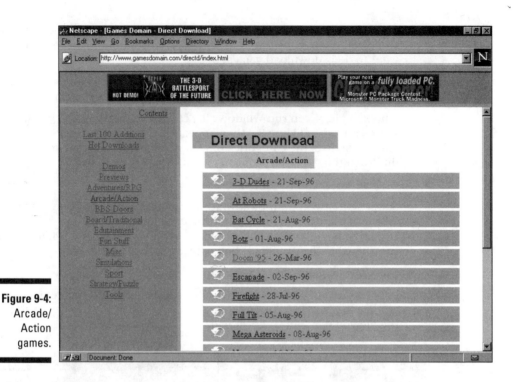

Figure 9-4:
Arcade/
Action
games.

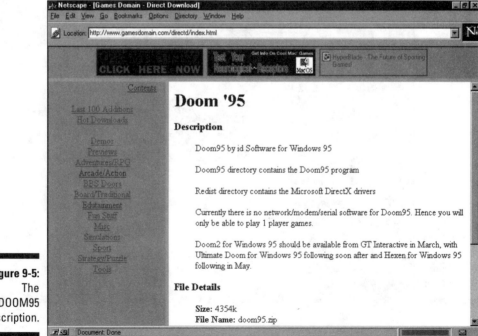

Figure 9-5:
The
DOOM95
description.

7. **Scroll to the bottom of the screen to see the links for downloading the file and click on the link for the location nearest to you.**

   If you're downloading from the U.S., for example, click on the link that appears next to U.S. The Unknown File Type message window shown in Figure 9-6 then appears.

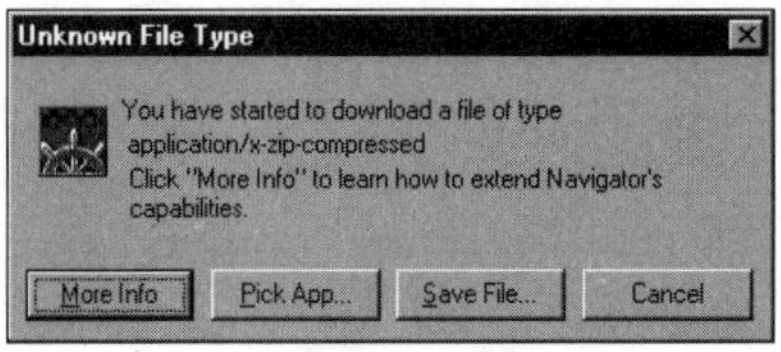

Figure 9-6:
How do you
want to
handle the
downloaded
file?

> **Unknown File Type**
>
> You have started to download a file of type
> application/x-zip-compressed
> Click "More Info" to learn how to extend Navigator's
> capabilities.
>
> [More Info] [Pick App...] [Save File...] [Cancel]

8. **Click on Save File.**

   The Save As dialog box appears, asking you to choose a folder in which to save the file.

   You should always have separate folders for every kind of software you download — to keep your hard drive clutter-free and organized. Soooo unlike your room.

9. **Click on the little down-arrow by the Save in text box and then select drive C to move to your root folder.**

10. **Click on the Create new folder icon and create a new folder named** DOOM.

11. **Double-click on the newly created folder to make it the current folder.**

    Your screen should look like the one shown in Figure 9-7. DOOM should now appear in the Save in text box.

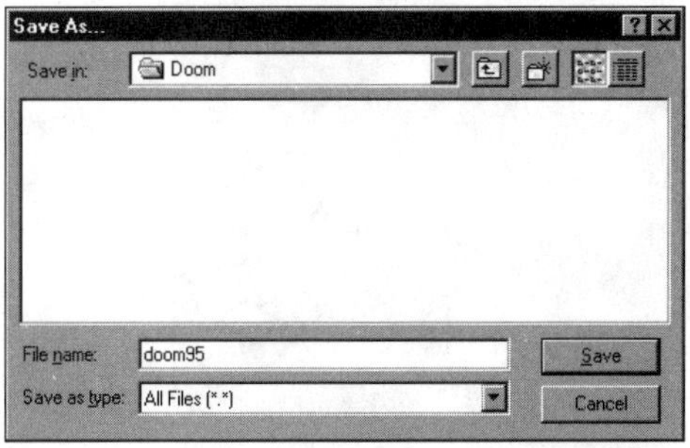

Figure 9-7:
Download
the file in
the new
folder.

> **Save As...**
>
> Save in: [Doom]
>
> File name: doom95   [Save]
> Save as type: [All Files (*.*)]   [Cancel]

12. Click on Save.

The download begins, and you see the screen shown in Figure 9-8. Notice the estimated download time shown in the window. Now go find something fun to do while the file downloads.

Figure 9-8: Downloading the file.

Saving Location	
Location:	ftp://ftp.gamesd...demos/doom95.zip
Saving	C:\Doom\doom95.zip
Status:	833K of 4354K (at 0.7K/sec)
Time Left:	01:15:29

19%

Cancel

13. When the download is complete, go to the DOOM **folder.**

You find a file there. That file is a *compressed* file that has within it many other files. Instead of downloading each of those files one by one, they're all squeezed or *zipped* into one file.

14. Double-click on the filename to unzip the files.

You should then see a window something like the one shown in Figure 9-9, with a whole bunch of files scrolling by. In a minute or so, they stop scrolling, and the files are unzipped on your hard drive.

TIP

If you don't have PKZip or WinZip, check out the CD. Appendix B gives the instructions for using it.

Depending on the program you use to unzip the files, you may need to indicate where you want them to be *extracted* (unzipped) and answer another question or two. It's easy. The window also may look a little different than the one in Figure 9-9. No biggie there, either.

Figure 9-9: Unzipping files.

```
Finished - Pkunzip                              _ □ ×
Auto        ▼
Inflating: RFMK2V.DLL
Inflating: RFMK2V.INI
Inflating: S3.DRV
Inflating: S3.VXD
Inflating: S376DD16.DLL
Inflating: S376DD32.DLL
Inflating: S3ADE.DLL
Inflating: S3DD16.DLL
Inflating: S3DD32.DLL
Inflating: S3MPG.DLL
Inflating: S3VDE.DLL
Inflating: S3_765.DRV
Inflating: S3_765.VXD
Inflating: SUPERVGA.DRV
Inflating: SXCTEXT.DLL
Inflating: TSENG.DRV
Inflating: TSENG.VXD
Inflating: TSNGDD16.DLL
Inflating: TSNGDD32.DLL
Inflating: VIDEO7.VXD
Inflating: WD.DRV
Inflating: WD.VXD
Inflating: TSS3_765.DLL
Inflating: S3_CP3CQ.DLL
```

15. **Close the window after the files unzip.**

16. **Go back to the** DOOM **folder and double-click on the icon named Doom95.**

    Ta da! There it is. You now have the DOOM95 game on your computer.

17. **Download as many games as you want (or until your hard drive is full, whichever comes first).**

Wait — there's more

Just when you thought it couldn't get any better, there's more good stuff to be found at Games Domain. What would you say if I were to give you all the hints you need to kick some alien hiney on your favorite game or solve that last step that prevents you from becoming Arch Angel on that game you've been playing for four months now, but still getting nowhere? You'd say "No way," to which I'd, of course, reply, "I have a way!!!"

Jump back to the main Games Domain screen shown in Figure 9-1. Then click on Games Info. You see the screen shown in Figure 9-10.

Click on Universal Hint System to open the screen shown in Figure 9-11.

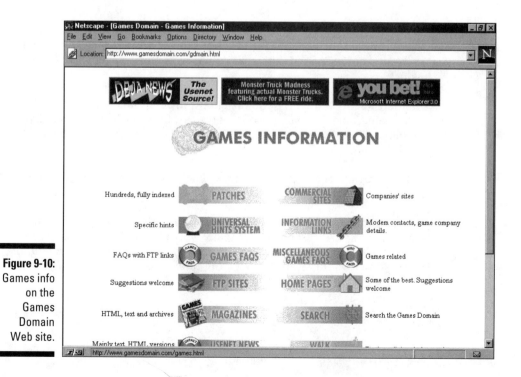

Figure 9-10:
Games info
on the
Games
Domain
Web site.

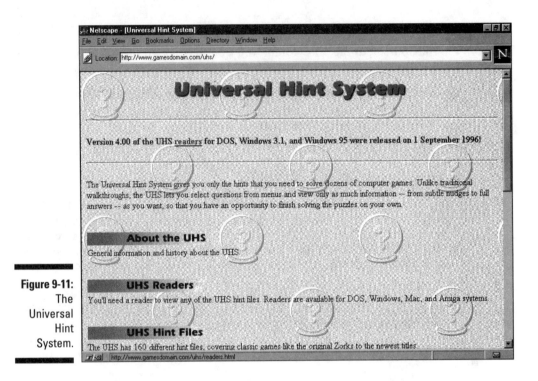

Figure 9-11:
The
Universal
Hint
System.

Click on UHS Hint Files. What you see is an alphabetical listing of over 160 games. How 'bout that, huh? I told you this was one awesome site, didn't I? Go ahead, knock yourself out . . . and then go to Duke Nukem 3D. Now we're talking!

And there's more still. After you take notes for your favorite game, go back to the main Games Domain page in Figure 9-1. Click on Top 5. This link takes you to the screen shown in Figure 9-12. This screen shows the top five most popular games.

To read a review of any of those games, click once on the game icon. For example, if you click on Quake, you see the screen shown in Figure 9-13.

This is a good place to come and check whether the game you're planning to buy with your hard-earned cash is really worth it. Or else the game store manager will again have to call Security on you when you ask for a refund. Now we don't want that to happen more than twice a week, do we?

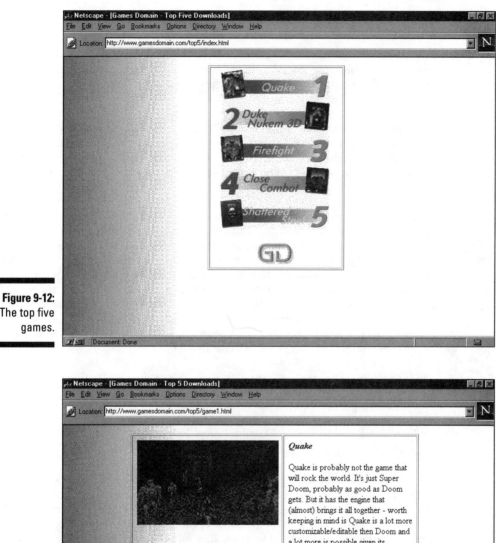

Figure 9-12:
The top five
games.

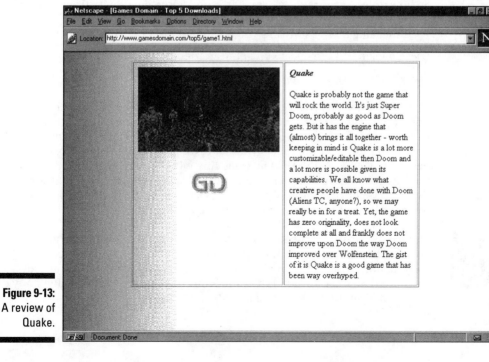

Figure 9-13:
A review of
Quake.

Viruses and other creepy things

We all know what it's like to catch the flu. The first thing you say when the doctor says that you have the flu is "Awesome . . . no school!" But that's not what you'll say when your computer catches a virus. Trust me. It's not a nice feeling.

A computer virus is just a piece of software (like your game software or your word processing software). The only difference is that a virus does harm to your computer. A virus can destroy all the data on your hard drive. One minute your data is there; the next minute it's gone. A virus is created by jerks who have nothing better to do.

Your computer can catch a virus just like you catch the flu virus — if you're not careful. How? Well, a virus hitches a ride on some good, clean software and gets into your computer. For example, a virus may be attached to the software you download to your computer from the Web. Then after the virus is on your computer, it attaches itself to all the other software on your computer. If you copy any software from your computer to a disk, the virus tags along. Then when you give that disk to a friend, the virus attacks your friend's computer, and from there spreads to other friends' computers. That's how it spreads. Viruses have been known to spread across the world, from one country to another in a matter of weeks.

So how do you stop a virus? You can stop a virus dead in its tracks by

- ✔ Checking all the software you download from the Web
- ✔ Checking all the disks you get from friends
- ✔ Periodically scanning or checking your entire hard drive for viruses

That's the only way to stop a virus from infecting your computer. If you don't regularly check for viruses, your entire hard drive can be destroyed by just one virus in a matter of seconds. Imagine, all the games you installed on your computer, all the reports you wrote for your school homework . . . everything gone. ZAPPED! In just one tiny minute. Why? Because you were too lazy to check for viruses. Have I scared you enough? Good. Better scared than sorry. I have friends who spent days trying to get their machines back to normal after they were attacked. Be smart; scan often.

McAfee Associates is the leader in virus-busting software. Forty thousand companies worldwide use their products. So they just may be good enough for you, don't you think? Their WebScan product automatically scans all software that you download over the Web. You can get an evaluation copy of WebScan from the McAfee Web site at www.mcafee.com.

Another cool product is Norton AntiVirus, made by Symantec Corporation. A free version of its DOS virus scanner is available from the Symantec Web site at `www.symantec.com`.

In Windows 3.1, you might check whether you have a file called `MWAV.EXE` or an icon named Microsoft Anti-Virus (or MWAV) in the Applications program group in Program Manager. Either of these refers to Microsoft's Anti-Virus software.

To scan for viruses, follow these steps:

1. **Open your virus-scanning software.**

   Figure 9-14 shows the Norton AntiVirus opening screen.

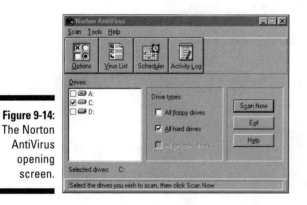

Figure 9-14:
The Norton
AntiVirus
opening
screen.

2. **Click on the icon for the drive you want to scan.**

3. **Click OK, Scan, Detect, Detect and Clean, or whatever command starts the scanning/fixing process.**

   The program reads the entire drive and shows the total number of folders and files it finds and alerts you if it finds any viruses. If you selected an option to detect and clean, the program should go ahead and clean up anything it finds, and may or may not tell you what's happening.

   Figure 9-15 shows Norton AntiVirus scanning drive A, my floppy drive. A virus was detected! The scary result is shown in Figure 9-16.

4. **If you didn't tell the program to clean up the virus automatically, kill the virus now. Viruses can be nasty; don't keep them around "just to see what they'll do."**

   Depending on what kind of virus you've got, your antivirus software may have to zap the file to clean the disk, so you may have to get another copy of the file.

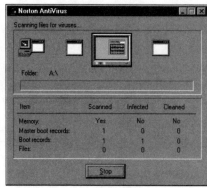

Figure 9-15:
Always
scan floppy
disks you
get from
other
people
before
copying the
disk.

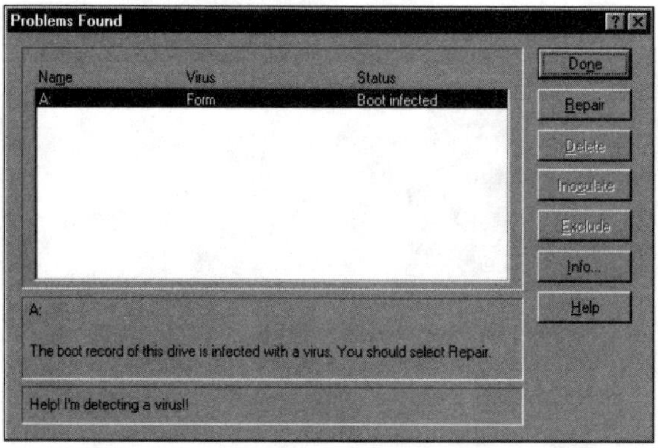

Figure 9-16:
Yikes! This
disk has a
virus!

5. **After the program finishes the scan, you see a summary screen that shows how many files and folders were checked, and what the results were. Close the summary screen, and you're done!**

   That's it. How much time did that take? Do you think you can do this about once a week? Is that too much to ask? I think not.

If a friend gives you a disk or file with a virus, kill it and then tell your friend immediately so he or she doesn't keep spreading it around. The flip side of that coin is admitting that *you* shared a disk or file that was infected. It may be embarrassing to admit, but it's pretty awful to let somebody's computer get fried by a virus when you could prevent it.

Most antivirus programs these days include an option to run the software all the time in memory, from the minute you start the computer. This option is a really good idea, because remembering to check every disk can be a big pain. And if you forget . . . When you have a virus checker running constantly, you get a warning message if you try to download or copy a sick file.

A few more shareware and freeware sites

Games Domain is a site solely devoted to games. But the Web has sites at which you can find shareware for almost everything. Downloading from other Web sites is no different from downloading from Games Domain. Following are some of the best sites to download shareware:

Name	Address	Type of Shareware
Shareware.com	www.shareware.com	Everything under the sun
The Shareware Page	www.concentric.net/ ~cameronb/	Windows 95
Happy Puppy	happypuppy.com	Games
Free On the Web	netutopia.com/ freebies/	Free stuff on the Web

For more ideas on the most jammin' software and shareware, you should also check out *Great Software For Kids & Parents,* by Cathy Miranker and Alison Elliott (IDG Books Worldwide). Remember to scan for viruses. You gotta zap those viruses before they zap you — or your computer.

Chapter 10

Listen to the Radio from All Over the World

*H*ow would you like to live in a place where you had only one radio station to listen to? Where I grew up, that's all we had — one radio station. One! Serious. But we still kept track of the Top 40 countdown — the top songs of 1940. And when we got tired of those, we turned on the TV and watched the one TV channel the country had! One! Oh, did I mention that TV broadcasts started at 6 p.m. and went off the air at 11:30 p.m.? And during those five-and-a-half-hours of viewing pleasure, we watched three news broadcasts and the usual spate of ultra-boring commercials, which left us with a solid thirty-seven minutes of non-news, commercial-free viewing excitement! Whoa! How could we handle all that fun? But we still watched reruns of Lucy. Only we didn't know they were reruns! Then I came to America. I couldn't believe that TV programs ran 24 hours a day! Wow! I loved A-may-rri-ka! Amerika vas kool! The first show I saw was the one with David Letterman. I then spent the first two weeks just trying to keep track of all the shows and wondering if Bob Barker and Pat Sajack really handed out those fabulous prizes. And then I found the radio stations — 50 in every city. This country was awesome.

I got that feeling again, awe at having this huge selection of music and radio stations to listen to, when I started listening to radio on the Web, and not just radio stations broadcasting from within the U.S., but from all over the world. These are not *recorded* broadcasts I'm talking about. This is *live radio*. You hear it as it happens.

Wanna listen to a station in England? Italy? Finland? Korea? Taiwan? Hungary? Canada? Switzerland? Hong Kong? Germany? Mexico? You can. You don't believe me, do you? I guess I'll just have to prove it to you.

What You Need

I've listened to radio on a 486-based PC and on a Pentium. I've used Windows 3.11 and Windows 95. In every case, the reception has been great. But I've run into my share of problems too, and so to prevent you from having to go though them, here's what I recommend:

___ Pentium-based PC

___ 28.8 modem

___ Sound card and speakers. Mac users need not worry about this.

___ Netscape 3.0 Gold running on Windows 95 or Internet Explorer

___ RealAudio software if you use Netscape. Internet Explorer comes with RealAudio software.

If you don't have this configuration, you still can listen to the radio, but the sound quality won't be very good. I recommend the above configuration because I've tried it and it works well. You set it up, you click your mouse, and you hear the music.

What's RealAudio and where can I get it?

RealAudio is a software program that works with a browser (like Netscape and Internet Explorer) to let you listen to the radio.

Time to get a parent! You usually have to answer some of the technical questions about your computer and your Internet connection before you can download software. If you don't answer those questions, you can't download. It's important to know the right answers so that you download the correct version of RealAudio for the type of computer you use. So go get 'em — a parent, I mean.

You can download a copy of RealAudio from the RealAudio Web site www.realaudio.com. Let's go to the Web site to download the software first. Follow these steps:

1. **Create a new folder named raplayer in your root folder.**

2. **Write down the name of the folder, so you don't forget it.**

   I know, you never forget a thing — except to carry out the trash or make your bed. Well, I do. I forget my own name half of the time, so I always write down names of folders and files. I'm not looking over your shoulder, though, so do what you wanna do.

3. **Open your browser and click on the Open button on the toolbar.**

The Open Location dialog box shown in Figure 10-1 appears. Cute little thing, isn't it? If you've been reading this book straight through, you've seen this dialog box more than once. But I included it here because you're probably a read-what-I-want-and-then-move-on type person, and I don't want you getting lost.

Figure 10-1:
The Open
Location
dialog box.

4. **Click in the Open Location text box, type the address** `www.realaudio.com` **and then click on Open.**

Away you go to the RealAudio Web site. When you get to the RealAudio site, you have the option of downloading RealAudio Player Plus or RealAudio Player. The Plus version has more features than the regular version has, but you have to pay for the Plus version. The regular version is free and is good enough to listen to the radio. I use the regular version, and it rocks.

5. **Follow the links for choosing the regular version, answering any technical questions that pop up on your screen.**

6. **After you've answered the questions about which version you want, continue following the links for downloading.**

Before the download begins, you have to specify where you want to save the file that you're about to download, as shown in Figure 10-2.

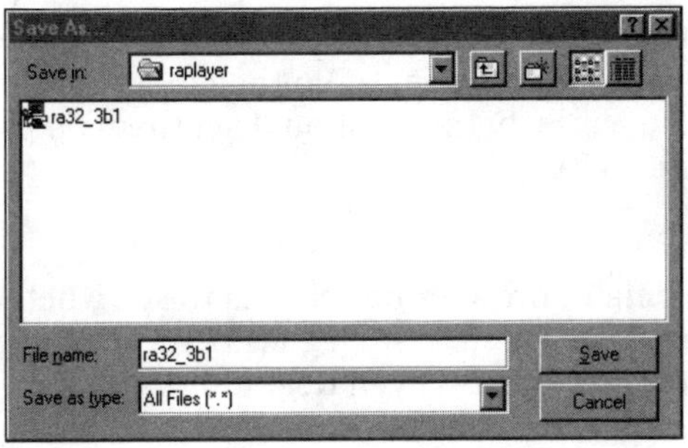

Figure 10-2:
The Save
As dialog
box.

7. **Write down the name of the file that automatically appeared in the File name text box.**

   Again, ignore me if you want; who am I anyway? Just the author of this book. I don't get no respect.

8. **Click on Save to begin the download.**

   Staring at the computer while the file downloads isn't much fun. So put yourself to good use. Get off your chair and help your parents with the dishes. You might have enough time to take the trash out, too. Awright, sit tight. See if I care.

Installing RealAudio to Work with Netscape

You probably spent what seemed like a lifetime downloading that file and are wondering, "How much more of this do I have to take before I can listen to the radio?" About 10 minutes, no more. We're almost there.

Parental assistance may be necessary here to answer a handful of technical questions.

Don't exit from your browser. Leave it running. If necessary, RealAudio will close it for you during installation and will prompt you before doing so.

1. **Open the folder in which you stored the file.**

   Aha! Aren't you glad you followed my instructions and wrote down that folder name? Wait'll you see the next step! You'll really be glad.

2. **Double-click on the filename you wrote down in the preceding set of steps.**

   The installation starts rolling. At first, you see a few screens with important licensing information. RealAudio then looks for the browsers on your computer and asks whether it should set them up to use RealAudio (see Figure 10-3).

3. **Click on Next.**

   RealAudio finds the default browser but checks to see whether it detected the right one (see Figure 10-4). I guess everyone needs a little positive feedback now and then — even RealAudio.

Figure 10-3:
Setup of
RealAudio
Player
window.

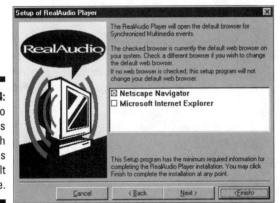

Figure 10-4:
RealAudio
guesses
which
browser is
the default
one.

4. Click on Next.

You're then asked whether the uninstall program for RealAudio
should be copied to the C:\Win95\SYSTEM\ directory if you have
Windows 95 — as if you'd ever want to uninstall RealAudio. Figure 10-5
shows the path. This varies from computer to computer. If you're a
Windows 3.11 user, that path may appear as C:\Windows\System.

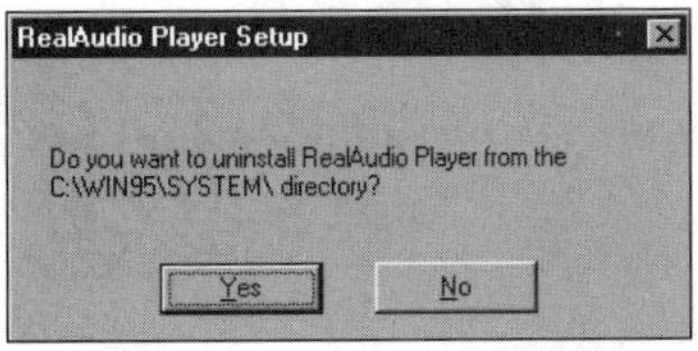

Figure 10-5:
RealAudio
asks for
your OK on
the path.

RealAudio Player Setup

Do you want to uninstall RealAudio Player from the
C:\WIN95\SYSTEM\ directory?

Yes   No

5. **If you do see the Unistall message box shown in Figure 11-5, click on Yes to accept the path.**

   You will then see a few windows fly by your screen at warp speed, making it seem as if your computer has gone nuts. Don't worry; RealAudio is just completing the installation. When it has finished, you see the message shown in Figure 10-6. Ta Da! We're finally done!

Figure 10-6: RealAudio congratulates you on the successful installation.

6. **Click on O_K.**

   You should now hear a welcome message from your speakers, and the RealAudio window shown in Figure 10-7 should pop up on your screen. Your installation was successful.

Figure 10-7: The RealAudio Player window.

7. **To play the message again, click on the Play button.**

   I just thought you should hear it once more. You worked so hard to get here.

Can We Get on the Air, Please?

Here we go. Follow these steps to listen to the radio via your computer:

1. **Start Netscape and click on the Open button.**

   The Open Location text box shown in Figure 10-1 appears. Aren't you glad?

2. **Type the address** ontheair.com **and click on OK.**

   The screen shown in Figure 10-8 appears.

3. **Save the address. You'll be coming back often.**

   If you don't know what I'm talking about when I say, "Save the address," check out the chapter about your browser — Chapter 1 or Chapter 3.

4. **Click on Non-US.**

   You just brought up the Non-US radio stations listing. Clever, huh? Scroll down the screen. What you see is similar to the screen shown in Figure 10-9.

   When you scroll down the screen, you see a list of radio stations. Some of the stations have the Listen RA28.8 icon next to them; others have the Xing icon next to them. These icons point out two separate audio formats. You should select only stations with the Listen RA28.8 icon next to them.

5. **Click on any icon with the Listen RA28.8 icon.**

Figure 10-8:
The
Ontheair.
com home
page.

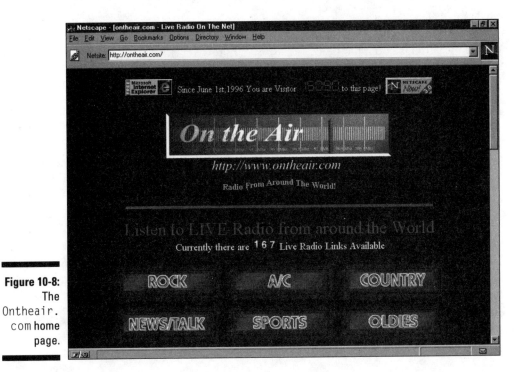

Netscape - [Non-U.S. Radio Stations on The Net]

File   Edit   View   Go   Bookmarks   Options   Directory   Window   Help

Netsite: http://www.ontheair.com/realfore.htm

Non-U.S. Radio!

Rock, AC, Pop, Dance, Blues, Classical

Listen   OZ FM New Foundland, Canada

Listen   Country, Rock, & Blues 1269 KICK AM Sydney, Australia

Listen   105.8 FM Virgin Radio London, England

Listen   1071 CFLG Toronto, Canada

Listen   Radio Italy

Listen   Radio Lancer Finland

Listen   Radio Padova Padova, Italy

Listen   Radio 105.5 Radio Bandit Sweden

Listen   Radio Comercial Lisboa, Portugal

Listen   Stefamikova, Czech Republic

Document: Done

Figure 10-9:
Non-U.S.
radio
stations.

Because not all radio stations are set up the same way, any of the following things could happen:

✔ The RealAudio window automatically comes up on the screen for a few seconds and then disappear. That's normal. No need for concern. If that happens, then you should start hearing the radio broadcast in a few seconds. One radio station that does the disappearing act is 105.8 FM Virgin Radio, London, England.

✔ If the RealAudio window doesn't automatically come up on the screen for a few seconds and then disappear, you probably will see the radio station's home page first. (This usually happens only on U.S.-based radio stations.) Somewhere on that home page, you should see a link for the station's live broadcast. Click on it. You then see the RealAudio window for a few seconds and then hear the broadcast.

After you hear the broadcast, you can continue surfing without fear of being disconnected. The music will continue in the background.

As you study different countries, connect to radio stations broadcasting in those countries. The kids will get a kick out of it and will also get to hear foreign tongues they might otherwise never hear.

How do I switch to a different station?

When I'm driving in my car, I'm constantly playing with the radio controls. As soon as a commercial comes on . . . ZAP! I tune to another station. On the Web, you can do the same.

When you listen to a regular radio and want to switch stations, do you turn off the radio first? Like duh. . . of course not. You just press the button for another station, right? It's no different with RealAudio. To switch stations, just click on another station's link. RealAudio automatically disconnects from the current station and connects to the new one. In a few seconds, you hear the new station.

Don't exit the RealAudio Player by bringing it up on the screen and then closing it. If you do, you may get error messages when you try to connect to a radio station the next time. If you accidentally closed the RealAudio Player and get error messages, exit your browser, start it again, and then try to connect to a station once more.

It's not loud enough!

To increase the volume of your radio-station-on-the-computer, follow these steps:

1. **Make the RealAudio Player window active.**

   In Windows 95, you make the window active by pressing Alt+Tab. If it doesn't show up on the screen right away, you may have to hold the Alt key down and repeatedly hit the Tab key till the RealAudio Player window is displayed. Then release both the Alt and the Tab keys.

2. **Move the mouse pointer to the volume control slide button, hold down the left mouse button, and drag the button up.**

   If you don't see a volume control slide button, your sound card doesn't support volume control, or you have asked RealAudio not to display it. To display the control, choose View from the menu bar and make sure that a check mark appears next to Info & Volume. If you don't see a check mark, click once on Info & Volume.

3. **If the volume still isn't loud enough, even though you've turned it all the way up, you can do three things:**

   • Turn up the volume on your speakers. Some speakers have a volume control knob on them.

   • Turn up the volume on the sound card. Some sound cards have a volume control knob on them. You have to turn the computer around to see whether your card has a knob.

Don't try to turn the computer around yourself, especially if it's too close to the edge of your desk. It could fall and then you will really hear a loud sound — EEEK! Ask your parents to help you. If the sound card doesn't have a volume control knob on it, its volume is probably controlled by its own software. Turn up the volume from the software controls.

To lower the volume . . . now do I really need to explain that? I think not.

How do I stop the music?

Sometimes you can listen to a foreign radio broadcast for only so long before you say, "Um . . . I haven't understood a word of what this DJ has said in the past two hours, and this English-Malay dictionary isn't much help either. I think I'll turn it off now." To stop the music, follow these steps:

1. **Make the RealAudio Player window active.**

   Don't look at me. You know what to do. You just did this in the preceding set of steps.

2. **Click on the stop button — the one with the black square.**

   You may continue surfing in silence now. How incredibly boring!

Listen to live concert clips from CDs: Are you ready to rock 'n' roll?

When you've had enough of radio stations and want to add to your fun, you can listen to clips from newly released CDs — *without having to buy the CD!* How often have you bought a CD, listened to it, and said, "I wish I hadn't bought that." Well, now you can listen before wasting your money. Ready to save some cash? Follow these steps to listen to clips from the CD of your choice:

1. **Start your browser and click on Open in the toolbar.**

   I'll bet you can write the text for this spot! Okay, okay. I will. The Open Location text box appears.

2. **Type the address** www.sony.com/music/ontap **and click on Open.**

   Guess where you arrived? You're right — the Sony Web site. (No, I don't get paid extra for using words that rhyme. That one just happened.)

3. **Click on Live Events.**

   You then see links to live concerts and to concert schedules. Rad! If you get an error message, click on Online Live Events at the bottom of the screen.

4. **Click on The Vault to listen to music clips from CDs.**

   You then see a screen with a juke box.

5. **Click on a letter to display an alphabetical listing of bands and then follow the links to the music clip you want to hear.**

   Doesn't the fact that you can listen to the music on your computer just blow you away? Is it possible that someday you'll do all your music shopping on the Internet?

Help! It's All Garbled . . . It's Not Clear . . . It's Not Working

No matter how well you set up your software and how good your speakers are, the sound coming from your RealAudio connection *may be* garbled, broken up, noisy, unclear, and crappy. I mean CRAPPY! It's horrible. It's sooo bad you wanna take a hammer and bust the screen. You wanna rip the speakers off and throw them off the roof. You wanna stop going to school and walk around in your jammies all day. That's totally unacceptable. Don't let it come to that. I promise to help you fix your problems if you promise it'll never come to that. Deal? Deal. Whew!!!

Following are some suggestions to try if your sound is bad:

- ✔ Some radio stations almost always have poor quality broadcasts. They probably have a bad connection to the Internet, or you're connecting at a busy time. Late evenings and nights are very busy because everybody and her or his brother is on the Web. To make sure that the problem lies with the station and not at your end, try connecting to the 105.8 FM Virgin Radio station (in London, England), the station that has good sound quality most of the time. (Sometimes even its broadcast drops from great to poor. When it does, it stays that way for only five to ten minutes. But it's a good station for testing your system.)

- ✔ If you did not download the latest version of RealAudio (Version 3.0) as mentioned earlier in the chapter, do so and try using that version. Some broadcasts are specifically made for Version 3.0 and will not work with older versions of RealAudio.

- ✔ Bring up the RealAudio window. Stop the broadcast by clicking the stop button. Make any of the following changes, one at a time or in combination. Try listening to a radio station after making a change to check whether it makes the broadcast any better or worse, and then try the other changes accordingly.

You can try two different methods to improve the sound quality in RealAudio. Try the easiest one first:

1. Choose View⇨Preferences from the RealAudio menu bar.

You then see a dialog box like the one in Figure 10-10.

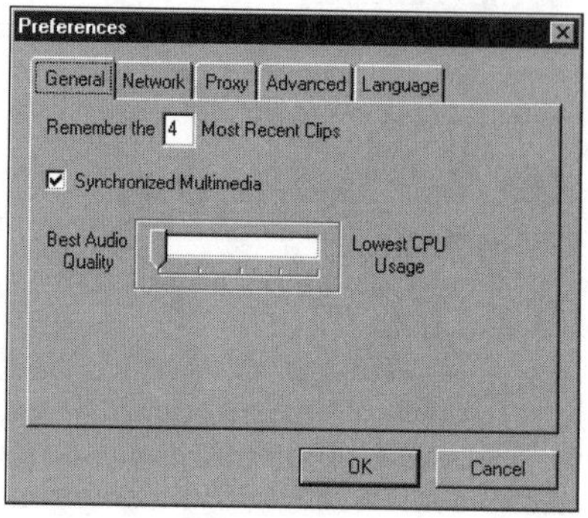

Figure 10-10: The General tab in the Preferences dialog box.

2. Move the slide control a notch or two to the right.

3. Click on OK.

If the preceding steps don't help, try the following method:

1. Choose View⇨Preferences.

There's the same dialog box shown in Figure 10-11. No duh! You just chose the same commands.

2. Click on the Network tab.

Guess what? You then see the Network page shown in Figure 10-11. Scary, isn't it?

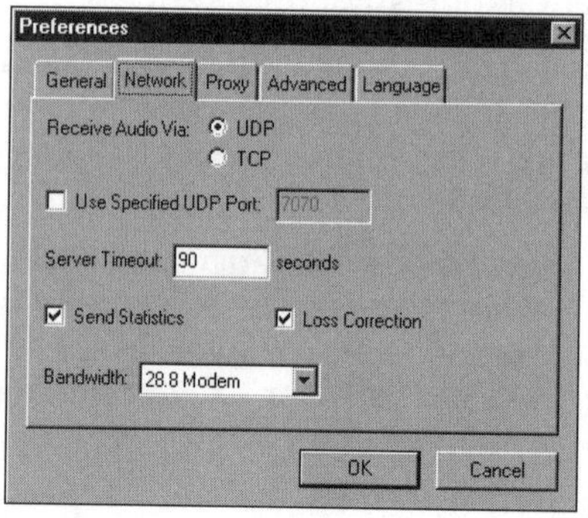

Figure 10-11: The Network page in the Preferences dialog box.

3. Make sure that the Receive Audio Via option is set to UDP, and the bandwidth is set to the modem you have — 14.4 or 28.8.

You don't have to understand this; you only have to DO it, and do it now! *Please.*

4. Click on OK.

You just set your options correctly for the Internet connection and modem you have — and you didn't even understand a thing about it, did ya? Cool, dude.

5. Click on the Advanced tab.

You then see the Advanced page shown in Figure 10-12.

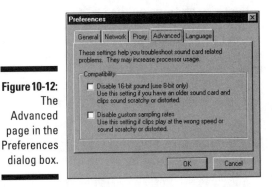

Figure 10-12:
The
Advanced
page in the
Preferences
dialog box.

6. Click on the check box next to Disable 16-bit sound.

A check mark should now appear in that check box.

7. Click on OK.

Can you believe it? You're there! You made it!

8. Try a radio station.

9. If the reception isn't any better, return to the screen shown in Figure 10-12 and put a check mark in the box next to the Disable custom sampling rates option.

10. Click on OK and try to connect to a radio station again.

If none of these solutions make the sound quality better, go to the RealAudio home page (www.realaudio.com) and refer to the detailed technical help available there. The suggestions given at that site are too numerous to mention here.

Radio Stations for Kids

Check out these addresses to some more awesome radio station sites:

Addresses	Organization
www.wrn.org	World Radio Network
www.abc.com	ABC Television Network
www.npr.org	National Public Radio

Happy listening!

Try a sampling of the more than 180 radio stations on the ontheair site, to make sure there aren't any stations that broadcast anything vulgar or inappropriate for kids. So far I haven't come across any, but you never know. So be alert. If you have one of the Internet filters on the CD described in Appendix A, you can easily restrict access to radio sites.

Chapter 11

Watching Video on the Web

● ●

In This Chapter

▶ What you do and don't need to watch video on the Web

▶ Installing the VivoActive software

▶ Watching video on the Web — I want my Web-TV

▶ Improving the sound and picture

▶ Checking out cool video sites

● ●

Can you imagine life without your daily share of TV? Naaaah! Can't live without it, right? Or without VCRs! When VCRs were first introduced many, many years ago — you weren't even born then — people were thrilled that they could watch movies at home. They didn't have to leave the comfort of their living rooms to experience the joy of a Friday night at the movies. The only things missing were the super-duper buckets of popcorn soaked in butter, Raisinets, Goobers, and, of course, that fresh feeling of feet sticking to the movie hall floor as you walked around looking for empty seats.

And now live TV and video have both come to the Web. The current state of Internet technology hasn't reached a point where you'd wanna fire up your computer to watch an episode of Beavis and Butthead. The quality of live TV broadcasts isn't something you wanna try at the moment, especially not with a 28.8 modem. Perhaps in the next year or so. But you can still watch video clips from your favorite movies and full-length, entire-song music videos. Are you doing anything right now? How about watchin' some videos?

What You Don't Need: A VCR Connected to Your Computer

Umm. . . . You really don't need to connect a VCR to your computer to watch videos. Your parents won't like that too much. Not because you might drop the VCR while carrying it to your desk, but because they might not think it's such an awesome idea to sit around your computer every Friday night.

So how *do* you watch videos on your computer then? You use software specially made for viewing videos. How easy is it to get your hands on that software? Very easy. As a matter of fact, if you're using Windows 95, you already have some of it on your computer. It's one of the Windows 95 multimedia features. But if you're not a Windows 95 user, don't despair. You can still watch videos. You might just have to use some other software.

You can find a whole bunch of video software out there, and many of them can be downloaded from the Web for free. But here's the catch: The video clips on the Web come in many formats — Video For Windows (discussed in Chapter 12), VDOLive, and VivoActive, just to name a few. Each format has its own special software for viewing videos. To view a video clip in VivoActive format, for example, you need the VivoActive software on your computer. VivoActive is my favorite video player, so I show you how to use it in this chapter. Why do I like it so much? With VivoActive, you can watch streaming videos.

No, no, no! Streaming audio and streaming video on the Web have nothing to do with those cassettes that play recorded streams or babbling brooks. Have you ever listened to those tapes? They're pretty realistic, aren't they? Only a year ago or less, if you wanted to hear audio or watch video on the Web, you first downloaded the audio or video file to your computer, fired up your audio or video software, and then listened or watched the video. Streaming audio or video lets you hear audio or view video as the audio or video file is being downloaded to your computer. In other words, you don't have to twiddle your thumbs as the file is being downloaded and then view it.

What You Do Need

If you have a modem slower than a 28.8 modem, you can waste a bunch of time trying to watch streaming videos on the Web. You might as well do your homework. You see, video clips have a lot of information in them. If you have a slow modem, not only does the download take forever, you also see interruptions and breaks as your modem tries to match its speed with the speed of the downloading information.

Here's what I recommend for successful video-playing:

    ___ Pentium-based PC

    ___ 28.8 modem

    ___ Sound card and speakers

    ___ Netscape 3.0 running on Windows 95

    ___ VivoActive Player software

Installing the VivoActive Player Software

I'm so happy that this book comes with a CD. On it, you can find a whole bunch of goodies that would waste your valuable time downloading from the Web. You see, I care about you. I know how much homework you gotta do. So I'm willing to save you as much time as I possibly can to give you ample time to do it. VivoActive Player software is one of the goodies on the CD. Appendix B tells you how to install the program.

Watching Videos: Are You Ready to Have Some Fun?

I know that you're ready to have some fun watching streaming video. You know by now what streaming video is, right? Cool. Then you oughta sprinkle it liberally in your daily vocabulary as you talk to your friends who think they're just way cool Web surfers. Here's an example: "Dude, the streaming video coming down a 28.8 on a Pentium Pro just blows my mind." Be prepared to get those stares that mean "What in the world are you talking about?" That's when you say, "You know what streaming video is, don't you?" You're just about to win the Nauseating Kids of the Year award.

To use VivoActive, follow these steps:

1. **Click on Open in your Netscape toolbar.**

   What do you have? Why, it's the Open Location dialog box that you've seen 900 times (see Figure 11-1).

Figure 11-1:
The Open
Location
dialog box.

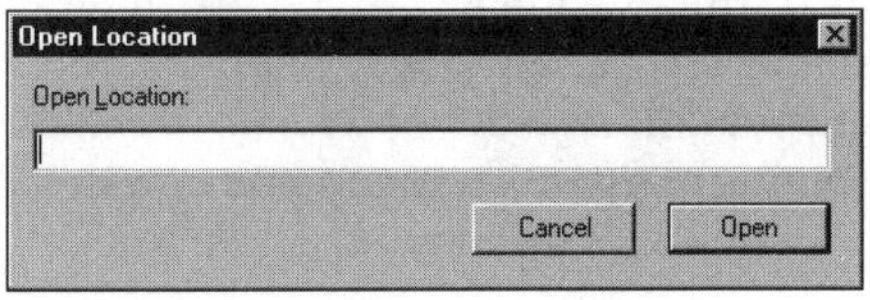

2. **Type** www.takeme.com/are-oh-vee **in the Open Location text box and then click on Open.**

   A window similar to the one shown in Figure 11-2 appears. It's the Web site of the folks at *Are oh Vee,* a wonderful site that contains jammin' rock videos.

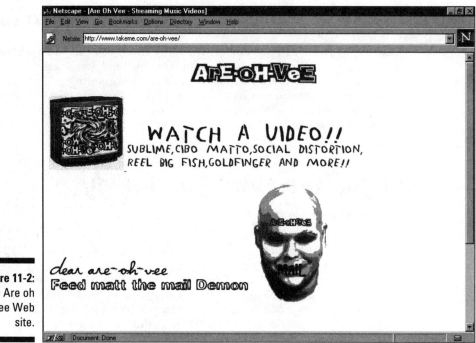

Figure 11-2:
The Are oh
Vee Web
site.

3. Scroll down the page and click on the Music Video link.

You see a screen informing you that you should have at least a 28.8 modem to view video, but you already knew that, didn't you? You're also asked to download VivoActive Player, but you have that too. Boy, you've come prepared, so let's continue.

4. Scroll down the screen.

You see a screen similar to the one in Figure 11-3, listing the current week's videos available for viewing. For each video, Are oh Vee gives you two choices for the speed: LOW (the option for a 28.8 modem) and HIGH (the option for a really, really high-speed line like the ones used in big companies).

5. Select LOW.

For a few seconds, it seems like nothing's happening. Then the TV on the screen disappears, and the title of the song you selected appears in its place. A few seconds later, you see a blank screen with a tiny triangle spinning in the bottom right corner: Vivo is downloading the initial segments of the video file.

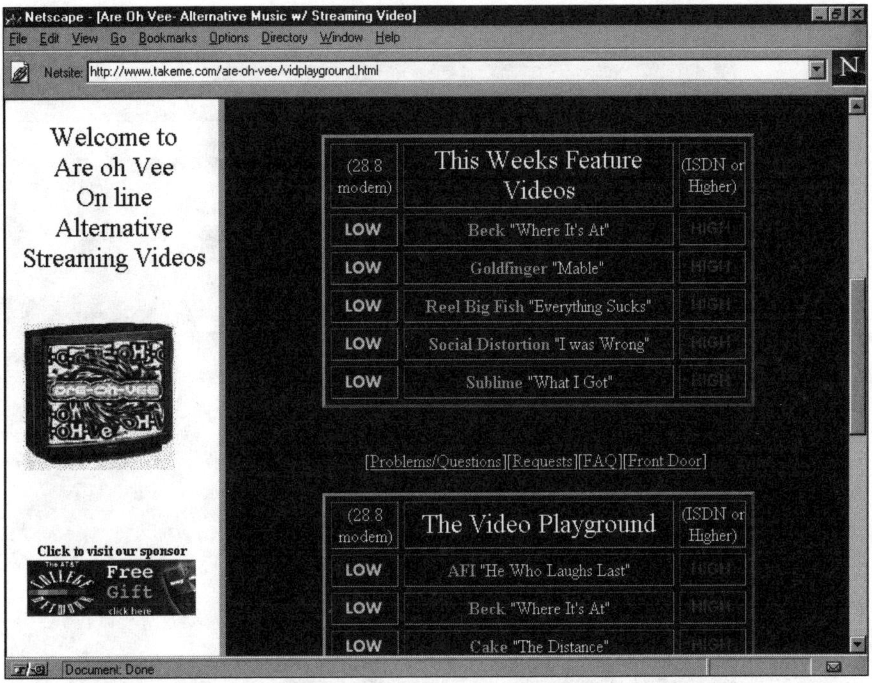

Figure 11-3:
This week's
listings.

Sometimes a few seconds could easily be a minute or more, depending on a variety of things, such as the amount of traffic at the music site or at the computers at your ISP. Imagine having a Porsche to drive around in. Nice thought, 'eh? Even though you may have a Porsche that easily does 150 mph, it's not much use if you're stuck in traffic, now is it? So even though you have a 28.8 modem and a screamer of a Pentium, you may have to wait a while for the video to begin playing. When it does, it looks similar to the screen shown in Figure 11-4.

When the video starts playing, a green play/pause button replaces the pink triangle. To pause the video, click on the play/pause button at the right bottom of the video screen. To resume playing, click on the play/pause button again.

Sometimes a blinking red and yellow triangle replaces the play/pause button: When that happens, Vivo is downloading additional segments of the file. If the video pauses for a second or two by itself, don't worry. The modem is just playing catch-up with the downloading file.

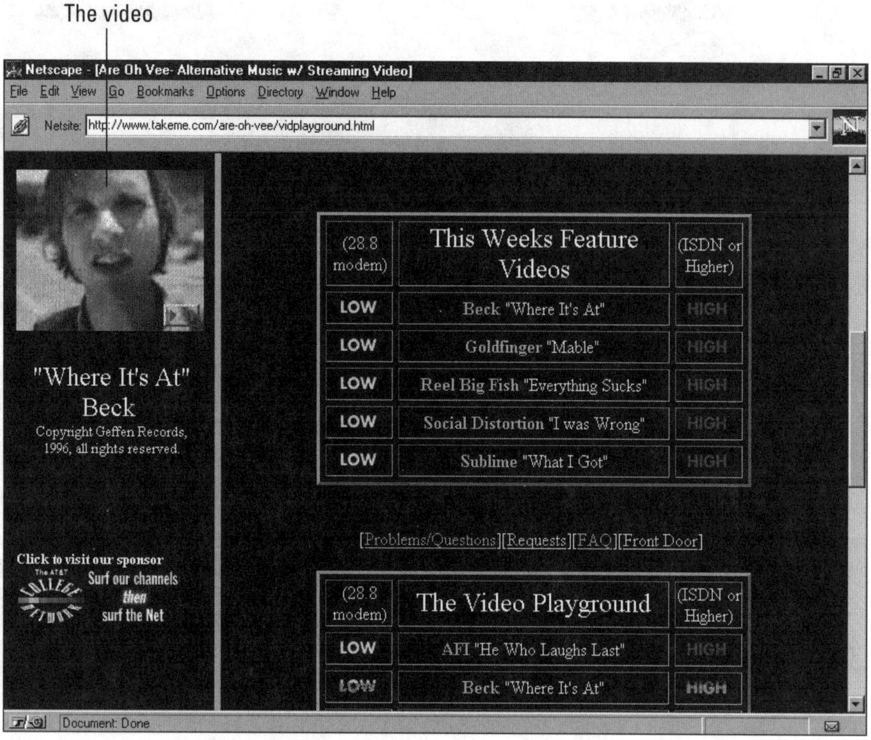

The video

Figure 11-4:
A music
video.

Netscape - [Are Oh Vee- Alternative Music w/ Streaming Video]

File Edit View Go Bookmarks Options Directory Window Help

Netsite: http://www.takeme.com/are-oh-vee/vidplayground.html

"Where It's At"
Beck
Copyright Geffen Records,
1996, all rights reserved.

Click to visit our sponsor
The AT&T
Surf our channels
then
surf the Net

(28.8 modem)	This Weeks Feature Videos	(ISDN or Higher)
LOW	Beck "Where It's At"	HIGH
LOW	Goldfinger "Mable"	HIGH
LOW	Reel Big Fish "Everything Sucks"	HIGH
LOW	Social Distortion "I was Wrong"	HIGH
LOW	Sublime "What I Got"	HIGH

[Problems/Questions][Requests][FAQ][Front Door]

(28.8 modem)	The Video Playground	(ISDN or Higher)
LOW	AFI "He Who Laughs Last"	HIGH
LOW	Beck "Where It's At"	HIGH

Document: Done

Sometimes the video just won't load, and you'll end up with a broken page or broken mosaic image, like the one shown in Figure 11-5. This image means that an error has occurred. Try the song again, or try another song.

Like all parents, you're concerned about the suitability of video clips on the Web and whether your child can access video with adult content. I haven't come across Web sites with adult-video content, but I'm sure that some sites contain such material. You can take action to prevent your child from being exposed to material you consider inappropriate. Appendix A contains information about Internet filters. They're easy to use and provide a fair amount of protection from unsuitable material. The sites mentioned in this chapter have the same kind of material that you would watch on MTV.

Broken mosaic

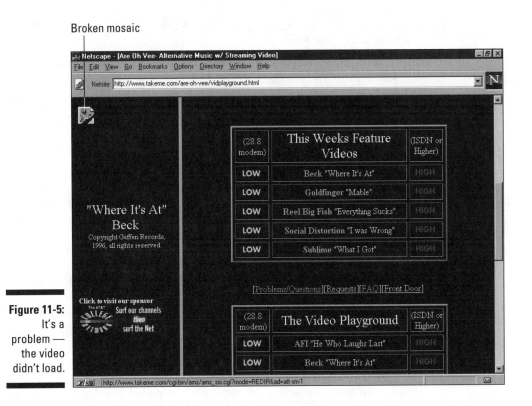

Figure 11-5:
It's a
problem —
the video
didn't load.

How good should the sound and picture quality be?

The videos at the *Are oh Vee* site produce great sound on my system. And I have pretty crappy speakers. The video is also of a good quality, but it varies from video to video. When rock videos are shot in dark settings or at concerts, for example, the quality of the video looks poor. If the quality looks grainy, even on a Yanni video (should you choose to watch one), try adjusting the colors within your computer. To adjust the color on a Windows 95 computer, follow these steps:

1. **Choose Start⇨Settings⇨Control Panel.**

   You will see the slightly frightening-looking Control Panel, with all kinds of technical stuff in it.

2. **Double-click on the Display icon and then click on the Settings tab.**

   A page with some pretty cool colors appears.

3. **Click on the list box arrow and select High Color (16-bit) in the Color palette drop-down list.**

4. **Adjust the slider (if possible) in the Desktop area, for a higher screen resolution.**

   It's kinda cool sliding that slider across the bar, isn't it? Who'd a thought computers could be so easy to adjust?

5. **Click on OK.**

6. **Exit and restart Windows 95.**

One other thing. Ever watch poorly-dubbed movies? You know how you hear the words about ten seconds after the actors' lips move? At times, that's what the video will look like, especially if you're on a super-slow connection to the Internet.

Want to try out another site?

Let's go to the site of the VivoActive player. It has a whole bunch of sites that carry VivoActive videos. To go to the site and watch some videos, follow these steps:

1. **Click on Open on your browser toolbar.**

   You know what opens — the Open Location dialog box. Hey, you could be writing this book! Where were you when I needed you?

2. **In the Open Location text box, type** `www.vivo.com` **and click on Open.**

   The screen shown in Figure 11-6 appears.

3. **Click on Gallery icon in the left margin of the screen.**

   Ta Da! There it is — a gallery of VivoActive video sites.

Another site where you can find videos is InterneTV at `www.internetv.com`. This site has video clips in a variety of different formats. Just make sure that when you select a video to play from the Choose and Click Play window, you select only the ones that have VIVO in their names or descriptions. VDO videos, for a format called VDOPLAY, are at the top of the list. You have to scroll down the list until you see the VIVO category, select the video you want to view, and then click on Play. This site even has film clips. Cool! Try them, too.

Happy Viewing!

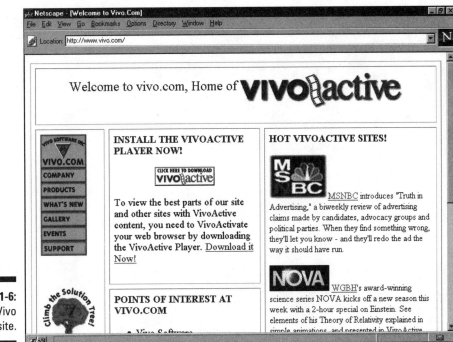

Figure 11-6:
The Vivo
Web site.

Chapter 12

Seeing You, Seeing Me on the Computer

*W*e all know what an air-guitar sounds like, don't we? We also know what it's like to sing in an arena filled with 80,000 screaming fans. Okay, so they're *imaginary* fans! We've all been rock stars in the privacy of our rooms, hairbrush in hand, driving roaches outta their holes with our ultra-horrible voices. Now how about recording that horrible stuff on video and sharing it with your friends on the Web? Scary Thought Alert! Yes, it's possible, and you don't need a TV crew or an *unplugged-on-MTV-* style studio.

What you need is a little camera called QuickCam, made by Connectix Corporation (`www.connectix.com`). The camera is about the size of a golf ball, is available in most computer stores, and costs about a hundred bucks. So start saving that allowance.

QuickCam — Small in Size, Big on Performance

QuickCam comes in two varieties: a gray scale (or black-and-white) version and a color version. The camera plugs easily into the back of your computer, using your computer's parallel port. (That's the port to which your printer is usually connected.) After you install the QuickCam software that comes with the camera, voilà! You have the coolest, hippest, niftiest little gadget to use on the Web. The first time I tried it, I was blown away by what this little thing could do. I mean, I was like, "WOW! This is rad." And I tried only the gray scale version! I've heard that the color version is even better — but it costs about twice as much, too.

Now before you get visions of sending live MTV-style video over the Web, peel yourself off the ceiling and gently float back to earth. Realistic motion video is possible with QuickCam — if you use a really high-speed connection to the Internet (the kind big companies use or cable companies will soon be offering to their cable subscribers). You probably will use QuickCam with a 28.8 modem, and this chapter shows you how you can use your modem to get the best quality video possible.

Live video is not the only thing you can do with QuickCam. You can record your very own video, store it on your hard drive, and then send it via e-mail to a friend. Your friend can then view the video — *even* without the VideoPhone Viewer software — because the files are produced in the .avi format; a format supported by most multimedia software, including the Windows 95 Multimedia Player.

But wait, let me tell you what else you can do with the camera. You can shoot photographs as if you were using a regular camera. You don't have to take film to a store to have it developed because the picture ready the minute you shoot it. You can then send pictures to your friends via e-mail or put them on your Web page and show your face to the entire world.

What your computer should have

Graphics sometimes take a l-o-n-g time to download on your screen from a Web site, don't they? That's because a picture is worth a thousand words, or more. Video, on the other hand, is worth a million words. For example, a twenty-second video clip can take up as much room on your hard drive as a three hundred-page novel. That's a lot of information to send across the Web. On a slow computer, transferring the file can take forever. Of course, you could always find something worthwhile to do during that time, like clean the kitchen. Yeah, rrrright!

The QuickCam works with IBM-compatible PCs and Macintoshes too. Each system has its own version of QuickCam, so make sure that you buy the one specific to your system. The minimum system requirements listed below are those that I recommend for good quality video using the gray-scale version QuickCam.

IBM-Compatible PCs

___ A Pentium — the faster, the better. I've used QuickCam on a Pentium 100, and it worked fine.

___ Windows 3.1 or Windows 95.

___ 16MB of RAM.

___ CD-ROM drive for installing the software.

___ 28.8 modem, if you want to transmit live video. (Not required if all you want to do is record movies and take pictures.)

___ Sound card, microphone, and speakers, if you want to use the VideoPhone audio feature.

___ Enough free space on your hard drive to store the videos you record.

___ One free 25-pin parallel port to connect the QuickCam to. If you don't have a free parallel port, you can use an A/B switch. Huh? A/B switch? Yeah, that's right. The switch has nothing to do with the quality of the video you see or record: The switch just relieves the pain and aggravation of using QuickCam and your printer together with your computer. You see, most computers have only one parallel port. That's the port your printer is usually connected to. But QuickCam needs to be connected to it, too. So what do you do? You can connect and disconnect your QuickCam and printer every time you want to use either of them — not much fun. You'll tire of that connecting and disconnecting pretty fast, trust me. And when you do, go buy this A/B switch. It's a little box with a knob, available at most computer stores for about fifteen bucks.

The A/B switch lets you use either the printer or the QuickCam with just the flip of a switch. You connect the printer and the QuickCam to this box and then connect the box to the parallel port on the computer. When you want to use the printer, you flip the switch one way. When you want to use the QuickCam, you flip the switch the other way. Very simple. I just had to tell you about this now because sooner or later you'd need it. If you don't mind waiting a week or so, I recommend that you buy this switch from Connectix itself, because they have built one specifically for this purpose, unlike the ones available at the computer store that are primarily for switching between two printers.

You can use the QuickCam with a laptop computer it has a keyboard port for connecting an external keyboard to it.

Macintosh computers

___ 68020 or faster Macintosh

___ System 7.0 or later software

___ 8MB of RAM

___ CD-ROM drive for installing the software.

___ 28.8 modem, if you want to transmit live video. (Not required if all you want to do is record movies and take pictures.)

___ Enough free space on your hard drive to store the videos you record.

___ **A free serial port.** If your computer has only one serial port and you already have a modem connected to it, you have to disconnect it every time you want to use QuickCam; to use QuickCam, you have to connect it to the serial port. Soooo, you can either use the modem or the QuickCam, but not both. Obviously, you can't transmit live video over the Web in such a situation. If you do want to transmit live video, you need to install a second serial port in your computer. If you've never seen what the inside of a computer looks like, I suggest that you let your computer-nerd friend take care of the installation. That way, it'll take only an hour, not the entire weekend. But if you don't intend to transmit live video and just plan to record home video clips or take photographs with the QuickCam, you can get by with just one serial port. Of course, this would mean that you'd have to constantly connect and disconnect the modem or the QuickCam from the serial port every time you wanted to use either of them. Unless you bought an A/B switch.

An A/B switch is a box that lets you alternate between two devices connected to one serial port. You first connect two devices — for example, a modem and a QuickCam — to the box, and then you connect the box to the serial port. Then with the flip of a switch on the box, you choose the device you want to use. Remember, the A/B switch will *not* allow you to use both devices together on the same port. You can only use one at a time. Make sure that the A/B switch box you buy is for serial port devices and for a Macintosh computer. A/B parallel port switches are avaiable, too. Pick the right one for your computer. Connectix makes A/B switch boxes specifically for the QuickCam.

The Mac Plus, Mac SE, PowerBook 100, and Mac Portable do not work with the QuickCam.

Installing QuickCam

Here's a piece of advice — if you ever see your parents in bell-bottoms, elevator shoes, and flashy jewelry, hanging around the QuickCam, RUN! They're probably making a video titled *Disco Fever* or something. Can you imagine being seen in that? How embarrassing. But here's why I'm telling you this. Since your parents will be using QuickCam anyway, why not give them the pleasure of installing it?

QuickCam installation is a snap. Connecting the camera and installing the software to your computer is simple and is covered in minute detail in the QuickCam user's manual. Actually two user's manuals are packed with the camera. One, the *QUICKCAM User Guide,* covers the installation of the camera. The other, *The Connectix VideoPhone User Guide,* covers the software setup. Both manuals are very detailed in their explanations, and the instructions couldn't be any simpler.

Setting up the camera

Hey, have you heard of those night-vision cameras that the U.S. Army uses to see in the dark?

The QuickCam is no night-vision camera. It needs a good amount of light to make a photograph. Following are some tips for using the QuickCam:

- ✔ Make sure that the lighting in the room and on you is adequate.

- ✔ Direct the light toward the ceiling or on the wall closest to you, but make sure that it doesn't reflect on your face. When the light *points* to your face and not away from it, your face gets a white, shiny glow, and the camera gets spastic.

- ✔ Place the camera on its stand, and then place the stand where you're least like to touch it when you get up and walk around. The QuickCam is not bounce-proof.

- ✔ Place the camera and its stand about two feet from your face.

Question: How do night-vision cameras work?

Answer: Regular cameras use light that's reflected off a person to make a photograph. Night-vision cameras use the heat given off by a person to make a photograph.

Live video on the Web — What you need to get connected

You can send live video from your computer to a friend who's connected to the Web. Although you need QuickCam connected to your computer to transmit live video, *your friend doesn't need to have a QuickCam camera to watch the video you're transmitting.* All your friend needs is a copy of Connectix VideoPhone Viewer software, a free software application available at the Connectix Web site at `www.connectix.com`. Your friend can either get the software from the site or copy it from the CD enclosed with his or her copy of this book.

To send a live video so that your friend can see you, you need to know the IP address of the computer your friend is using. Following are important points to remember about IP addresses:

- ✔ To have an IP address, you must log on to the Internet.
- ✔ Each time you log on to the Internet, a new IP address is assigned to your computer.
- ✔ Each computer connected to the Internet has its own IP address, or number, that identifies it among the millions of computers connected to the Web at any given time.
- ✔ No two computers on the Internet can have the same IP address.

The easiest way to find your IP address is from the QuickCam software, as you see in the next section.

Lights, camera, live video — Roll that camera

First things first. Have you brushed your hair? Have you wiped the sleep out of your eyes? Blown your nose? Cool! Just making sure. You don't want to appear messy, now do you?

1. **Log on to your Internet Service Provider.**

   For me, the Internet Service Provider is AT&T WorldNet Service.

2. **Double-click on the Cvphone icon in Connectix folder.**

   You should see the screen similar to the one shown in Figure 12-1. Notice that the status bar says Disconnected. Your screen is showing whatever your camera is focused on.

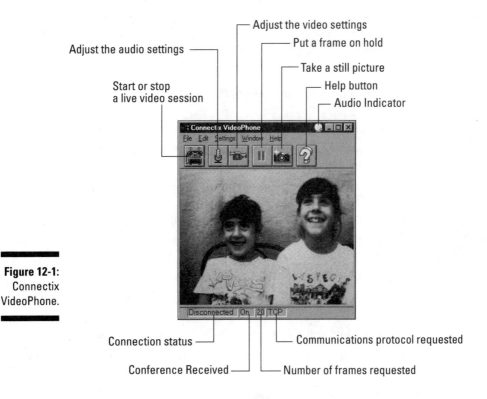

Adjust the video settings
Put a frame on hold
Adjust the audio settings
Take a still picture
Start or stop a live video session
Help button
Audio Indicator
Connectix VideoPhone
File Edit Settings Window Help
Disconnected On 20 TCP
Connection status
Communications protocol requested
Conference Received
Number of frames requested

Figure 12-1: Connectix VideoPhone.

3. **Choose Help➪About this machine's address from the Connectix VideoPhone menu bar to find your IP address.**

   You will see a screen similar to the one shown in Figure 12-2.

This Machine's Addresses
207.146.135.76
V's computer
OK

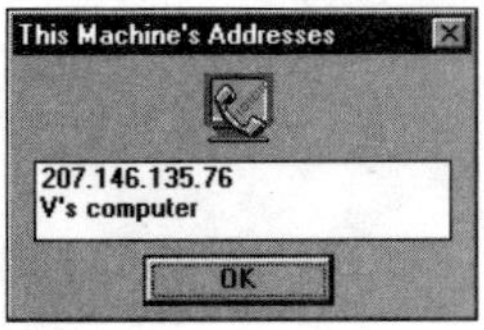

Figure 12-2: The IP address for my computer.

The number you see — 207.146.135.76 — is the IP address. Remember that this is the IP address for *my* computer. You can't have it. I won't, no, I can't, share it. I would if I could. You know that. Your IP address is different.

4. Write down the IP address on a piece of paper.

Knowing your handwriting, maybe you should print it. Just remember that the IP address never has any spaces or letters in it — only numbers and dots.

5. Click on OK.

6. Send your IP address to your friend via e-mail.

That's the cheapest way to send it, because if your friend is in Calcutta, your parents won't be exactly thrilled if you use the phone.

7. Have your friend log on and find the IP address for his or her computer.

While you are sending your IP address, your friend should also be sending the IP address of his or her computer to you.

Every time you connect to the Internet, you get a new IP address. So you have to do what you just did to find your IP address each time you log on. It's no big deal, right? I figured you weren't a whiner.

8. Adjust the camera so that the image is clear.

The excitement is building. Your hands are probably trembling with anticipation.

9. Click on the Phone button on the VideoPhone toolbar.

The Call dialog box shown in Figure 12-3 appears. You're almost there!

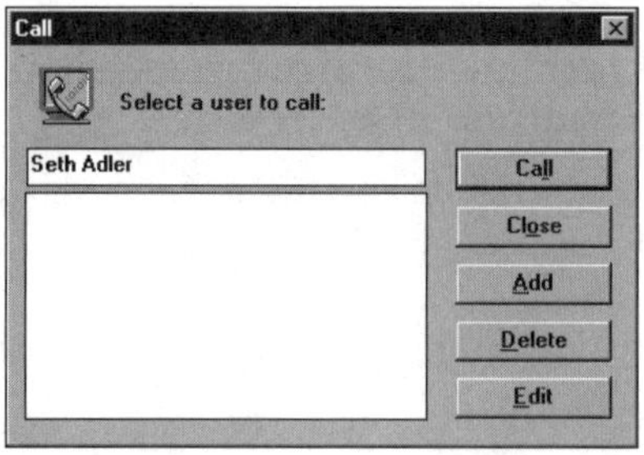

Figure 12-3:
The Call
dialog box.

Call

Select a user to call:

Seth Adler

Call
Close
Add
Delete
Edit

10. Type your friend's name.

In case you can't tell, I'm calling Seth Adler.

11. Click on Call.

Figure 12-4 shows the Add Address dialog box that appears.

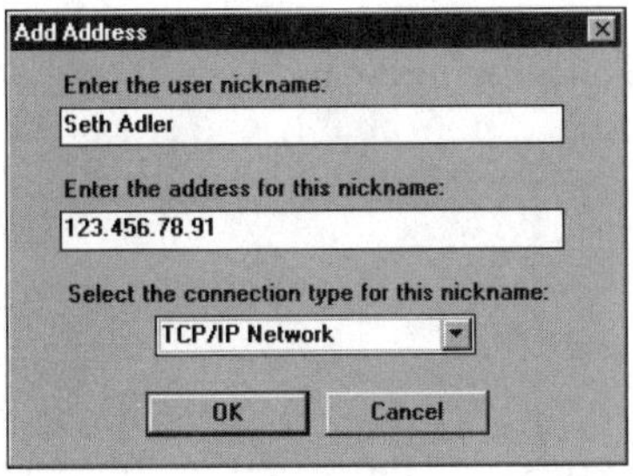

Figure 12-4:
The Add
Address
dialog box
for adding a
friend's IP
address to
the
VideoPhone
directory.

Add Address
Enter the user nickname:
Seth Adler
Enter the address for this nickname:
123.456.78.91
Select the connection type for this nickname:
TCP/IP Network
OK   Cancel

12. **Type your friend's IP address in the text box under Enter the address for this nickname.**

Be careful. Don't make mistakes. Nothing will explode if you make a typo, but you'll be plenty disappointed when your call doesn't go through — and so will your friend, who's waiting for you with baited breath.

Although you can add your friend's address to the VideoPhone directory, remember that every time the two of you log on to the Internet, your IP addresses change. So you have to edit the IP addresses in the VideoPhone directory each time you go live. What good is the directory then, you wonder. Well, big companies that don't need to dial an ISP to get onto the Internet have a permanent connection to the Internet. Some of those IP addresses never change. If you add one of these companies to your VideoPhone directory, you don't need to keep changing the IP address each time you connect to them.

13. **Click on OK and watch the status bar at the bottom of the video screen.**

You should see messages saying that VideoPhone is making a connection. If, instead of making a connection, you get a This address is invalid message, check the IP address for errors, and then try again. You may have typed the address exactly as your friend gave it to you, but your friend may have made a mistake in it somewhere. If you're not connecting, make your friend check the address given to you. We both know that *you* can't be the one making the mistake!

As soon as a your computer establishes a connection with your friend's computer and your status bar displays the message Connected, your display screen will go blank for a few seconds and then display video images of what your friend's QuickCam is focused on. Now isn't that just way cool! What'd I tell you? I don't joke about high-tech stuff.

Fine-tuning for better video quality

Before long, you may realize that, although you and your friend can see each other, the pictures are barely moving. You probably can see one picture every half a minute or so. That doesn't even qualify as slow-mo. It's more like no-mo. Not good. Not good at all. So why don't you fine-tune this puppy?

Reduce the picture size

Remember these words of wisdom: Big picture — bad. Small picture — good. The bigger the size of the picture, the more data it contains. And we know that more data takes longer to send than less data. Duh! So follow these steps to reduce the size of the picture:

1. **Choose Settings⇨Video⇨Image Size and Quality.**

   The Image Size and Quality dialog box shown in Figure 12-5 appears.

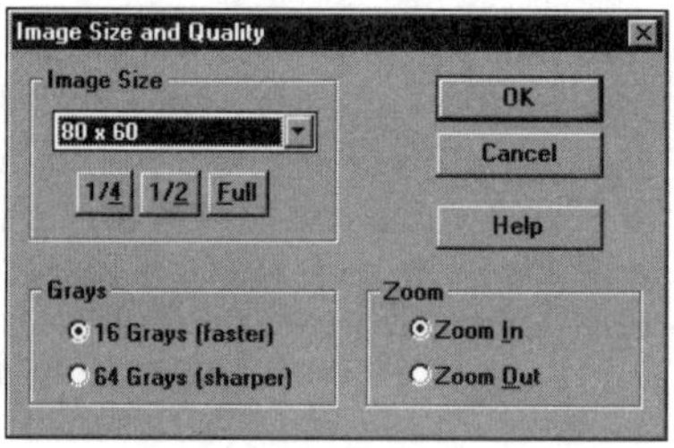

Figure 12-5:
The Image
Size and
Quality
dialog box.

2. **Click on the 16 Grays [faster] option if it doesn't have a dot in the circle.**

   Clicking on a dot until the circle is filled is called *selecting*. But you didn't really want to know that, did you?

3. **Click on the down arrow in the Image Size drop-down list box and then click on 80 x 60.**

   This too is called selecting. Whoop-de-doo.

4. **Click on OK.**

   You just reduced the size of the image to that of a postage stamp. I know it is rather small, but aren't the pictures at least moving a little faster now?

Turn audio off

During a live video transmission, VideoPhone always gives more importance to the audio portion of your transmission than the video portion, making the video even slower. If you don't care about the audio, follow these steps to turn the audio off:

1. **Choose Settings⇨Audio.**

   If you see a check mark next to the Enable option, your Audio feature is active. If you don't see the check mark, it's not active.

2. **Click on Enable until you don't see a check mark next to Enable to turn Audio off.**

   You just deactivated Audio. The next time you choose Audio⇨Settings, you shouldn't see a check mark next to the Enable option.

When you want to reactivate the Audio feature, click once on the Enable option.

Adjust the transmission bandwidth and frame rate

Now is that title a mouthful, or what? Don't worry. You don't have to call the CarX Man. We're not taking about that kind of a transmission. The *transmission bandwidth* is the speed (measured in *kilobits per second* or KBits/Second), at which a computer transmits the audio and video signals. A higher bandwidth means that the signals are sent faster to the other computer. The higher the transmission bandwidth, the faster your computer sends the information.

The *frame rate* is the rate at which your computer wants to receive the transmission from your friend's computer. Frame rate is measured in number of frames per second (Frames/Second). The higher the frame rate, the smoother the motion of the video you see. The lowest value is 1, and the highest value is 20.

The transmission bandwidth and frame rate settings go hand-in-hand. The exact values for these settings vary from one connection to another and also depend on the speed of the computers at both ends of the connection. You need to experiment with these settings to determine the settings that are best for your connection. However you and your friend both must make the changes to your computers; if you change only one computer, nothing is different.

Even though you may have set your frame rate as high as you possibly can (20), you may not see any change in the quality of the video. It may still appear choppy because the video quality largely depends on the transmission bandwidth of the computer at the other end of the connection. If the transmission bandwidth of your friend's computer is low, then a high frame rate setting in your computer doesn't make a difference. Your computer still receives video at a slow rate. This is why it's important that the settings on the computers at both ends of a connection be adjusted simultaneously.

To adjust transmission bandwidth, follow these steps:

1. **Choose Settings⇨Preferences⇨Bandwidth from the VideoPhone menu bar.**

   The Transmission Bandwidth dialog box shown in Figure 12-6 appears.

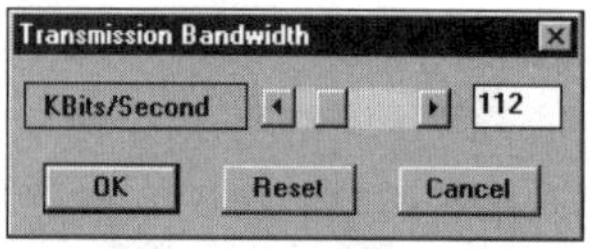

Figure 12-6:
The Transmission Bandwidth dialog box.

Transmission Bandwidth	✕
KBits/Second ◄ ▢ ►	112
OK	Reset	Cancel

2. **Increase the bandwidth value by typing a higher number in the text box or by moving either the scroll box or scroll arrows to the right.**

3. **Click on OK.**

To adjust the frame rate, follow these steps:

1. **Choose Settings⇨Preferences⇨Frame Rate.**

   The Adjust Frame Rate dialog box shown in Figure 12-7 appears.

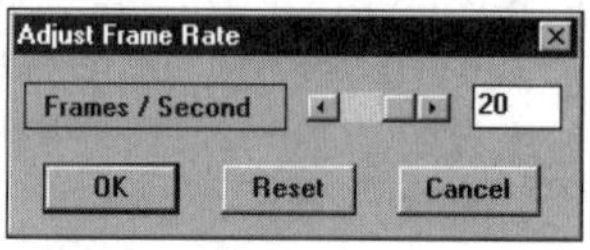

Figure 12-7:
The Adjust Frame Rate dialog box.

Adjust Frame Rate	✕
Frames / Second ◄ ▢ ►	20
OK	Reset	Cancel

2. **Increase the value to 20 — if it isn't 20 already.**

3. **Click on OK.**

Check the modem connection speed

If none of the above settings make a difference in your live videos, check the speed of your connection to the Internet Service Provider. Open the Connected to AT&T Worldnet dialog box. If you have a Pentium-based PC and a 28.8 modem, your modem connection speed shown in the window should be 24000 bps (see Figure 12-8). If it is anything less than that, you aren't making the fastest possible connection to your Internet Service Provider. If this happens frequently, you should contact your ISP and report the problem.

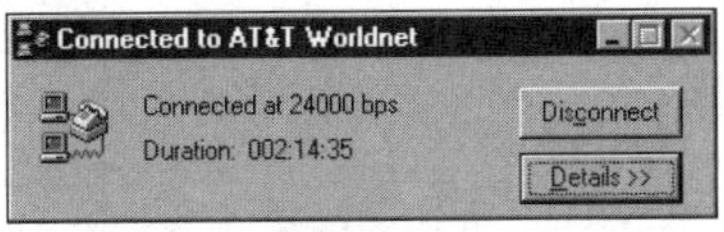

Figure 12-8:
The
Connected
to AT&T
Worldnet
dialog box.

Check whether your parallel port is bidirectional or unidirectional

The speed of the parallel port to which the QuickCam is connected can also affect the quality of the video you see. This speed is almost always determined by the type of parallel port you have. A bidirectional port is a lot faster than a unidirectional port. To check what type of port you have, follow these steps:

1. **Exit VideoPhone.**

2. **Double-click on the QuickPict icon in the Connectix folder.**

   QuickPict loads on your machine and displays the QuickPict screen.

3. **Choose Help⇨About in the QuickPict window.**

   The QuickPict information box shown in Figure 12-9 appears.

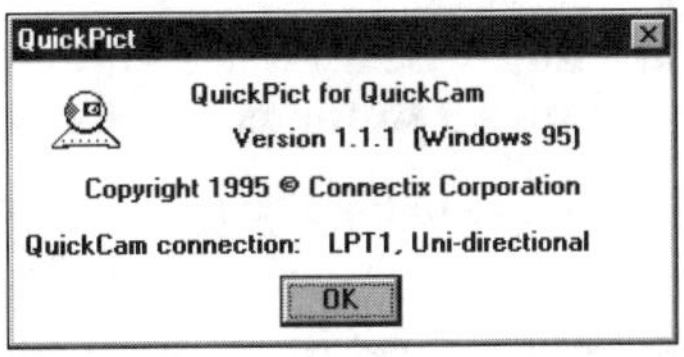

Figure 12-9:
The
QuickPict
information
box.

You can pick up a faster bidirectional parallel port at a computer store for about thirty bucks. If you've never opened a computer before, however, you're better off asking your computer-jock friend to install it. Otherwise, what should take an hour may end up being a weekend of frustration for you.

Recording a Video

Remember the *Friends* episode about Ross and Rachel's prom? The one in which Ross gets dressed to go to the prom, and Rachel leaves without him? Did you check the 'do on Ross's head? Whoa! Don't you wish you could have a video of *your* brother in a 'do like that? Boy, that sure would be a gem you could share with your family and friends for years to come on Thanksgiving. What's more, you could even share it with your friends around the world. How? It's simple. You first record the video with the QuickCam and then store the recorded file on your hard drive. Then you can send the file via e-mail to anyone who has an Internet connection. And the greatest thing about storing the video on your hard drive is that the quality of the video never gets worse even if you watch it a million times — unlike what happens when you watch your favorite movie on your VCR over and over and over again.

Recording a video with sound is very easy. Here's how you do it:

1. **Double-click on the QMovie32 icon in the Connectix folder.**

   The QuickMovie window shown in Figure 12-10 appears.

2. **Focus the camera and adjust the lighting appropriately.**

3. **If necessary, fine-tune the camera settings by choosing Settings⇨Video⇨Camera Adjustments.**

4. **Click on the Preview button (the button with the QuickCam on it) on the QuickMovie toolbar.**

   The button should now appear to be pressed or pushed in. It may already be in that mode, so you may not have to do it anyway.

5. **Choose Settings⇨Video⇨Capture Rate⇨Best Frame Rate to make sure that you have the frame capture rate set to the correct setting.**

   This setting ensures that the software is using the frame capture rate most suited to your computer.

6. **Press the space bar on your keyboard once, or click once on the red square under the display window when you're ready to begin recording.**

   The Capture Dialog dialog box shown in Figure 12-11 appears.

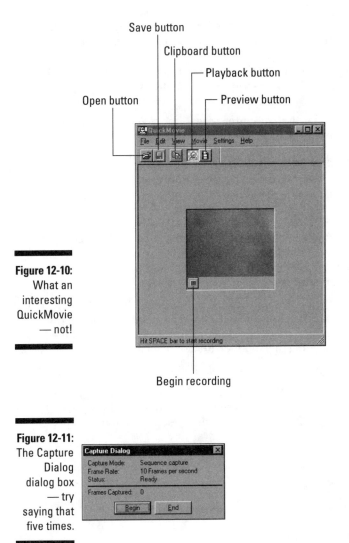

Save button

Clipboard button

Playback button

Open button

Preview button

Begin recording

Figure 12-10:
What an
interesting
QuickMovie
— not!

Figure 12-11:
The Capture
Dialog
dialog box
— try
saying that
five times.

7. Click on Begin to begin recording, keeping in mind these points:

- Don't record for more than 20 or 30 seconds at a time because video clips take up a lot of room on your computer, and they take forever to download via e-mail as well. It's better to record a few small clips than one very large clip. That way you can send your hip, Web-cruisin', e-mail-chattin' Grandma one small clip every day. Large files take forever to download. You want to make Grandma happy, not have her bawl you out for wasting her time downloading stuff. Also, if a file is too large, her computer may not have sufficient memory to load the file and view it.

- You don't have to leave the camera stationary on your desk. The cable attached to the camera is only about ten feet long, but you can get an extender cable to attach to the first cable so that you can move further away from your computer as you record. You can move the camera around just like you would a regular video camera.

- Keep looking at the computer screen to make sure that the camera is pointing where you want it to point.

8. **Turn on your microphone if it has an on/off switch.**

9. **Point the microphone in the same direction that you point the camera.**

10. **Enable the Capture Audio option.**

   Choose Settings➪Audio and then click on the Capture Audio option *if it doesn't have a check mark next to it already.* If the option already has a check mark next to it, click on Settings again and the drop-down settings list box disappears.

   If you accidentally clicked on Capture Audio even though it had a check mark next to it and the check mark disappeared, click again on the Capture Audio option to turn Audio Capture on. And don't ask me why I thought about including this Blooper. Remember, I'm the King of Bloopers.

11. **Click on the End button when you're ready to stop recording.**

   You might see the QuickMovie Windows Application message box shown in Figure 12-12. It tells you the number of frames dropped from the recording. The fewer frames dropped, the smoother the recorded video.

Figure 12-12:
Number of
frames
dropped.

QuickMovie Windows Application

Dropped 6 of 16 frames (37.5%) during capture.

OK

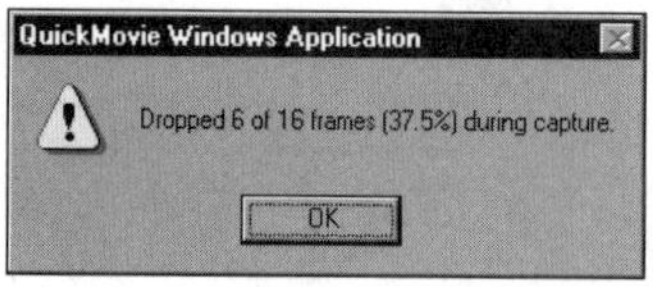

12. **Click on OK.**

13. **Click on the Save button (the button with the floppy disk on it) on the QuickMovie toolbar.**

   The Save As dialog box shown in Figure 12-13 appears.

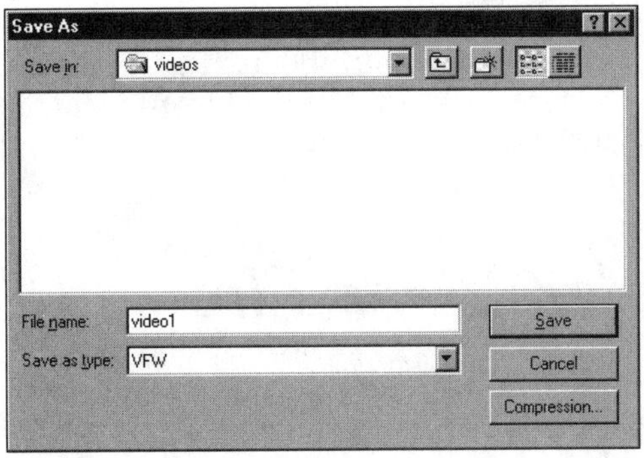

Figure 12-13:
Saving a
recorded
video.

14. Type a name in the File name text box and click on Save.

That's all there is to recording a video. The file is saved in the .avi —
also called Video For Windows — format.

A Few Recording Suggestions

You might want to follow these few suggestions while you record your video:

- ✔ Close the AT&T WorldNet Service software if it's running.

- ✔ Turn off your modem.

- ✔ Close any applications you're not using.

- ✔ Don't move your mouse while you're recording.

- ✔ Make sure that you have sufficient light, especially when you're chasing
  your sister under the table.

- ✔ Use a small picture window. Remember — big picture, bad; small
  picture — good.

- ✔ Make sure that you have the frame capture rate set to the correct
  setting. Choose Settings⇨Video⇨Capture Rate⇨Best Frame Rate. This
  setting ensures that the software is using the frame capture rate most
  suited to your computer.

Teachers, QuickCam opens up a world of possibilities to bring out the
dormant creativity in your students. If your students are a part of an international pen pal program on the Internet, you can have them record a short
movie clip, explaining a little about themselves. The clips can then be sent
over e-mail to the students' pen pals. If your students maintain home pages,
shoot pictures via QuickCam and add the pictures to the pages. You don't

need to have a QuickCam connected to each of the computers in the computer lab. Connect it to just one computer, and use that computer for recording movies and pictures. Then transfer the recorded files to the computer the student is using to send e-mail.

Viewing a Recorded Video Clip

Viewing a recorded video is extremely easy; easier than recording one. Unless, of course, you get embarrassed easily, in which case it's not easy to watch your dorky self in full-motion glory. To view a clip that you just finished recording, click once on the Playback button on the QuickMovie toolbar. To view a clip that you may have recorded earlier and saved on your hard drive, follow these steps:

1. **Select File⇨Open from the QuickMovie menu, or click on the Open button (the one with the yellow file folder on it) on the QuickMovie toolbar.**

2. **Select the file you want to view and click on Open.**

    The file loads into memory, and you see the QuickMovie playback window shown in Figure 12-14.

Play button

Figure 12-14: Viewing a video in QuickMovie. Who is that star?

Hit SPACE bar to play

3. Click on the Play button (the right arrow under the video) or press the space bar on your keyboard to play the video.

Hey, have you ever watched movies that were shot 70 or 80 years ago — the ones in which everybody and everything seems to be moving around really fast? Do you want to see what your video clip would look like if you were to play it at super-fast speed? Cool. Here's what you do. Move your mouse pointer to the playback status indicator (the bar next to the Play button). Start dragging the indicator to the right. As you do, you'll see the video being played. The faster you drag the indicator, the faster the video plays. You can even do that in reverse. Just drag the playback indicator to the left.

Don't Have QuickMovie to View a Video? No Problem

QuickCam is cool in more ways than one. Here's an example: What if the person to whom you plan to send the video you recorded doesn't have QuickCam or QuickMovie? No problem at all. Since QuickCam records videos in the .avi format, they can be viewed using a variety of software packages, not just QuickMovie. The *Media Player* included with Windows 95 is sufficient, too. To use the Windows 95 Media Player, choose Start⇨Programs from the Taskbar. Then choose Accessories⇨Multimedia⇨Media Player. Whew! Then click on the Play button.

Taking Still Photographs

When your family has had just about enough of your newly discovered video direction and production talents, you can introduce them to still more fun with the QuickCam. Show them how you can take still photographs with the QuickCam. What good are black-and-white pictures on the computer, you ask? Well, for one, you can take a picture, and a minute later, add it to any document you create with your word processing program; or put it on the flier you create for your next party; or put it on your home page — the possibilities are endless. QuickCam lets you take pictures in two ways: using either the QuickPict program or using VideoPhone.

Using QuickPict to take still photographs

QuickPict lets you take pictures of what your QuickCam sees. Duh! When you take any photograph, you're capturing only what the camera sees. But with QuickCam, you can take pictures of *what your own* QuickCam sees and also *what your friend's* QuickCam sees, assuming that your friend is transmitting live video to you. Using QuickPict is easy. It's like using a regular camera. To take still photographs using QuickPict, follow these steps:

1. **Open the Connectix folder, and double-click on the QuickPict icon.**

   The QuickPict window shown in Figure 12-15 appears.

2. **Make sure that your subject is willing, though. Tying up a brother or sister is generally not acceptable behavior. Focus the camera on your subject.**

3. **If necessary, adjust the brightness by using the sliding brightness knob under the display window.**

Figure 12-15:
Taking a
picture with
QuickPict.

4. **If you need to make further adjustments, choose Settings⇨Camera Adjustments and experiment with the Brightness, Contrast, and White Balance settings until you get them right.**

5. **Click once on the Save button (the one with the disk on it) on the toolbar to save your photographs on your hard drive.**

   When you click on the Clipboard button, QuickPict saves your photograph in memory, and then you can transfer it to a document or flier you're working on — or to any other application.

   Only one photograph is saved in memory at any give time in the Clipboard. Every time you click on the Clipboard button and then take a picture, the picture currently in the Clipboard is replaced by the new one.

6. **When you're ready, say "Cheese," and click on Take Picture.**

   Did you hear the camera click? Cool, isn't it? Those guys at Connectix thought of everything. The Save As dialog box shown in Figure 12-16 then appears.

Figure 12-16:
Saving a
QuickPict
picture.

7. Click once in the Save as type text box at the bottom of the window.

A drop-down list appears. You can save the image in one of three formats: Bitmap, TIFF, or JPEG.

8. Select the format you want.

If you want to add the picture to your home page, for example, select the JPEG format. The Bitmap format allows you to use the picture as a wallpaper within Windows. TIFF is another format that many graphics software can use.

9. Type a name for the picture in the File name text box. No, My Ugly Brother is not a good filename.

10. Click on Save.

QuickPict saves your picture in less than a second. Unlike paper photos that rip, get discolored, crumpled, or lost, this electronic photo will look just the way it does today, even 10 years later.

Cropping unwanted stuff from a QuickPict picture

Sometimes you want to save only a portion of the entire picture displayed in the display window. QuickCam allows you to do that. Here's how:

1. Move the mouse pointer to the display screen.

The pointer changes to a plus sign with a dotted square next to it.

2. Position the plus sign at the point in the display window where you want to begin cutting out (called *cropping*) the picture.

3. **Hold down the left mouse button and drag the mouse.**

Notice that as you drag the mouse, a square begins to form and becomes larger as you drag it across the display screen. Everything within the square is included in the final picture (see Figure 12-17).

4. **Release the mouse button when you've cropped the image to your liking.**

Everything that was outside the square has been erased.

Oooops! You erased a little too much. Now what? Well, you see the hand that used to be the mouse pointer? Just move the hand to the picture and double-click anywhere on it. Voilà! The whole picture is back.

Cropping window

Figure 12-17:
Cropping a
picture in
QuickPict.

Using VideoPhone to take still photographs

The VideoPhone software reminds me of the Swiss Army knife. It's small and packed with many useful things, one of which is the capability to take pictures. VideoPhone lets you take pictures of whatever is displayed in the display window. When you're not receiving live video from another QuickCam somewhere in cyberspace, the display window shows what your own QuickCam is focused on. When you're receiving live video, the window shows what the QuickCam at the other end of the cyber-connection is focused on. To take pictures using Video Phone, follow these steps:

1. Start a connection with a friend as described in the "Lights, camera, live video — Roll that camera" section, earlier in this chapter.

Your screen will look similar to the one shown in Figure 13-18. Notice that the status bar displays the word Connected. What the figure shows is what my friend's camera is focused on.

Figure 13-18:
Two little callers show up in the Connectix VideoPhone window.

2. Focus the camera, if necessary.

3. Choose Settings⇨Video⇨Camera Adjustments to make adjustments to the Brightness, Contrast, and White Balance settings, if necessary.

4. Choose Settings⇨Video⇨Image Size and Quality to select the size of the picture, if necessary.

5. Click once on the Camera button on the VideoPhone toolbar to take a picture of what's displayed on your display screen.

A Picture Roll window like the one in Figure 12-19 appears. Isn't it cool?

Figure 12-19:
Storing pictures in VideoPhone's electronic film roll.

6. Click on Save.

The picture is stored in an electronic film roll. You can save a maximum of 36 pictures in the film roll. When you save picture number 37, VideoPhone deletes picture number 1. Then when you save picture number 38, VideoPhone deletes picture number 2, and so on. That way, only 36 pictures are in the roll at any time.

7. Click once on Export to move the picture from the film roll to your hard drive.

The Save As dialog box shown in Figure 13-20 appears.

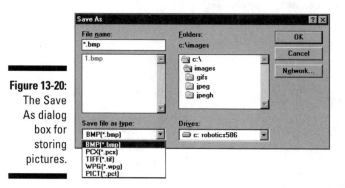

8. Click once in the Save File as type text box to select a format for the picture.

9. Type a filename for the picture in the File name text box and click on OK.

Your picture is saved.

10. Click on Close.

Now that you can produce your own videos, don't you think the whole world oughta know about it? Feel free to flood your friends' mailboxes and fill their hard drives with your Oscar-worthy productions. Who knows — one of your friends' parents just might be in showbiz and will hire you as the next *Home Alone* kid. Here's your chance to become a star.

Chapter 13

All the Phone, None of the Bills

*W*hat would you say if I told you that you can talk on the phone as long as you like, with friends across the globe — all for the cost of a local call? No long-distance charges. None whatsoever. You'd say there must be a catch. Nope, no catch. You call, you talk, you hang up, and you pay nothing. And . . . get this . . . you can do all this no-charge long-distance calling right over the Web.

How easy is it? Fairly simple. While I can't lie to you and say that the sound is as clear or that it's as convenient as a regular phone, talking over the Web really works a lot easier than you may think. But hey, give the Web a break — it's only been 125 years since Alex first sent sound over a wire and said to his colleague, "Awesome, Dude. Look what I have here." Alex who, you ask? Whaddaya mean, "Alex who?" Alexander Graham Bell, that's who. It's taken 125 years to get our phone system to the level it is today, so don't expect to get crystal-clear sound when talking over the Web — this new technology is barely a few years old. But even though this Web-talkin' technology is relatively new, you'll be surprised at how well it works. It's not as convenient as a regular phone call, but it works.

Question: In addition to Alexander Graham Bell, one other person also invented the telephone. Who was he?

Answer: Elisha Gray. He filed for a patent for his invention a few hours after Alexander Graham Bell did.

Although this chapter is primarily devoted to talking on the Web, which by itself is enough to keep a student thrilled for hours, I also include a discussion on using a *white board*. When users connect to a white board, all of them see the same screen. Using highlighters, they can mark areas of the screen and carry on a discussion in real time. If you have a class project in which you connect with kids from around the world, a white board can be a wonderful tool for creative interaction.

What You Need to Talk on the Web

To get started talking on the Web, you need the following:

___ An Internet connection

___ A sound card and speakers on your computer (Mac users don't need to worry about these.)

___ A microphone (Macs have microphones)

___ A software program such as CoolTalk

These days most computers come equipped with a sound card and speakers. Some computers even come equipped with a microphone. If your computer doesn't have a microphone, your parents can pick one up at the local computer store for under ten bucks.

Some computers work only with the microphone supplied by the computer manufacturer. Although such cases are rare, I have come across a few. Check your computer's user manual for guidelines on using a microphone. After you buy the microphone, switch off your computer, turn it around, and plug the microphone into the sound card — in the hole marked MIC. If you don't see a hole marked MIC, you may see a plug marked IN. Try plugging your microphone into that hole, instead. That's all the hardware installation you need to do. Simple, huh?

Talking Cool with CoolTalk

CoolTalk is one cool application. Not only does CoolTalk let you talk to another person as if you're talking on the phone, it also has an answering machine. You can leave an outgoing message like "Hi! Nobody's here to take your call right now because we're all busy cruising the Web. But if you'd like to leave a message . . . Beeeeeep!" CoolTalk lets callers leave messages if you don't pick up the phone.

No microphone? No problem. You can still communicate with a friend by typing messages using CoolTalk's Chat feature. I'll show you how. You can even draw pictures and have your friend color them at the same time, even though your friend may be in a faraway country. As long as the two of you are connected via CoolTalk, both of you can see the same picture on your screens and work on the picture together. In short, CoolTalk's real cool.

Getting all set up

Before you make your first call, you need to make sure CoolTalk is set up correctly. You need to tell CoolTalk a little bit about the kind of equipment (your modem, sound card, and so on) that you will be using to communicate with your friends. If you need to, you can download CoolTalk from the InSoft Web site at `www.insoft.com`.

Installing CoolTalk is a snap — just run the setup.exe program, which you can find in the folder where you downloaded CoolTalk.

To start CoolTalk, go to the folder where you downloaded it and find the CoolTalk icon, shown in Figure 13-1.

Figure 13-1:
Click on the
CoolTalk
icon.

Follow these steps to check your CoolTalk settings:

1. Double-click on the CoolTalk icon.

CoolTalk pops up with the window shown in Figure 13-2.

Figure 13-2:
The
CoolTalk
window.

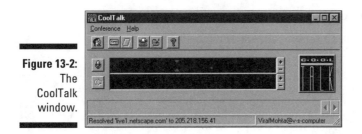

2. Choose Conference⇨Options.

You see the Options screen shown in Figure 13-3. If the Conference tab is not already selected, click on it to display the Conference options page.

Options

Conference | Answering Machine | Audio | Business Card

411 Server

Host Name: live.netscape.com

☑ Make me available through server

Do not request more than [500] entries.

Search for substring: [   ]

Bandwidth
○ 14,400 bps
● 28,800 bps or LAN

Accept Invitation
○ Never
● Ask
○ Always

OK | Cancel | Help

3. Select the speed of your modem in the Bandwidth section.

If you're not sure what type of modem you have, you can always ask the *walking encyclopedia* in your house, otherwise known as the *parent*. Parents have this uncanny ability to know all that's going on; whether it's happening at school, inside the house, or inside your head. Scary, isn't it?

4. Select Always in the Accept Invitation section.

Selecting Always is like saying, "Whenever my friend calls me on CoolTalk, I always want my CoolTalk to accept the call without waiting for my approval." When your friend calls you in CoolTalk, this option lets CoolTalk answer the call automatically.

5. Click on the Audio tab in the Options window.

You see the Audio screen, shown in Figure 13-4.

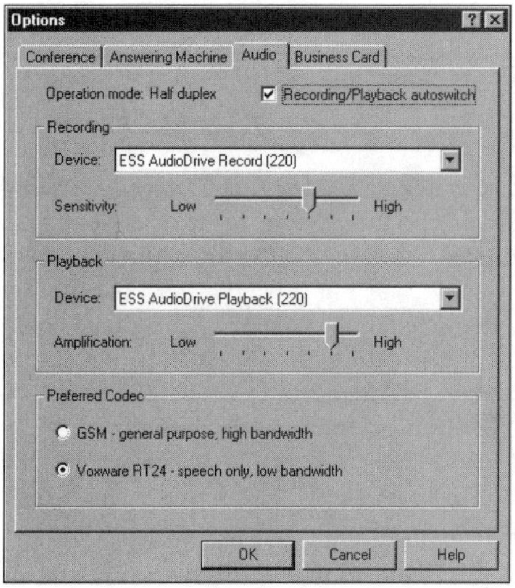

Figure 13-4:
Checking
the
CoolTalk
audio.

6. **Click on Recording/Playback autoswitch if the first line says Operation mode: Half duplex.**

   You then see a check mark in the Recording/Playback autoswitch check box.

7. **In the Preferred Codec section at the bottom of the Audio Options page, click on the Voxware RT24 option *only* if you have a fast machine such as a Pentium. If you're not using a Pentium, select the GSM option.**

   The Voxware option offers better sound quality than the GSM option, but only if you have a fast machine. A black dot appears next to the option that you select.

8. **Click on OK.**

Hang in there; you're almost ready to call someone.

Finding your IP address

Can you call someone without first knowing the person's phone number? Duh! Of course not. Similarly, before you can call someone using CoolTalk, you first need to know the person's *IP address,* a number assigned to your computer each time you log on to the Internet. An IP address is kinda like your post office address — people who know your address can send messages to you. To find out your current IP address, you first need to be

Roger, I copy . . . Over and out

If your sound card is a *half-duplex* card, you can't listen and talk at the same time like you can on a regular phone. Think of a half-duplex card as a tunnel through which traffic flows in only one direction at a time; first one way, then the other, then the first, and then . . . you get the idea. So if you have a half-duplex sound card, you talk first, and then you listen; then you talk and then you listen. To see if your sound card is half-duplex, choose Conference⇨Options and then click on the Audio tab. The Operation mode line at the top of the Audio window should mention your card type.

Now here's the catch. Sometimes, even though your card may be a full-duplex card (which allows you to talk and listen at the same time), the Operations mode line may show that you have a half-duplex card. If this is the case, the sound driver used by your card may not be communicating the correct information to Windows 95. Check with the manufacturer of your sound card for the latest sound drivers.

If you have a half-duplex card, try to end all your sentences with the word *Over* (like they do in war movies). This way, your friends know when you're finished talking so that they can get in their two cents worth. Remember, although CoolTalk can automatically switch between receiving sound and sending it with a half-duplex card, the switching depends on many factors and may not switch smoothly every time.

assigned an IP address — that is, you must connect to the Internet. If you're running Windows 95, you can check your IP address by following these steps (Windows 3.1x instructions follow these):

1. **Log on to your Internet Service Provider.**

   When you log on, you are assigned a unique address — your IP address.

2. **Choose Start⇨Run from the taskbar.**

   The Run dialog box appears.

3. **Type winipcfg in the Open text box and then click on OK.**

   The IP Configuration dialog box appears, as shown in Figure 13-5. Don't freak out over all the numbers and stuff. Just go to the next step.

NERD ALERT

Checking out your IP address

IP stands for *Internet Protocol,* which is a set of rules determining the way that information is sent and received over the Internet. One such Internet Protocol rule is that every computer connected to the Internet *must* have an IP address. Think of an IP address as a postal address. Without an address for your house, the post office can't deliver mail to you. In the same way, if your computer doesn't have an IP address, how can your friends send information to your computer?

An IP address has the following format: 207.116.44.16. Each of those numbers has a special meaning, but you don't need to be concerned with all those details. What you do need to know is that unlike your postal address, which remains constant, *your IP address changes each time you log on to the Internet.* For example, suppose that your current IP address is 205.118.75.19. When you log off the Internet and log on again, your IP address may change to something like 205.118.75.73. Notice that the last two digits of the IP address have changed? Each time you log on to the Internet, you get a completely different IP address from the previous time you logged on.

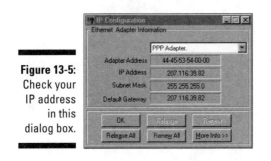

Figure 13-5:
Check your
IP address
in this
dialog box.

BLOOPERS

4. **Write down your IP address exactly as it appears in the window.**

   If you're not logged on to the Internet, your IP address shows as a bunch of zeroes. If you see all zeroes, go back to Step 1 and log on. You need to use your IP address when you start up CoolTalk.

5. **Click on the Close button to close the IP Configuration dialog box.**

   You return to the screen where you were before you ran the winipcfg program.

If you're running Windows 3.1, you can check your IP address by following these steps:

1. **Log on to your Internet Service Provider (ISP).**

   My ISP is AT&T WorldNet Service. You should log on to whatever service you use to get on the Web.

2. **Press Ctrl+Esc.**

   The Task List box appears, in which you see a list of the programs currently running under Windows 3.1.

3. **Double-click on AT&T Dialer, which appears in the Task List box.**

   A message window with a Statistics button on it appears, as shown in Figure 13-6.

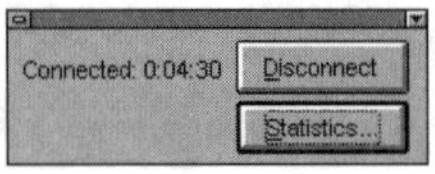

Figure 13-6:
The AT&T
Dialer
message
window.

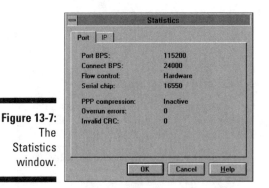

4. **Click on the Statistics button.**

   You see the Statistics window, as shown in Figure 13-7.

Figure 13-7:
The
Statistics
window.

5. **Click on the IP tab.**

   Your IP address appears on the last line of that window, as shown in Figure 13-8.

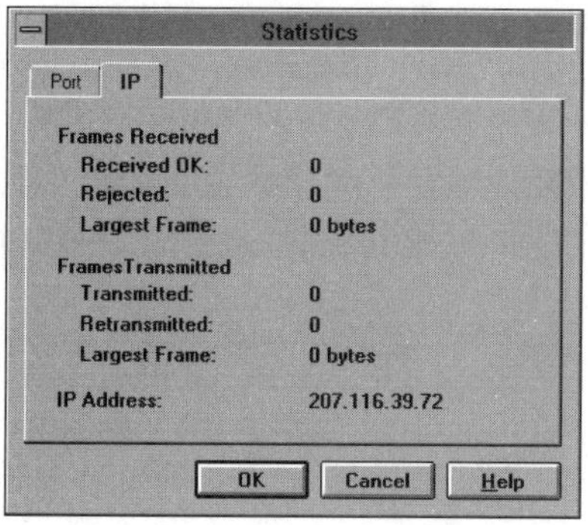

Statistics

| Port | IP |

Frames Received
 Received OK: 0
 Rejected: 0
 Largest Frame: 0 bytes

Frames Transmitted
 Transmitted: 0
 Retransmitted: 0
 Largest Frame: 0 bytes

IP Address: 207.116.39.72

| OK | Cancel | Help |

Figure 13-8:
The IP tab
shows your
IP address.

6. Write down your IP address exactly as it appears.

You're gonna need to know your IP address when you get CoolTalk up
and running.

7. Click on OK.

You return to the screen where you were before you activated the AT&T
Dialer.

If your computer is a Mac, you need to use one of two ways to check for
your IP address. If your Mac is running MacTCP to keep track of your
Internet connection, the MacTCP control panel is in your Control Panels
folder. Follow these steps to find the address:

1. Log on to the Internet.

2. Open the MacTCP control panel, using the Apple menu.

You may see the IP address in the window that appears.

3. If you don't see the IP address, click on the More button.

This window shows the current IP addresses. The address is probably
shown under Gateway Address.

If your Mac is using Open Transport to keep track of your Internet connection, TCP/IP is in your Control Panels folder. Follow these steps to find the
address:

1. Log on to the Internet.

2. Choose TCP/IP from Control Panels in the Apple menu.

The current IP address probably appears in the window. If you do not
see the IP address, your Mac may be using a different configuration.

3. Choose File⇨Configurations to change the current configuration so that the control panel shows other connection settings you may have on your computer (particularly if you have another ISP).

4. Look for the IP address in the window that appears.

There it is! There's that weird-looking number that controls so much of what you do on the computer.

Because anyone who wants to talk to you with CoolTalk needs your IP address, you need to let them know what your address is. How do you tell someone your IP address? Easy. You can just send them a quick, one-line e-mail message that says something like "Hey, Homie. My IP address is 123.456.78.90. So call me!" Then one of you calls the other. How? I'll show you how. That's real easy, too. Time to get talking!

Reaching out and calling someone

Have the IP address of the person you want to call handy. (If someone is calling *you*, make sure that he or she has *your* IP address.) Follow these steps to start talking on the Web:

1. Log on to your Internet Service Provider.

Although my ISP is AT&T WorldNet Service, you should log on to whatever service you use to get on the Web.

2. In the CoolTalk window, choose Conference⇨Start.

The Open Conference dialog box appears, as shown in Figure 13-9.

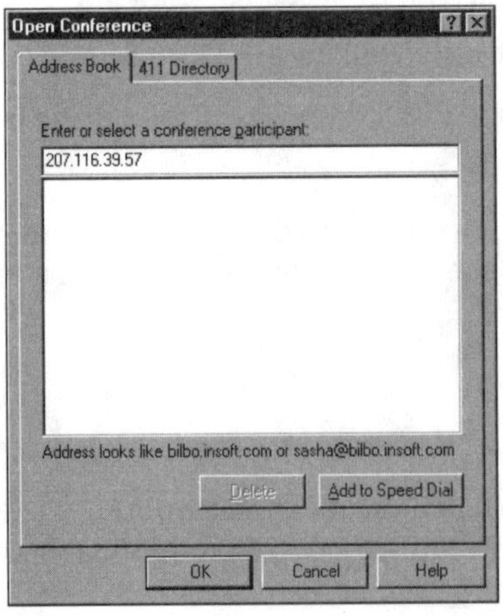

Figure 13-9: The Open Conference dialog box.

Open Conference

Address Book | 411 Directory

Enter or select a conference participant:

207.116.39.57

Address looks like bilbo.insoft.com or sasha@bilbo.insoft.com

Delete | Add to Speed Dial

OK | Cancel | Help

3. **In the Enter or select a conference participant box, type your friend's IP address. Duh!**

Make sure that you that you type the IP address correctly — don't add spaces or extra periods between the numbers in the IP address. If you make a mistake, CoolTalk makes you enter the address all over again. Bummer!

4. **Click on OK.**

CoolTalk starts dialing. On the other end, your friend should hear the phone ring. (Well, actually, it's CoolTalk that's ringing through the sound card.) A dialog box like the one shown in Figure 13-10 appears on your friend's screen. If the Accept Invitation setting on your friend's Conference options is set to Always, your friend's CoolTalk automatically picks up the phone and the two of you can start talking. If your friend's Accept Invitation setting is not set to Always, your friend must click on Accept to let your call come through.

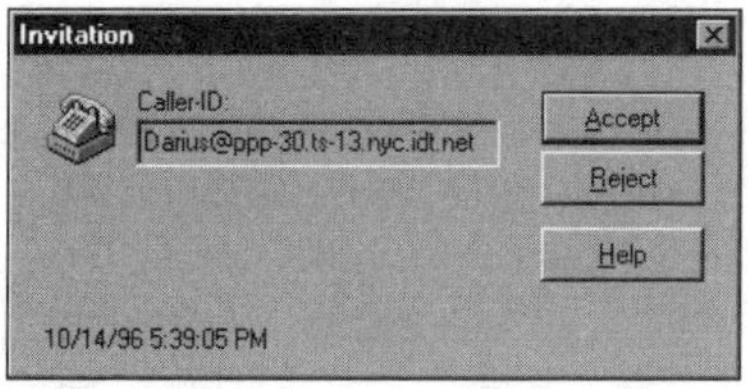

Figure 13-10:
The
Invitation
dialog box.

> **Invitation**   ☒
>
> Caller-ID: Accept
> Darius@ppp-30.ts-13.nyc.idt.net
>   Reject
>
>   Help
>
> 10/14/96 5:39:05 PM

5. **Say hello, my friend: You're talking on the Web!**

Talk it up — it doesn't matter if you're talking to a kid in India or a kid in Alaska. You're talking long-distance on the Web — and it doesn't cost you a penny extra.

6. **When you're all talked out, choose Conference⇨Leave to hang up the connection with your friend.**

How could it be easier?

Troubleshooting with CoolTalk

The first time I used CoolTalk to talk on the Web, I couldn't believe the clarity — I was truly impressed. I called my friend on the regular telephone, and on the Web simultaneously. That way, I could tell how much longer it took my voice to travel over the Web than it did by using the regular phone. The Web only took about a second and half longer than the regular phone did — that was the only difference; nothing else.

I'd *like* to tell you that you'll have absoooooluuuutely no problems using CoolTalk if you've followed my instructions. But then I'd be lying. You see, I've used all kinds of software over the years, and I hate it when, in spite of everything I do, the software doesn't run the way the manufacturer says it should. That really ticks me off. So I call the software hot line, and what do you think happens next? Right . . . I get put on hold and have to listen to the latest classical CD. Now, I don't know about you, but if I want to torture myself, I can slam my fingers in the door (I *hate* it when that happens). I don't need the torture of listening to some software support hot line's hold music. Come to think of it, some software support hot lines should change their phone numbers to something more meaningful such as 1-800-Who-Cares, 1-800-Go-Fish, 1-800-Take-A-Hike, or 1-800-No-Answer.

If you do have a problem with CoolTalk, don't panic — I've had my share of problems, and I'm sure that you may, too. Before calling the software support hot line and getting tortured by hold music, try these tips on CoolTalk troubleshooting:

- ✔ **Flip the switch.** People usually overlook the simplest fixes to a problem. For example, once I couldn't get my microphone to transmit anything. I tried everything and then realized that I hadn't turned the microphone switch ON. Duh! Some microphones have this switch, but not all of them do. Check for an ON switch if your microphone doesn't transmit. Also check the ON switch and volume setting on your speakers.

- ✔ **Get plugged in.** Make sure that you plugged the microphone in the right hole on your sound card. Make sure that you plugged the mike into the hole that says MIC. If your sound card doesn't have a hole that says MIC, try the hole that says IN. Also check whether you've plugged in your speakers properly.

- ✔ **Set the Silence Level.** If your sound card *is* half-duplex, it's important that your card sends a signal only when you speak and not otherwise. You don't want CoolTalk to send the sounds of your pet's panting as it lies next to you. Those background sounds trash your CoolTalk call. To prevent background sounds from messing up your conversation, you need to adjust the Silence Level. Follow these steps:

  1. **On the CoolTalk screen, point the mouse pointer to the Silence Level indicator.**

     The Silence Level indicator is shown in Figure 13-11. The mouse pointer becomes a double-headed arrow.

  2. **Hold down the left mouse button, drag the Silence Level indicator a little to the right, and then release the mouse button.**

     The status bar at the bottom of the CoolTalk window shows the new silence level.

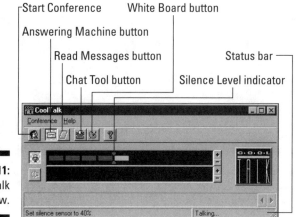

Figure 13-11:
The CoolTalk
window.

If you set the Silence Level too low by moving it too far to the left, your microphone picks up all kinds of little sounds. But if you set the Silence Level too high by moving it all the way to the right, you have to yell in the microphone for it to pick up your voice. *It's very important that the Silence Level be set correctly.* Most problems can be solved just by fine-tuning this setting. The best way to adjust the Silence Level is by talking into the microphone in a normal voice and then marking the position of the light green indicator on the Record Panel as you speak (just where the bright green one begins). Then set the Silence Level marker slightly to the right of that mark. Figure 13-11 shows the Silence Level indicator positioned exactly where the light green indicator ends and the dark green one begins. This setting gives you the best transmission and reception clarity.

✔ **Hello, hello, hello. . . ? Echo, echo, echo. . . .** If your sound card is the *full-duplex* type, you see a white Echo Cancellation marker near the Silence Level indicator. If the person you're talking to hears an echo when you speak (because the sound coming out of your speakers goes right back into your microphone), you can adjust the white Echo Cancellation marker. Set the Echo Cancellation marker to the right of the Silence Level marker. You can even try moving it all the way to the right. **Note:** If you have a half-duplex card, you don't see an Echo Cancellation marker — this marker appears only if you have a full-duplex card.

Picking the right time to talk on the Web

The amount of traffic on the Internet greatly affects the sound quality. When lots of people use the Internet (between 8 p.m. and midnight, for example), the CoolTalk sound quality is far worse than at other times of the day (although I've sometimes had good reception even during those busy evening hours).

The best time to use CoolTalk is early on a weekend morning when the rest of America is asleep. You see, because America generates the largest amount of Internet traffic, you get much better reception by talking during *off-hours*. Even though the *rest* of the world may be wide awake and using the Internet on an early Saturday morning, you're likely to get much better sound quality during those early hours. When America wakes up, Internet traffic increases manyfold.

Letting CoolTalk Do the Answering

You know what a pain it is to record messages on your regular answering machine, right? You record your message, you rewind to hear your message, you realize that you didn't press the right buttons — no message. You record again; you rewind again, you listen again, you realize you recorded over the message that Grandma left for your parents. You record again; you listen again; you go get the baseball bat. That's the way it goes. With CoolTalk, however, you're in luck. CoolTalk has an answering machine that's really simple to use.

Follow these steps to set the greeting (or outgoing message) that people hear when they get your CoolTalk answering machine:

1. **In the CoolTalk window, choose <u>C</u>onference⇨<u>O</u>ptions.**

   The now-familiar Options dialog box appears.

2. **Click on the Answering Machine tab.**

   The Answering Machine page appears, as shown in Figure 13-12.

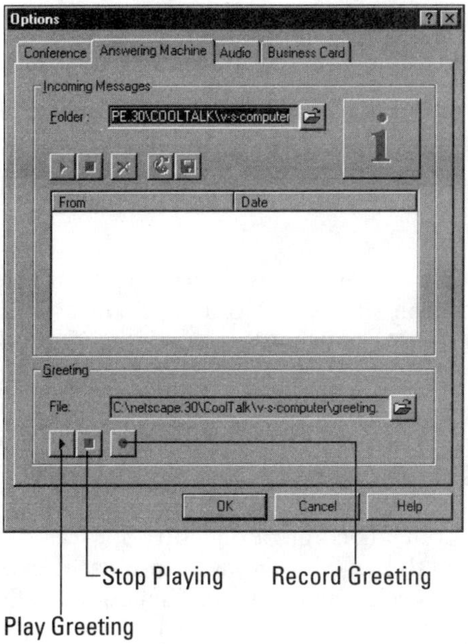

Figure 13-12:
Answering
Machine
options.

Stop Playing   Record Greeting

Play Greeting

3. **Before you record an outgoing message, listen to the one that's already in there. In the Greeting box at the bottom of the Answering Machine window, click on the Play Greeting button to hear your outgoing message.**

   You may like your current message, or you may want to update it.

4. **Click on the Record Greeting button to record your message. Wait a second and then begin speaking into your microphone.**

   You know the routine. Say something like, "Hi, you've reached my answering machine. I'm probably Web-surfing or something, so leave me a message and I'll get back to you."

5. **Click on the Stop Playing button when you finish recording your message.**

6. **Click on the Play Greeting button to listen to your recording.**

   Don't like the sound of your voice? No problemo. Go back to Step 4 and just record your greeting again.

7. **Click on OK when you're done.**

   This action returns you to the CoolTalk screen.

8. **To turn on your answering machine, click on the Answering Machine button, which has a picture of a cassette on it (refer to Figure 13-11).**

   To turn the answering machine off, click on the Answering Machine button again.

You can tell whether you have any messages if the Read Messages button has a number on it. If the button shows that you have a message, click on the Read Messages button to hear your message (refer to Figure 13-11).

Typing Your Message with the Chat Tool

After you've established a CoolTalk connection with your friend, you can even type messages and *chat* that way — typing your messages back and forth, instead of speaking into your microphone. This CoolTalk feature is especially useful if your phone connection is really bad or if the person you call doesn't have a microphone. On the other hand, if your phone connection is good, I don't recommend that you use the Chat Tool because you just add to the data CoolTalk has to send. Sending voice data is heavy-duty work. Check out Chapter 14 for more info about chatting.

To start chatting, follow these steps:

1. **Click on the Chat Tool button on the CoolTalk menu bar.**

   The Chat Tool button has the typewriter on it. The Chat Tool window appears on your screen, as shown in Figure 13-13. The same window also appears on your friend's screen. That's CoolTalk's way of saying, "Yo! Enough talking . . . start chatting."

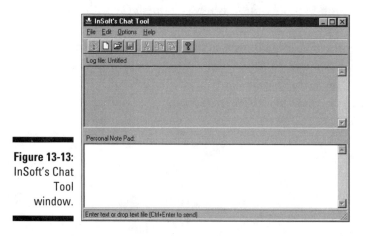

Figure 13-13: InSoft's Chat Tool window.

2. **Type away in the Personal Note Pad section. After you type each sentence, press Ctrl+Enter to send your message.**

   The Chat Tool displays everything that your friend types in the Log file section (above the Personal Note Pad section).

3. **Choose File⇨Close to end the chat session.**

   Pretty easy, wouldn't you say?

Hanging Ten with Your White Board

Of course you know what a white board is — no, it's nothing like a boogie-board or a snow-board. A white board is that thing that hangs in the front of the class, sometimes in place of a blackboard, where you have to go and pretend to solve the math problem you haven't a clue how to solve, in full view of the entire class, half of whom don't have a clue about the problem either. Sound familiar? Thought so. Actually, in CoolTalk, the White Board is similar to that classroom blackboard except that you don't have a room full of people watching you make a fool of yourself.

I think white boarding is rad. I can't get enough of it. With a white board, you can draw just like you do in Paint (or Paintbrush). You can display pictures you have on your hard drive. You can even display a screen from some other program that you're using. But here's the awesome thing about the White Board. As you draw or display a picture on the white board, your friend's screen displays the same images — what your friend draws, you see; what you draw, your friend sees. Only you and the friend you're communicating with via CoolTalk can see the White Board.

Like the Chat Tool, as soon as you click on the White Board button, it appears on your screen — and your friend's computer screen, too.

1. **In CoolTalk, click on the White Board button (refer to Figure 13-11).**

   The White Board button has the palette and paint brush on it. You and your friend both see a screen much like the Paintbrush or Paint screen you're used to (like the one shown in Figure 13-14). Now both of you can draw or type in the white space. Your friend can see everything you draw or type, and you can see everything your friend draws or types.

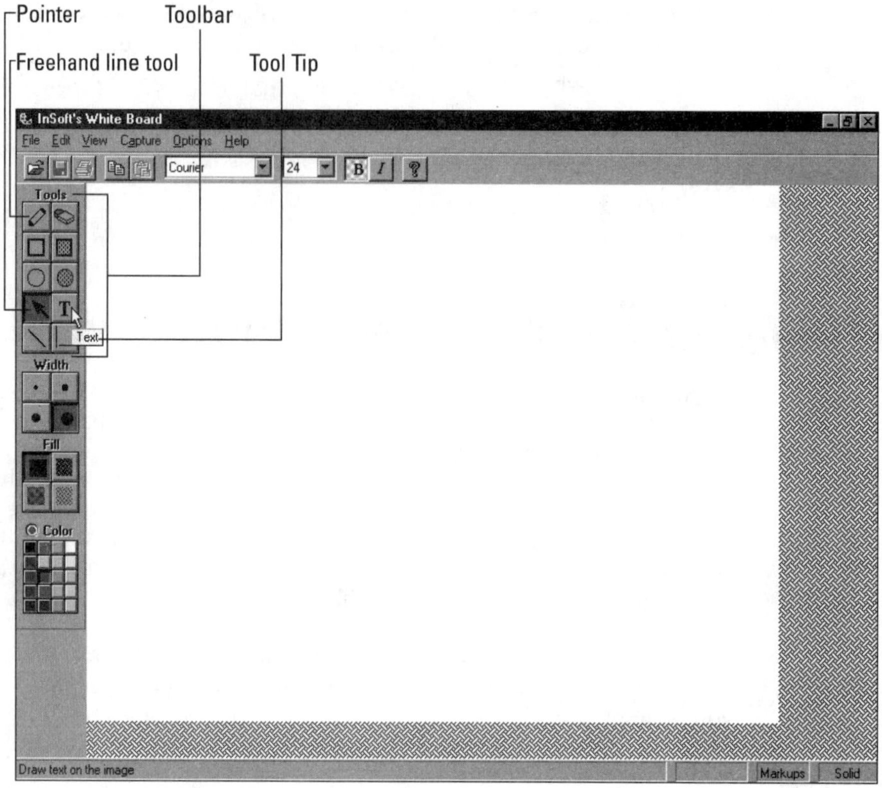

Pointer   Toolbar

Freehand line tool   Tool Tip

InSoft's White Board

File Edit View Capture Options Help

Courier   24   B I   ?

Tools

Width

Fill

Color

Text

Draw text on the image   Markups   Solid

Figure 13-14:
CoolTalk's
way-cool
White
Board.

2. Move the mouse pointer to any button on the toolbar (along the left margin of the screen), and leave the pointer there for a second. What do you see?

A little Tool Tip pops up with a description of the button you're pointing at. For example, Figure 13-14 shows the Text Tool Tip. Move the pointer to another button and leave it there for a second. You then see the description for that button.

3. Click the Text button on the White Board toolbar.

This button has the big *T* on it. The mouse pointer now has the letter *A* attached to it.

4. Move the pointer to any place on the White Board, and click once.

You now see a blinking cursor at the position you clicked with the mouse. That's where your text appears when you begin typing. If you want to move the cursor elsewhere on the screen, just move your mouse to the new position, and click once. Simple, isn't it?

5. Start typing. Your text appears on your screen as you type.

Now here's the cool part — whatever you type on your screen appears immediately on your friend's screen, regardless of how many thousand miles may separate the two of you.

Drawing on the White Board is similar to typing on it. Instead of clicking on the Text button, like you did when you wanted to type, click on one of the other tools. For example, click on the Freehand Line tool (the one that looks like a marking pen). Your mouse pointer changes to look like the marking pen. Hold the left mouse button and start drawing.

If you have a picture that you want to display on the White Board and then discuss with your friend, that's easy too. All you have to do is open the graphics file (those picture files that end with letters like .jpg, .gif, or .bmp) on the White Board screen. Then both of you can see the picture on your White Boards at the same time. You can even highlight those portions of the picture that you want your friend to pay special attention to. For example, I can open a picture file on the White Board, and then draw on the picture to show my friend who's who in the picture. Here's how you can mess around with pictures on the White Board:

1. **Choose File⇨Open and then select a picture file that you want to display on the White Board.**

   If you have a folder where you store picture files like .gifs and .jpgs, go to that folder and pick a file to display on the White Board. When the file appears on your White Board, it appears on your friend's White Board, too.

2. **From the toolbar, click on the Freehand Line tool (the one that looks like a marker), and use it to highlight and mark the portions of the picture you want your friend to notice.**

   As soon as you draw on the screen, what you draw shows on your friend's screen, too. Use the marker to draw arrows on the picture. (You can also draw mustaches, Groucho glasses, or Spock ears — whatever you want.)

3. **Click on the toolbar Text button, click the pointer where you want to put some text, and then type your note on the picture.**

   You can type stuff that tells what that arrow is pointing to. For example, my sister used the text button to add the words and then sent the picture to her friend in India (see Figure 13-15). Go ahead, Picasso. Knock yourself out.

Now that you have white-boarding at your fingertips, I wonder how you could make real good use of it? Oh, I know just the way! Here's the scenario: It's Monday morning, and you realize that you forgot to write that paper for Mr. Greb's history class. Ooooops. How could you have forgotten? As always, you try to feign sickness and stay home. You fool your parents into thinking that you're really, *really* sick. Your parents buy your story, and you secretly pat yourself on the back. You're getting good at this, aren't you?

But listen up, Einstein. You overlooked one little detail. You forgot that only last week you were bragging to Mr. Greb about what a whiz you were with the Web and how cool the CoolTalk White Board was. So when Mr. Greb hears of your sickness, he says, "Noooo problem." He calls you up and asks you to fire up CoolTalk to show him that paper. Get the picture? He wants to discuss your history paper with you on the White Board. Now isn't that a cool use of CoolTalk? I knew you'd like this story. Happy white-boarding.

Figure 13-15:
Marking up pictures on the White Board.

Chapter 14

Let's Chat

As if the phone weren't enough to keep in touch with your friends, now you have the Web. Isn't the Web way cool? I think it's the greatest thing to hit the world of computers . . . ever! And it just keeps getting better. New things pop up all the time. You stay away for a week and when you come back, the Web is like a whole new world — new things to do and new people to meet.

One of the best ways to meet people and make friends on the Web is by chatting. Yup. Chatting. Most people refer it to as IRC, or Internet Relay Chat, but that's not the chatting this chapter presents. Using IRC for chatting is borrring. That's all you need to know about IRC.

If IRC is your parents' Chevy station wagon, the chat stuff I'm gonna show you is a Jag. Which would you rather have? I thought so. But before you go any further, lemme tell you that if you think chatting is the same as talking on the phone, it is and isn't! Huh?

If Chatting Isn't Talking, What Is It?

Now I've confused you, haven't I? Coooool. That's exactly what I wanted to do. Juuuust kidding. You see, when you chat on the Internet, you're talking to another person by typing messages on your computer. You type a message, you click your mouse, and BAM! . . . your message immediately goes to whomever you're chatting with. You can chat with ten, twenty, even a hundred people at the same time. Everyone sees your message on his or her computer screen at the same time. Now because you're using your keyboard and not your phone, chatting's not talking in the strictest sense. But you're still communicating with people, right? Which is just like talking. So now do you understand what I mean when I say that chatting is and isn't the same as talking? I knew you would.

To get a better picture of chatting, imagine a huge house somewhere in cyberspace. An electronic house, if you will. Within this house are many, many rooms. And within the rooms, people use their own computers to send messages to each other. Some of the rooms are lame; some are cool, so people wander in and out of rooms. If they like the conversation in a room, they stay and chat with the people there. If they don't like the conversation or the people, they leave and begin chatting in another room. Some rooms have twenty, thirty, fifty people, all talking at the same time. Others can have only two people at a time. Not all rooms have people in them, though; some are totally empty.

What's So Cool about Chatting Anyway?

The greatest thing about chatting is that you make new friends from all over the world. Because of the way the Web works, you can log on to a chat room from anywhere in the world — which means that the people you're chatting with can be in your town or in a city across the oceans on another continent. It doesn't matter where they are. As long as they can get on the Web, they can log on and chat. Here's an example: Say your dearest and closest friend, the one with whom you've been since kindergarten, the one who took the blame when you stuck chewing gum in Ms. Teitelbaum's hair in first grade, the one whose T-ball glove you lost, is moving to Antarctica. You wonder how in the world the two of you are going to talk like you do every night. Those long distance calls can be mighty expensive, you know. They can wipe out all your savings . . . all seven dollars in one shot . . . Poof! Gone! Every dime.

Well, all the two of you need to do is start *chatting*. Here's how: You both agree on a time and day during which you will log on to a chat service and then you start a conversation using your computers, typing away and wasting hour after precious hour. That way, the cost to each of you is only a local call to your Internet Service Provider, unless, of course, your service provider charges you by the hour. In that case, your parents need to work on getting a service provider that doesn't charge by the hour. If they complain, just tell them I said, *"Plllease."*

Enough about talking. It's time to chat.

Are you ready to chat? Are you ready to shoot the breeze? Just follow these steps, and make sure that your friend follows them, too:

1. Start your browser and click on the Open button on your toolbar.

The Open Location dialog box appears, as it always does when you click on Open on the toolbar (see Figure 14-1).

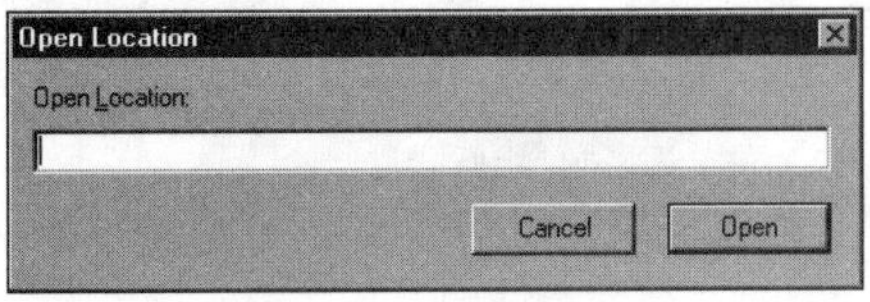

Figure 14-1:
The Open
Location
dialog box.

2. Type `freezone.com` **in the Open Location text box and click on Open.**

The browser flies you over to the FreeZone home page, shown in Figure 14-2.

3. Click on the <u>spiral</u> that has the sign Enter FREEZONE here pointing towards it.

A screen with a bunch of icons appears.

4. Click on the Chat Box icon.

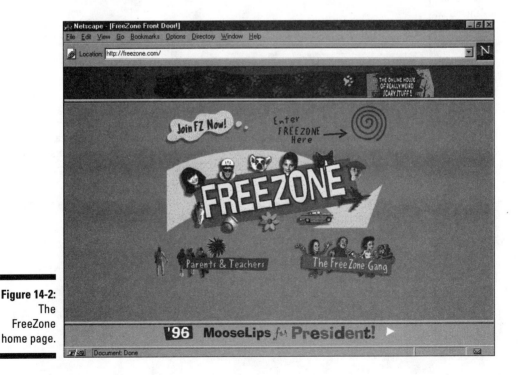

Figure 14-2:
The
FreeZone
home page.

The registration form shown in Figure 14-3 appears. All new users are required to register before they can start using the Chat Box.

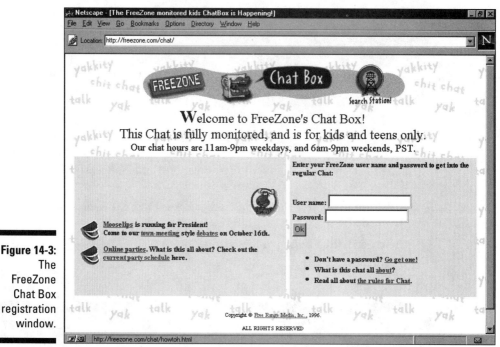

Figure 14-3:
The
FreeZone
Chat Box
registration
window.

5. Register in the registration window.

Remember, you don't need to use your real name in the User name text box. Come up with something imaginative — something unreal like Snoop Doggy Dog. I'm sure SDD himself spent many a sleepless night to come up with that gem. Or something like Coolio. Nothing's cooler than Coolio.

After you register, you see the Code of Conduct that you have to follow to be allowed to use the chat area, shown in Figure 14-4.

6. Read the rules carefully.

You don't want to be asked to leave for bad behavior, now do you?

7. Click on Enter Chat.

You're ready to yackety-yack, yackety-yack all you want.

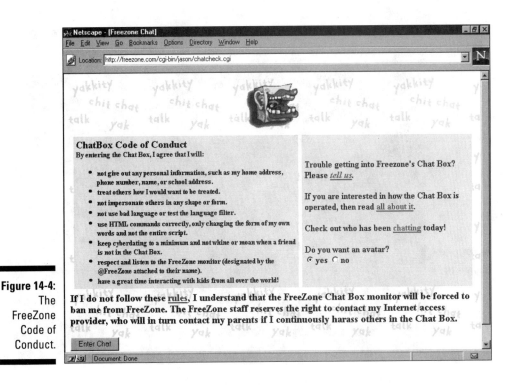

Figure 14-4:
The
FreeZone
Code of
Conduct.

This site rules. It allows you to become an *avatar,* an imaginary character in the chat area. The avatars available in FreeZone all have pictures to go with them. So if you're feeling out of this world today and want to be an alien, choose from the four or five alien pictures. Then, when you send a message in the chat area, your name (which appears next to your message) has a picture of an alien next to it. That's rad! If you don't want one of the avatars available on FreeZone, you can use one of your own. The site has easy instructions on how to do that. In fact, one of the reasons I like this site so much is because instructions for everything are really simple and easy to follow. Figure 14-5 shows a sample message screen with avatars.

FreeZone also hosts online parties. Have a birthday coming up? A gradua-tion? Just wanna celebrate for the heck of it? Let the folks at FreeZone know a week in advance, and they'll set up a cyberparty. Invite your friends, and have a blast. FreeZone also has a penpal (ooops! I should say e-pal) match-ing service, and a bulletin board section in which kids discuss stuff, leave questions (called *posting*), vote on issues, and so on. FreeZone is one cool site.

Figure 14-5:
The
FreeZone
message
screen with
avatars.

Other Cool Sites for Chatting

Yet another jammin' site is JAM!Z at www.jamz.com (see Figure 14-6). Like
FreeZone, JAM!Z too has live chat and bulletin boards. The site has separate
chat and bulletin boards for each of its many areas — sports, science, and
arts. As always, you must register before you can use either chat or post to
the bulletin boards. Registration is a breeze and takes no more than five
minutes.

One other Web chat site that you *must* visit is the WebChat Broadcasting
System at wbs.net. The site is wonderful, it is hip, and it kicks. It's the
future of chat areas on the Web. Trust me. You read it first here; you heard it
from me. This site is the one that other chat areas will use as an example in
setting up chat areas for themselves. WBS has many more people visiting it
than either FreeZone or JAM!Z because it is for kids *and* adults. WBS has
more kids' chat rooms that are divided into categories — pre-teens, teens,
girl chat, guy chat, and so on — than I've seen on any other Web site (see
Figure 14-7). And the rooms discuss a variety of different subjects. The site
even has a *private* feature that allows you to send private messages, messages only the person you're sending to can read. You can even create a
private room where only you and the person you want to chat with can sit
comfortably and keep chatting away for hours. You gotta check out this site.

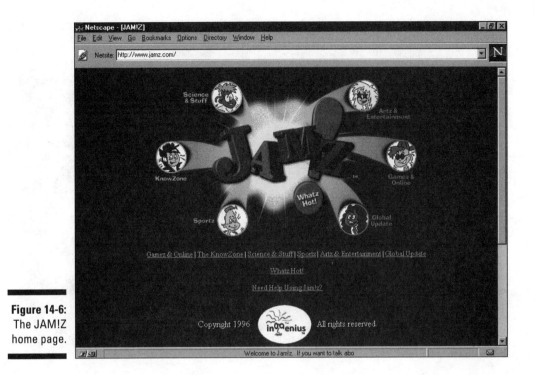

Figure 14-6:
The JAM!Z
home page.

The chat rooms in the WBS site *may* not be monitored as closely as the ones in FreeZone or JAM!Z. The site does have rules, though: Discussions should be acceptable to family members of all ages, and material indecent to minors is prohibited and will not be tolerated. I have not seen much that I consider indecent, but I want you to visit the site first to check it out before your child visits it. The site also has rooms for entertainment, current events, community-related stuff, sports travel, business, and much more. It's a cool place for parents to hang out, too — if you can ever get to the computer!

You're now free to yackety-yackety-yack to your heart's content. Just remember to keep an eye on the clock. Time flies when you're having fun.

Figure 14-7:
The WBS
categories.

Chapter 15

Playing in the MUD

· ·

In This Chapter

▶ What's a MUD?

▶ Suggestions, advice, and commands for novice MUD players

▶ Playing in the MUD — getting down and dirty

· ·

*E*ver play *Dungeons and Dragons*? How good were you? Good? *Very* good? Oh, really? So good that you were *bad*. *Real* bad? Ooooo, I'm scared! Well, how would you like to eat a slice of humble pie and get your toosh kicked. How? By playing against other players on the Web. Excuse me, that should be ". . . other players on a MUD." Yeah, on a MUD. Never heard of a MUD? Never even heard of *Dungeons and Dragons*? So, what's it like living on Mars? Okay, quiet down. Even if you've never played D&D, you'll get the hang of MUDs in no time at all. So don't worry.

What's a MUD?

Depending on who you ask, *MUD* could stand for Multiuser Domain, Dungeon, Dimension, or Dialogue. Confused? Don't worry. It's not important. All you need to know is that a *MUD* is a computer game played by multiple users at the same time. They all connect to one computer — called the *MUD server* — and the game is on. The players are all in cyberspace, but they could be anywhere on the globe. There is no set time for all players to log on. You can join a game in progress and leave it any time you jolly well please, without the risk of being called a crybaby — unless you're playing against me, in which case I'll drive you to tears when you come back. Just kidding. You also can be the only player playing the game at any given time and still have fun.

Although MUDs are text-based games — no graphics or sound in them — they do have a hint of violence. Perhaps *more* than a hint in some MUDs. Some parents believe that kids shouldn't be playing in MUDs because of this. If you buy your kids any of the hundreds of Nintendo or Sega Genesis games in which violence seems to be the norm, or you let your kids go to video arcades to play those gory games, you have nothing to worry about in MUDs. MUDs are timid in their violence content compared to those other games. But you may still want to check out a few MUDs yourself, just to be sure. Note that not all MUDs have violence in them. Some have no violence whatsoever.

A MUD is no video arcade game — it's better

If you imagine a MUD to be a shoot 'em, nuke 'em, blow 'em outta the sky kinda game, you're a little off track. Okay, you're waaaaay off track. As a matter of fact, a MUD doesn't make use of any graphics at all. It's a purely text-based game. Hey, wait up! Where do you think you're going? So what if it doesn't have graphics? It's still tons of fun. Hundreds of thousands of people wouldn't be addicted to MUDs if they weren't so much fun.

You can find many kinds of MUDs. Two common ones are social MUDs and adventure MUDs. In social MUDs, players are friendly to each other; they chat, gossip, share jokes, and discuss everything under the sun. In adventure MUDs, players assume fantasy characters, fight each other and demons and monsters, collect treasures, solve puzzles, and earn points. If you make an error, you get points taken away. If you die in an adventure MUD, you're automatically thrown off the game and disconnected from the MUD server. While playing, if your parents interrupt you to do some lame thing like taking out the garbage, you can log off the server, later log back on, and continue right where you left off. If you get bored with the MUD you're currently in, you can log off, connect to a different MUD server, and continue where you left off when you last logged off that MUD.

While you can find hundreds of MUDs on the Web, some are so good and so popular that you have to add your name to a long waiting list to be allowed in.

How do you move around in a MUD?

All MUDs use similar commands for players to get around. The commands may differ a little here and there, but they're basically the same. Learning to use these common commands should take you, uuhhhh, all of ten minutes. Read that last sentence again. I said, "Learning to use these common commands" should take you about ten minutes, which is not the same as "Becoming a *skilled player* should take you ten minutes." Becoming a skilled player takes a lot more than just knowing the commands. It's knowing what to look for as you move around the MUD. Moving around? Ummmm . . . can I be a little more vague? Puuuhleeeeease! Okay, lemme use an adventure MUD as an example.

A MUD sometimes has forests, streams, caves, castles, pits, and, of course, all kinds of creatures who'd like to have you for dinner. When you start, you get a description of your current surroundings. For example, "You are standing in a large clearing. You see a castle in the north, a stream in the east, and a path that leads into a forest in the west."

You can then choose where you want to go. If you want to go to the castle, you type North at the command prompt. You end up at the castle. Once there, you use the LOOK command for a description of what's around you. You may be told, "There is a sword lying on the ground." To take the sword, you use a command, such as Take sword. You might get 50 points for that. Now, had you not used the LOOK command while standing outside the castle, you wouldn't have known that a sword was lying there, just waiting to be picked up. You'd have passed by without picking it up and wouldn't have gotten the 50 points. Get it?

The object of the game is to collect all kinds of stuff in your adventure, not get killed (that's sort of important, duh), get as many points as you possibly can, and end up becoming a Wizard on that MUD. A *Wizard* is one who has mastered the game. No one is above the Wizard on the MUD — with the exception of God. The *God* is the person who created the MUD. A God has total control of the MUD.

Any Words of Advice Before I Play in the MUD?

Yeah, I have one word of advice: win. Other than that, I don't need to say anything. "But isn't that obvious? Like . . . duh!!" you say. All right, smarty pants, here's some real advice:

✔ **MUDs are addictive.** Very addictive; just like Web surfing is addictive. What? You're *not* a Web addict! You spend *only* six hours on it every evening? Uh . . . huh! Uh . . . huh!

✔ **Read the rules, the Help section, and the list of commands.** Remember that when you sign on to play on a MUD, you're a guest on someone's computer. So respect the rules that the God created for using the computer and for playing in the MUD. The MUD usually has a set of instructions that you should read before you get started. If you don't read 'em and then end up doing something really dumb (for example, asking the other players how to go north, which you could have avoided had you only read the Help file), you're going to get flamed. A *flame* is a few unkind words sent your way by someone who disagrees with what you said, what you did, or sometimes, just doesn't like the way you smell. So read the instructions, read the Help section, read the list of commands that could be specific to that MUD, and you'll be in good standing . . . until a monster shows up and cuts you in half. Then you start all over again. That bites, doesn't it?

✔ **Be polite and be patient.** People won't mind helping you if they feel that you've made an honest attempt to look for answers yourself first. If you still have problems, then by all means ask the other players or the Wizard, but be polite about it. Sometimes the Wizard is also God, and you don't want to face the wrath of God. If the Wizard isn't busy helping someone else, he or she may help you right away. If the Wizard is busy, you'll have to wait. Be patient. Remember, 50 players may be asking the Wizard for help. The Wizard couldn't possibly help all of them at the same time.

✔ **Don't automatically assume anything.** Just because you might be playing in an adventure-based MUD, don't assume that you can kill other characters or players. Some MUDs don't allow that. God could kick you out if you do that. Once again, read the rules of the MUD before you start.

Can I pleeeeaaaase start now?

Sure, you can start, but before you connect to a MUD, you need to set up your browser to work with a software program called *Telnet,* which is part of Windows 95. Telnet lets you use your computer to give commands to a different computer. Here's how to set it up:

1. **Choose Options➪General Preferences from the Netscape menu bar.**

   You should see a dialog box similar to the one shown in Figure 15-1. If you don't see anything remotely close to it, it's because the Apps page is not the active (selected) page in the Preferences window. Click once on the Apps tab to bring it to the front of the dialog box. If you're a Windows 3.1*x* user, you can find the Telnet software WinTelnet on the CD.

   If you're a Mac user, choose Options➪General➪Applications.

2. **Click on the Browse button next to the Telnet Application text box. You should see a dialog box similar to the one in Figure 15-2.**

   Don't worry if your screen shows folders other than Java, plugins, and netscape as shown in the figure. It's not important.

3. **Click the down-arrow next to the Look in text box and go to your Windows 95 folder.**

   Your Windows 95 folder may be named something other than Windows95. For example, it's called Win95 on my machine.

   You should now see a whole lot of files and folders where you once saw Java, plugins, and netscape in Figure 15-2.

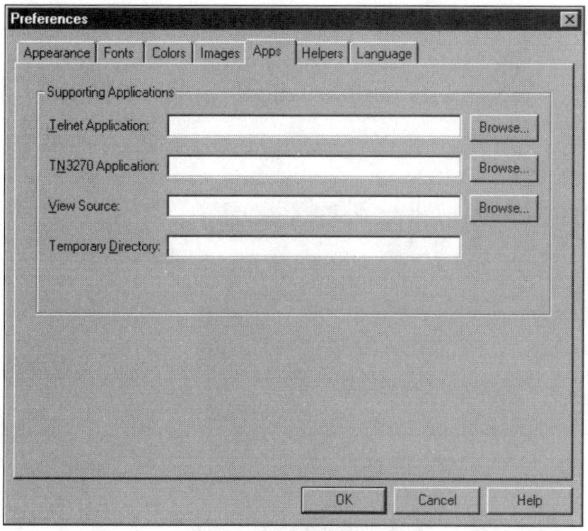

Figure 15-1:
The
Netscape
Options
dialog box.

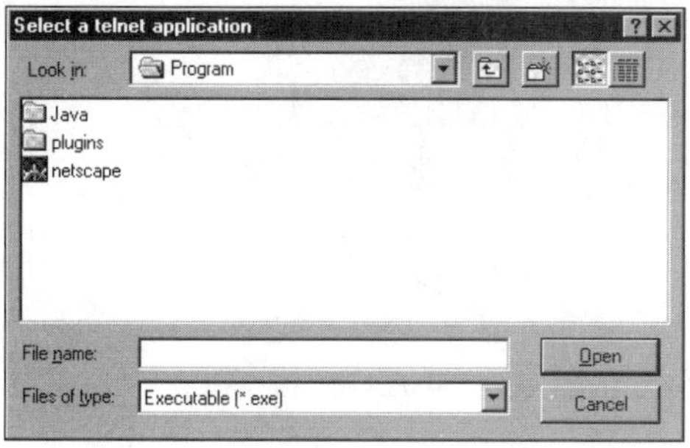

Figure 15-2:
Selecting a
Telnet
application.

**4. Scroll through the Windows 95 folder until you see a file named
Telnet (see Figure 15-3).**

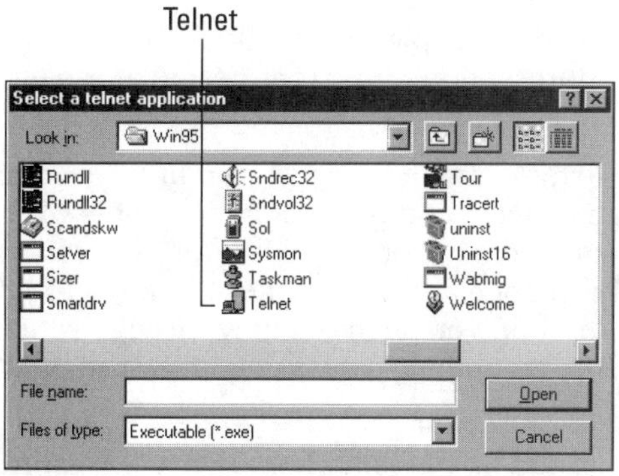

Telnet

Figure 15-3:
The Telnet
icon in my
Windows
95 folder.

5. Double-click on the Telnet icon.

You should now see Netscape's Preferences screen again, but this time, the Telnet filename and its path are displayed in the Telnet Application box (see Figure 15-4).

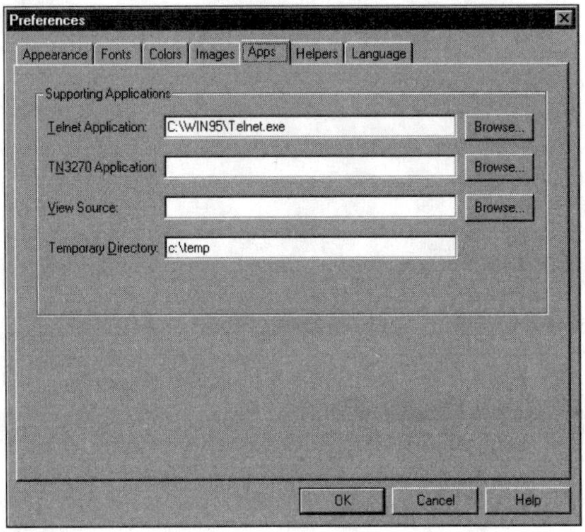

Figure 15-4:
Telnet.exe
is selected
as the
preferred
Telnet
application.

6. Click on OK.

You're set. You can now connect to a MUD server. Finally!

Connecting to a MUD

To connect to a MUD, you need to know four things about it:

___ A MUD address — for example, `aber.ludd.luth.se`. (When you enter the MUD address, don't type that period at the end — that's my period.)

___ A port number — for example, `6715`. A *port number* on a computer is a *door* through which a computer communicates with the outside world. The person in charge of the computer determines which port (door) to keep open and which ones to close. To join a MUD running on a computer, you need to know through which port (door) to enter the computer. Unless you know the right number, you can't join in the fun.

___ The MUD address and its port number are usually expressed together, as in `aber.ludd.luth.se:6715`.

___ You use Telnet to access the MUD address `aber.ludd.luth.se` on port number `6715`.

To connect to a MUD, follow these steps:

1. **Click on Open on your browser toolbar.**

2. **In the Open Location dialog box, type** `telnet://` **followed by the MUD address and the port number.**

   In this example, you're going to the Northern Lights MUD, which is an adventure-based MUD. Type telnet://aber.ludd.luth.se:6715 (We're using the Telnet application to access the MUD, so that's why you type the telnet:// bit in front of the address.)

3. **Click on Open.**

   Your Telnet program starts up, and you connect to the Northern Lights server in the blink of an eye. You should now see the screen shown in Figure 15-5, asking you for a name.

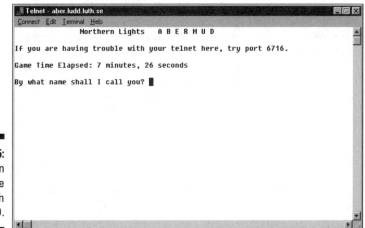

Figure 15-5:
Logging on to the Northern Lights MUD.

If you get an error message instead, check whether you typed the address correctly. You shouldn't have any spaces in the address, and you need a colon (:), not a semicolon (;), before the port number.

4. **Choose a fictitious name and press Enter.**

   MUDs are games in which you have the pleasure of becoming your favorite comic book character . . . a fictitious character you always wanted to be: Xena, Superman, Spock, Princess Leia, Tarzan, whoever.

5. **Make up a password and press Enter.**

   You should now see the welcoming screen shown in Figure 15-6.

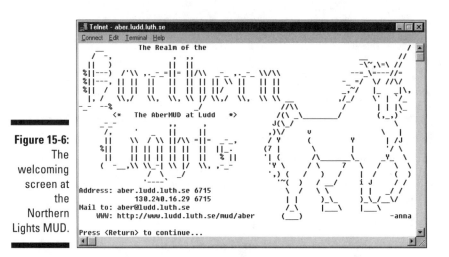

Figure 15-6:
The welcoming screen at the Northern Lights MUD.

Some computers are very finicky about your name and password. When they ask you for your name and password, they want you type them without any mistakes. Sometimes, even the uppercase and lowercase letters have to be typed exactly. For example, let's say the password you selected is *opensesame.* The next time the computer asks you for your password, if you type *OPENSESAME* — all in uppercase — the computer will deny you entry. You can get down on your knees and beg all you want; the computer won't budge. So remember your name and password because you may have to leave the game temporarily to do the dishes or something.

You go do the dishes in three and a half minutes flat, you rush back to your computer to log on to the MUD and continue where you left off — just one step from becoming a Wizard. And then disaster strikes, the sky turns gray, your fingers go numb . . . you can't remember your password!!!!! You type every combination of letters that you think make up your password, but none of them work. This can't be happening. You're so close to paradise, but you can't get back in. If only you had written your password down and stored it in a vault. Now you have to begin as a new player, from scratch.

So the moral of this tip is . . . ? No, it's not "Write down your password." It's "Do the dishes before you start playing." Okay, okay, the moral really is to write down your name and password and store it in a safe place.

6. Press Return or Enter as instructed.

You then see the screen shown in Figure 15-7. Notice that the screen tells you to Read INFO, INFO POLICY, and BULLETIN regularly! It also has a HELP facility. New users should always read these files before entering a MUD. They offer valuable advice on using the MUD.

Always read these before you play

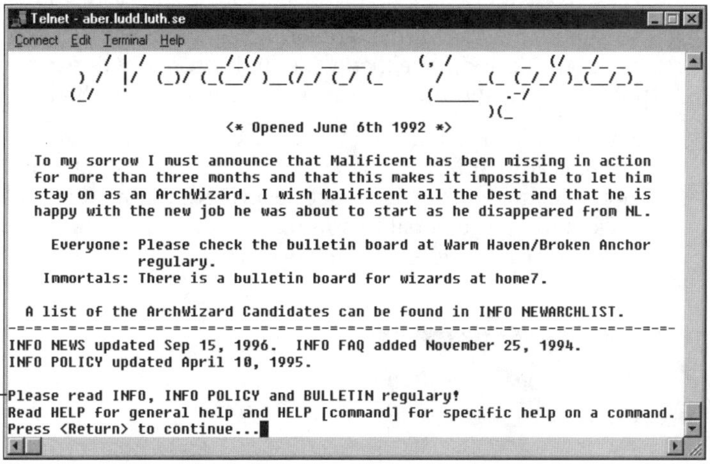

```
      / | /  ___ _ / /_/ /__) _/ /__ _        ( , /   _( _(_/ )_(_/)_
     ) / |/  ( )/ (_ /)_ /_/ /_/ (         (____ .-/
    (_/  !                                    )(_
                    <* Opened June 6th 1992 *>

   To my sorrow I must announce that Malificent has been missing in action
   for more than three months and that this makes it impossible to let him
   stay on as an ArchWizard. I wish Malificent all the best and that he is
   happy with the new job he was about to start as he disappeared from NL.

     Everyone: Please check the bulletin board at Warm Haven/Broken Anchor
               regulary.
     Immortals: There is a bulletin board for wizards at home7.

   A list of the ArchWizard Candidates can be found in INFO NEWARCHLIST.
 -=-=-=-=-=-=-=-=-=-=-=-=-=-=-=-=-=-=-=-=-=-=-=-=-=-=-=-=-=-=-=-=-=-=-=-=-
 INFO NEWS updated Sep 15, 1996.  INFO FAQ added November 25, 1994.
 INFO POLICY updated April 10, 1995.

 Please read INFO, INFO POLICY and BULLETIN regulary!
 Read HELP for general help and HELP [command] for specific help on a command.
 Press <Return> to continue...
```

Figure 15-7:
The
information
screen at
the
Northern
Lights
MUD.

7. Press Enter to continue.

You see the screen shown in Figure 15-8, asking you to type **E** to take a tour. I highly recommend that you take the tour; that way you get to try some commonly used commands for moving around the MUD and learn how to use it. Take the tour and come back to this point. If you don't want to take the tour, skip Step 8.

Notice the command prompt > at the bottom of the screen, followed by a cursor. You interact with the server and play the game by typing commands at that command prompt. Everything else you see on the screen is a message from the MUD server.

The command prompt

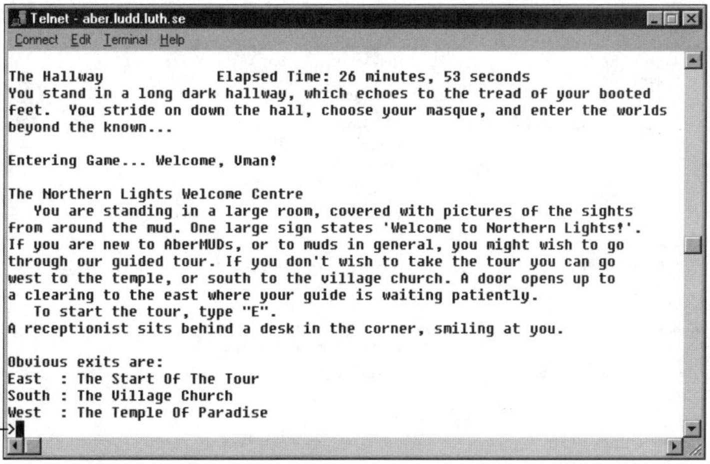

```
The Hallway              Elapsed Time: 26 minutes, 53 seconds
You stand in a long dark hallway, which echoes to the tread of your booted
feet.  You stride on down the hall, choose your masque, and enter the worlds
beyond the known...

Entering Game... Welcome, Uman!

The Northern Lights Welcome Centre
   You are standing in a large room, covered with pictures of the sights
from around the mud. One large sign states 'Welcome to Northern Lights!'.
If you are new to AberMUDs, or to muds in general, you might wish to go
through our guided tour. If you don't wish to take the tour you can go
west to the temple, or south to the village church. A door opens up to
a clearing to the east where your guide is waiting patiently.
   To start the tour, type "E".
A receptionist sits behind a desk in the corner, smiling at you.

Obvious exits are:
East  : The Start Of The Tour
South : The Village Church
West  : The Temple Of Paradise
>
```

Figure 15-8:
Are you
ready to
tour the
MUD?

If you press a key on your keyboard, but the letter doesn't display on your screen, choose Terminal⇨Preferences from the Telnet menu bar. You should see the screen shown in Figure 15-9. The Local Echo check box should have a check in it. It probably doesn't, so click in that box . You should now see a check mark in it. Click on OK.

Sometimes, instead of the character you type not appearing on the screen, it appears twice. It seems as if you're seeing double. In that case follow the same procedure just described, but instead of leaving a check mark in the Local Echo box, take the check mark out by clicking on the box once and then clicking on OK.

Figure 15-9:
Turning off
the local
echo.

8. **To start your tour, type** E **at the command prompt and then press Enter or Return.**

You're taken on a tour of the MUD and then dropped off at the command prompt again.

9. **Type** info **at the command prompt and then press Enter or Return.**

You see the screen shown in Figure 15-10, displaying the various topics on which information is available.

```
Telnet - aber.ludd.luth.se
Connect  Edit  Terminal  Help
Information can be found on several different subjects.

Subjects:

  - GAME AND QUEST INFO      - MISC INFO            - FUN STUFF
      * game                    * frobs                * color
      * quests                  * motd                 * dead
      * qlist                   * messages             * stats
      * altquests               * news      <960915>   * ftp       <941118>
      * faq       <941120>      * oldnews              * www
      * spells                  * oldnews1             * moose
                                * oldnews2             * bed
  - IMPORTANT INFO              * mudlist              * food
      * policy                  * mlist                * fish
      * important               * powers               * maur
      * telnet                  * zones                * muffins
      * copyright               * please               * story
      * philosophy              * rooms     <960820>

Type 'info [subject]' to read the info texts.

Type HELP for a brief list of commands, type HELP [command] for detailed help
Press [Return] to continue, `q' to quit or `?' for help...
```

Figure 15-10:
Information
topics.

10. To quit this screen, type q **and then press Enter to return to the command prompt.**

Now let's get some info on the game itself and see what it's all about.

11. Type info game **and press Enter.**

You see the screen shown in Figure 15-11.

```
 Telnet - aber.ludd.luth.se                                    _  □ ✕
Connect  Edit  Terminal  Help
>info game

The idea of the current game is to score 300,000 points, to solve some "quests
and become a wizard.

Points are scored for dropping treasure into the sacrificial pit at the temple
the village church, the forest chapel or the dancing stones. Points can also b
scored for killing monsters and solving puzzles.
Remember to use the VALUE command to check the worth of items you find before
you pit them; some objects actually have negative values...

The game has a complete combat system, one that considers weapons and shields,
and also allows people to FLEE from fights.  To complement this the game also
has a magic system with several spells of both informational, combat and
utility nature.

All this adventure and mayhem is fine, but there is one important problem with
life in the game, that is dying.

There are two ways of dying in the game.  Dying through little accidents with
puzzles is a non-fatal event that simply kicks you off the game, while dying i
a fight is fatal (you lose half of your score).  Most players will rapidly
Press [Return] to continue, `q' to quit or `?' for help...
```

Figure 15-11:
Information
on the
game.

12. Read the information and then press Enter to return to the command prompt.

If you look closely at Figure 15-10, you notice that one of the topics on which information is available in the GAME AND QUEST INFO section is *FAQ* — Frequently Asked Questions. This list contains questions that the Wizards have gotten tired of answering. So they put all the questions in one place for newbies like you and me.

13. Type info faq **and press Enter.**

You're given a choice of two kinds of FAQs: one for the game and the other for quests. A *quest* is a puzzle. MUDs have puzzles all over the place, but they're hidden. You first need to find them and then solve them. That's how you win points. On certain MUDs, that's the only way you can become a Wizard — by solving all the puzzles.

Read the FAQs. They take about fifteen minutes to read, but they give you more tips for playing the game than you would find out on your own in fifteen hours. But if you don't, you might get massacred by a monster in your fifth hour. (Boo hoo! Let me bring out my violin.)

14. Type info game-faq **and press Enter.**

You see the screen shown in Figure 15-12.

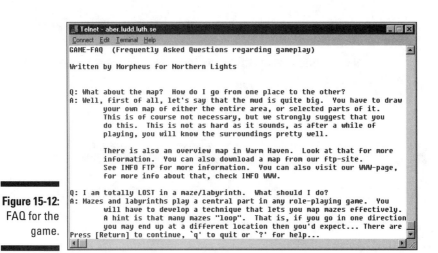

Figure 15-12:
FAQ for the
game.

15. Keep pressing Enter to move through the FAQ or type q **to quit.**

When you're finished, the MUD returns you to the command prompt.

16. Type info quest-faq **and press Enter to read the FAQ about quests.**

You see the screen shown in Figure 15-13.

Figure 15-13:
FAQ for
quests.

17. Scroll through the list by pressing Enter or type q **to quit.**

When you're finished, the MUD returns you to the command prompt.

Now you're armed with quite a bit of information to begin playing the game. The following section on common commands should help you get started.

Some common MUD commands

Commands vary a little from MUD to MUD, but they're fairly standard in the MUD world. It's always a good idea to read the online documentation on the MUD server itself to know what works and what doesn't. The following commands work on most MUDs.

Command	*What It Does*
Who	Lists the players
Look	Describes your surrounding
Examine	Describes a particular object
Say	Sends a message to everyone
Shout	Same as Say
Tell	Send a message to a particular player — not to all the players
Get	Pick up an object
Drop	Drop an object you're carrying
Drink	Drink
Eat	Eat
North/South/East/West	Go north/south/east/west (sometimes you can just use N/S/E/W)
Inventory	Shows all the loot that you have (sometimes you can just use I or inv)
Exits	Shows all the exits available to you
Autoexits	Constantly displays all the available exits so that you don't have to type exits over and over again. To turn this feature off, type autoexits again.
Quit	Disconnects you from the MUD server

With the exception of certain command like LOOK or WHO, you have to follow the command with the object or item you're performing the command on. For example, DRINK by itself means nothing. But if you have coffee in your inventory, you type DRINK COFFEE. Want another example? GET by itself means nothing. You type GET SWORD if you want to pick up a sword. Get it? Simple? Fun? Then get started. Remember, when you want to quit playing, just type QUIT and press Enter.

After you quit the MUD

After you end your MUD session, you see a blank Telnet window with a blinking cursor. If you quit the MUD accidentally and want to return to it, follow these steps:

1. Click on Connect on the Telnet menu bar.

The Connect menu shows the address of the MUD you had just been connected to (see Figure 15-14).

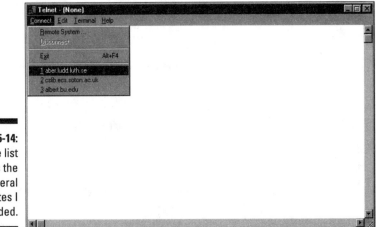

Figure 15-14:
The list shows the last several sites I invaded.

2. Select the address of the MUD and click once.

You automatically connect to that server.

If you want to leave the MUD, just close the Telnet window.

Although you may disconnect from a Telnet application, your Web connection may still be active in the background. Therefore, you can continue surfing the Web. Just return to your browser to do so. When you finish surfing, remember to disconnect.

Some other MUD references on the Web

Cool Web site

You can find so many MUDs on the planet that it's hard to have one comprehensive list of them all. But if I had to recommend one Web site for you to go to — just one — it would have to be the *Index of The MUD Resource Collection* at the University of Pennsylvania. Lydia Leong maintains the site, a one-stop shop of MUD info. The site has lots, I mean LOTS, of MUD information. It also has links to FAQs, Web sites, documents, manuals, archives . . . you name it. The address is `www.cis.upenn.edu/~~lwl/mudinfo.html`.

Newsgroups

The following newsgroups are all MUD-related:

- ✔ `rec.games.mud.announce`
- ✔ `rec.games.mud.admin`
- ✔ `rec.games.mud.diku`
- ✔ `rec.games.mud.lp`
- ✔ `rec.games.mud.misc`
- ✔ `rec.games.mud.tiny`

If you want to know more about newsgroups, check out Chapter 8.

Go ahead, wallow in the MUD. Nobody's looking!

PART V
Building Castles in the Air

"Hold your horses. It takes time to build a home page for someone your size."

In this part . . .

Now that you've visited other peoples' home pages on the Web, it's about time to stake a claim to a piece of cyberspace yourself, right? This part is where you can find out how. And, unlike what you may have heard, you don't need to know anything about programming. Not a word of cryptic code. None . . . nada . . . zip. Get the picture? Good. Now it's time to convert that picture into a home page.

Chapter 16

Building a Home on the Web

*H*ave you wondered how all those home pages on the Web are created? Especially the ones that make you go, "WOW! That one kicks! How'd they do that?" Ever thought of having your very own home page, too? Sure you have! Wouldn't that be cool? You could then tell your classmates, "Even *I* have a Web site now! Here's the address. Check it out." But you probably thought that setting up a Web site was just way, way too much work. Besides, you never, ever, EVER took a class in computer programming. So how are you going to know how to set up the site? And how much time will you have to spend on it? You probably just shelved the idea because you thought you needed to take a whole year off from school to work on it, and although you wouldn't mind that at allll, somehow your parents wouldn't be too thrilled about it. Well, think again! Creating a Web page my way is a piece of cake. If you don't believe me, come along. I'll show you.

Do Home Pages Have Homes, Too?

Sure, home pages have homes. They're called Web servers. A *Web server* is a computer for storing home pages. The computer looks like a regular computer, but its only purpose is to store peoples' home pages. When you click on a link as you cruise the Web, going from one home page to the next, what you're actually doing is jumping from one Web server to another. The Web is a bunch of Web servers linked together.

So, when you want to see a page and you click on its link, you're telling your browser, "Yo! Netscape Dude or Yo! Internet Explorer, go to this Web server and get me this page." Your browser then tells the Web server, "Send me that page . . . and hurry up, will you? I haven't got all day." More than one person can ask for the same page, and like a good server in a restaurant, the Web server tries to serve everybody as quickly as possible. Sometimes the service is just a little slower than at other times. Can't help it.

Here's a startling thought. Even though you can create your own home page on your own computer, it cannot live on your computer if you want the world to see it. If your page stays on your computer only, you and you alone will be able to appreciate it. Nobody else. You have to place your page on a Web server somewhere in cyberspace so that others can get to it.

Okay, so do you know anybody with a Web server who'll let you put your home page on it after you create it? For free? No problem, 'cause I have some good news for you. I know of a company that lets you put your page on its Web server for free, without charging you a dime. Go tell your parents that there are some things in this world you can get for free!

Laying the Foundation of Your Home Page

First, you're going to the company that gives free home page space, get yourself a vacant house for the home page, and then create the home page. You'll be amazed how little time all of this takes. Just follow these steps:

1. Fire up your browser and click on Open on the toolbar.

The Open Location dialog box appears (see Figure 16-1).

Figure 16-1: The Open Location dialog box.

2. Type www.geocities.com **and click on Open.**

Figure 16-2 shows the GeoCities home page, the home for your Web page. The page has a link for <u>Free Home Pages & Free Member Email</u>.

The link that starts it all

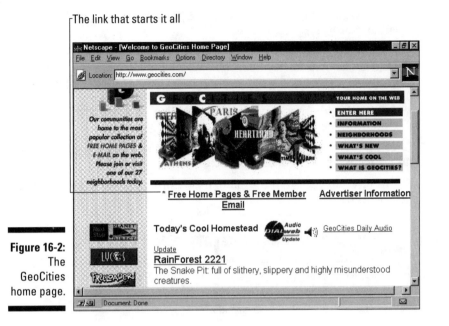

Figure 16-2:
The
GeoCities
home page.

3. Click on the <u>Free Home Pages & Free Member Email</u> link.

The Homesteading Program screen shown in Figure 16-3 appears.

The link you're looking for

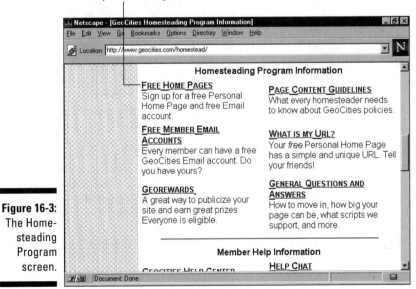

Figure 16-3:
The Home-
steading
Program
screen.

4. Scroll down until you see a link for <u>FREE HOME PAGES</u> and then click on that link.

The next screen explains how to select an address for your home. GeoCities has over 27 neighborhoods in which you can live (or store your home page). Each neighborhood has a theme. For example, if you like movies and television, you can live in the Hollywood neighborhood. The SoHo neighborhood, on the other hand, is an area for people who are interested in the arts.

5. Click on the <u>Neighborhood Directory</u> link to see a list of all neighborhoods from which to make a selection.

Figure 16-4 shows part of the list of neighborhoods and a brief description of each.

Figure 16-4: The list and description of GeoCities neighborhoods.

6. Click on the neighborhood in which you'd like to live.

I'm clicking on SoHo. You can click the neighborhood you want. You may want to check out the Enchanted Forest, but be careful. You never know what lurks behind those trees. Figure 16-5 shows the page that appears. You've just picked a neighborhood, but you can't pitch a tent on just any street in the neighborhood and move in. That's a no-no! You need to join the neighborhood before you can move into a vacant house with an address.

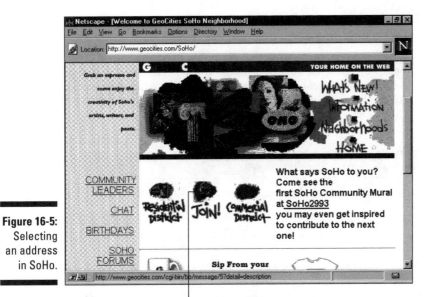

Figure 16-5:
Selecting
an address
in SoHo.

Click on Join

7. Click on Join.

The next screen asks you to confirm that you really want to move into
SoHo (see Figure 16-6).

Figure 16-6:
The screen
for saying,
"Yep. I was
in my right
mind when
I chose that
neighbor-
hood."

8. Click on Yes.

The *vacancy locator* screen shown in Figure 16-7 appears. Since each neighborhood has about 10,000 people in it, you may think that the best way to find a vacant house is to pick a number and see if the house on that lot is vacant. But you can't just pick a number. Nooo. You have to pick a range of numbers to see all the houses that are vacant in that range.

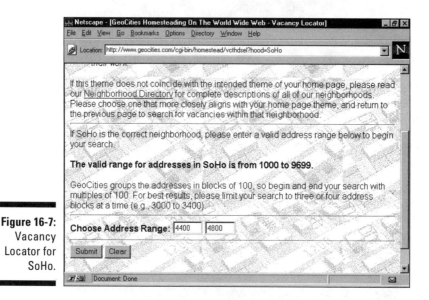

Figure 16-7:
Vacancy
Locator for
SoHo.

9. Type any two numbers in the Choose Address Range text boxes at the bottom of the screen and then click on the Submit button.

Figure 16-7 shows the numbers I picked. You don't need to copy mine. GeoCities then tells you whether any vacant houses are in that range. If you do find a vacancy, you see a screen similar to the one shown in Figure 16-8.

If the range doesn't have any vacancies, click on the Back button on your browser toolbar (which takes you to the previous page) and type another range of number. Keep trying until you find a vacancy. If you try several number ranges and still can't find a vacancy, you don't need to follow that "Try, try, try till you succeed" routine. Just select another neighborhood. That works fine — and it also saves a lot of time! To select another neighborhood, click on Neighborhood Directory and start from there.

Available addresses links

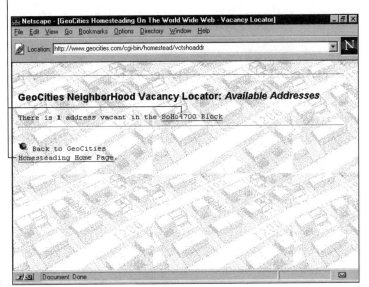

Figure 16-8:
Available
addresses.

**10. Click on any of the Available Addresses links (like the one in the
page shown in Figure 16-8).**

The next screen appears, displaying the home pages in your range (see
Figure 16-9). Just as you see all kinds of houses in your real neighborhood, this one too has a variety of them. But you need to look for a
house with the Available sign in the front yard. Fortunately, I found one.

Home sweet home

	4791	raapr	Post It stickers
	4792	vacant	Apply for this address
	4793	petra1	I Love Art, Skiing and my children
	4794	ggiacomo	All free Warez Software Giacomo's Home Page The Best in the World
	4795	oaom4e	Lyrics and so! Check out the lyrics I have written I also greet my friends
	4796	night_writer	Prose, Poetry, and Personal Hum
	4797	a1c_loring	This is my first page
	4798	zobavan	Daytraced art, moving in

Figure 16-9:
Whaddaya
know? A
vacant
house.

11. Click on **Apply for this address**.

A page asking you for personal information appears (see Figure 16-10).

12. Fill out all the blanks on the page, giving information about yourself, and then click on the Submit button at the bottom of the page.

Don't type what you see in Figure 16-10; use your own information — except that you get to choose a nickname. If someone else has already claimed the name you wanted for your nickname (Member Name), you are asked to give another one. No big deal. Use another one. If on the other hand, GeoCities accepts your information, you get a page that says, "Way to go!" Notice that some of the spaces on this page have an asterisk (*) beside them — you must fill those spaces in. The others are not absolutely necessary in order for you to get a space for your home page.

That's it. You're done. You have got your house. But to start building a home page, you need a password; GeoCities sends it to the e-mail address you listed in their form. You should get your password within a few minutes of completing the preceding steps. Sometimes it takes a couple of hours, but that's rare — and only if the computers at either your ISP or at GeoCities are having a problem.

13. **But wait just a minute. Before we do anything else, write down your password or print the message that contains your password because you'll need to refer to it. Keep it in a safe place; if you forget the password, you have to get new one. Bummer.**

If you don't get your password within a day, something is definitely wrong. In that case, go back to the Free Home Page & Free Member Email page, scroll down until you see a link for FAQ Pages. (*FAQ,* pronounced *fak,* stands for Frequently Asked Questions. You see this term all over the Web). In the FAQ section are instructions on what to do to get your password and how to alert GeoCities of the problem. Also, as a last resort, you can call the GeoCities technical support number at (310) 270-0400.

Can I Please Make My Home Page Now?

Web pages look like they do because they have a few codes (or *tags*). The tags are written with something called Hypertext Markup Language (HTML). Not to worry! HTML is easy, easy, easy to learn — if you want to — and you can find HTML editors around that make the whole process even easier. Also, the CD that comes with this book has an HTML editor, HomeSite. Check it out. However, in this chapter you build your home page without needing to know any HTML at all.

Calling in the construction crew

Okay, here you go. It's time to put GeoCities to work building your home page. Just follow these steps:

1. **Return to the main GeoCities home page at** `www.geocities.com`.

   If your browser is still open, you can get to the home page by clicking on Back until you reach it. The easiest way, however, is to look at the bottom of the GeoCities screen you're on for a link to the main page.

2. **Click on <u>Information</u>.**

   Guess what? The Information screen appears (see Figure16-11). Can you believe it?

3. **Scroll down the page until you get to the Member Information section and then click on <u>Member Utilities</u>.**

   You have now entered the Homesteaders Utilities page (see Figure 16-12).

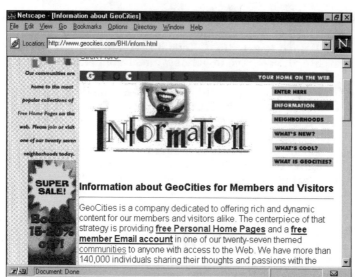

Figure 16-11:
The
GeoCities
Information
screen.

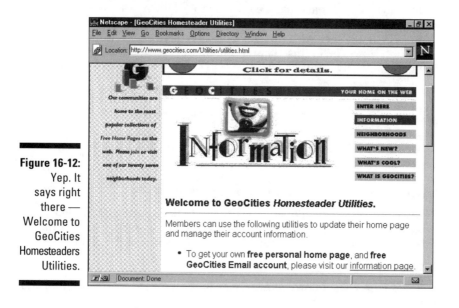

Figure 16-12:
Yep. It
says right
there —
Welcome to
GeoCities
Homesteaders
Utilities.

4. Scroll down the page until you see the Member Utilities section, and then click on <u>Home Page Editor and HTML Editor</u>.

The screen that appears mentions the Basic Home Page Editor (see Figure 16-13). Can you see that Profile Information section trying to peek over the lower edge of the screen?

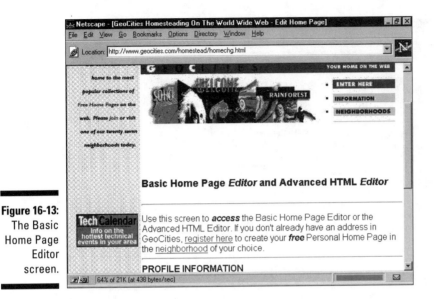

Figure 16-13:
The Basic
Home Page
Editor
screen.

5. **Scroll down the screen until you see the Profile Information section and fill it out.**

   Figure 16-14 shows the empty Profile Information section, in which GeoCities says, "Yo! Before I let you go any further, I need some ID." This section is just to make sure that you're changing your home page only, not someone else's. Your Member Name is not your real name. It's the name you made up when you filled out the form for a vacant house. Make sure that you type the password *exactly* as you see it in the e-mail message you got. You have to type lowercase letters (*a*, for example) in lowercase and uppercase letters (*A*, for example) in uppercase. When you type the password, it shows up as asterisks (*) in the Password text box.

6. **Click on the Choose Your Editor Here button.**

   Now you've reached it — the page for choosing GeoCities Home Page Editor, shown in Figure 16-15.

   If you get an error message, you probably mistyped something. Because you don't actually see the password when you type it in (only a line of ****) be sure to type very carefully. Click on the Back button on your toolbar, correct your mistake, and click on the Choose Your Editor Here button again.

7. **Click on the tiny circle beside the option Basic Personal Home Page Editor so that it fills in with a dark circle.**

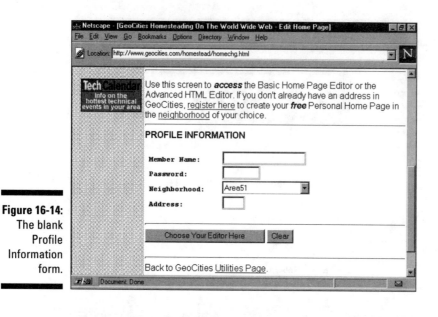

Figure 16-14:
The blank
Profile
Information
form.

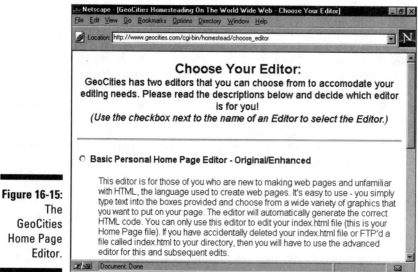

Figure 16-15:
The
GeoCities
Home Page
Editor.

8. Scroll down the screen and click on Goto Selected Editor.

Do not change anything in the Filename text box at the bottom of the screen. This part of the Web doesn't accept mistakes. But first go ahead and change the filename back to Index and make sure that html is selected, not htm. (The html should have a black dot next to it.)

Telling GeoCities how to build your home page

If you've been wondering when you actually get to put your home page together, the time has come. The screen shown in Figure 16-16 is what you've been waiting for. This screen is where you get to play Picasso and pick the colors and pictures. This is where you get to decide what you want people to read on your page. Go ahead; get to work. Here's an explanation of some of the things you see in the Home Page Editor screen.

✓ **Background Color:** You can make the background color any of the colors on the drop-down list if you click on the arrow to the right of the default color (gray) — which is really pretty boring! White, while not particularly exciting either, does make a good background that you can be sure won't look terrible with those nifty graphics you're probably already planning to add to your page.

✓ **Text Color:** Well, for sure you don't want it to be the same color as the background color you've chosen. No way! No one would ever be able to read it!

✓ **Unvisited Link Color and Visited Link Color:** You've probably noticed this, but . . . when you go to a home page, all the links are one color, usually blue. When you click on a link, go to its page, and then return to the page with the link you clicked, the color of the link has changed to a different color, usually red. Your browser's telling you which links you've visited and which you haven't. Like you'll forget. Yeah, right!

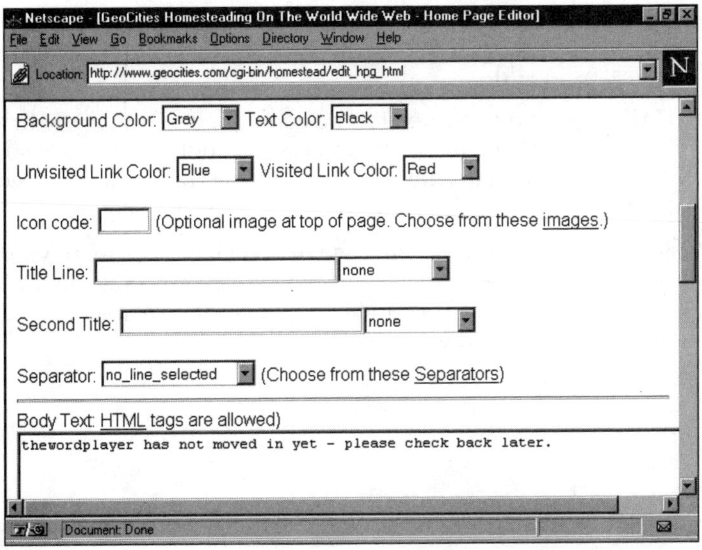

Figure 16-16: The top portion of the Home Page Editor screen.

Make sure that the colors of the links and text on your page are not the same as the background. If the colors are all the same, you won't be able to read anything on your page.

✔ **Icon Code:** GeoCities provides some icons that you can use. They're, frankly, pretty lame, but you may want to use one of them at least for now. Just click on the link to images to the right of the blank for the code. The code you're looking for will be the two-letter code that's beside the image you choose.

✔ **Title Line and Second Title:** These entries will be the very first lines on your page. You can select the size of the type for each of them by clicking on the check boxes next to them.

✔ **Separator:** *Separators* are graphical lines that separate portions of your page — just like the name sounds. Just click on the arrow beside the space to see the list that's available. Some of them are okay.

✔ **Body Text:** In the Body Text, you can delete the line that says you haven't moved in yet. That line is the standard message Geocities puts on all newly created home pages. If someone visits your home page before you've decorated it, they at least see the message. It's better than having a totally bare page, don't you think?

When you type in that Body Text box, you don't need to press Enter when you reach the right edge of your screen, although you can if you want to. Even if you continue typing beyond the right edge, your browser automatically starts the text at the beginning of the next line when it displays the text: Geeks call this *wrapping text*.

✔ **Link to URL:** In this section, shown in Figure 16-17, you list the home page addresses of the places you like to go to — places you think are cool and want to share with others. If you don't know of any sites now, you can leave the section blank and come back later and fill it up. Figure 16-17 shows what this section looks like if you have some addresses to add.

✔ **HTML tags:** You don't need to be concerned with the HTML tags yet but you're probably going to want to know about them pretty soon. They can make your page a lot more interesting than this one is going to be at first.

✔ **Include E-Mail Address on Page:** If you want visitors to your page to be able to send you e-mail, click on that check box (see Figure 16-17). Your e-mail address will automatically appear on your page, and anyone who clicks on it can send you e-mail.

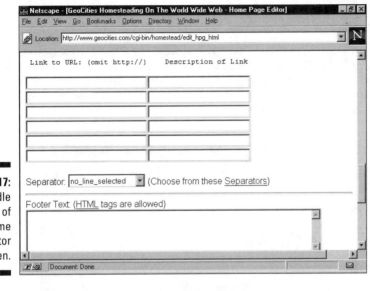

Figure 16-17: The middle portion of the Home Page Editor screen.

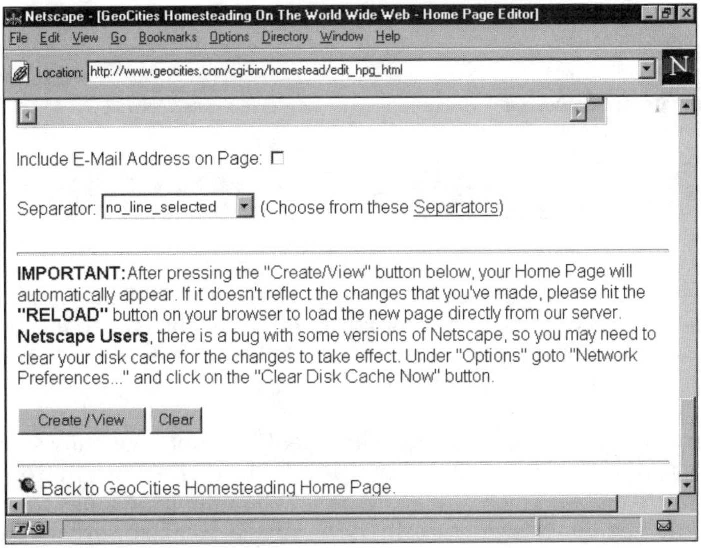

Figure 16-18: The very last portion of the Home Page Editor screen.

What Does My Page Look Like?

To see what your page looks like, click on the Create/View button, shown in Figure 16-18. Figure 16-19 shows a sample page. Note the address that appears in Location text box. If you do happen to forget the address, it's in the mail message that you received from GeoCities when you registered your page.

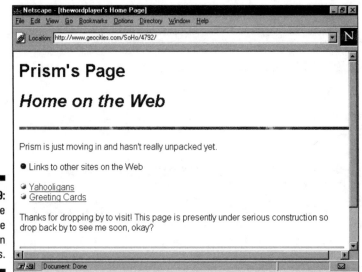

Figure 16-19: A sample Web page created in GeoCities.

You don't need to fill out the form completely to see what your page will look like. You can see how it looks as you make changes to it. Just scroll down to the bottom of the screen and click on Create/View to see what your page looks like at any point.

Every time you click on Create/View, GeoCities automatically saves your changes. To continue editing your page, click on the Back button on your browser toolbar. The editor reappears. When the page looks the way you want it, you don't have to do anything special to make sure it's saved. Just view it one last time and then go surfing on the Web.

Now, how difficult was that? Easy as 1-2-3, right? Go ahead; tell the world about it. By the way, do you still want to take that year off from school to work on that *home* of yours? You'd better check with your parents first, or else you may find yourself in need of a real home instead of this virtual one in cyberspace. At least the rent's not too steep on this one.

Now you've got this one pretty okay page, and I know you're going to want to improve on it. You can do lots of things to make it even more fun and interesting. And I bet you're going to want to learn something about HTML tags so you can really make some heavy-duty changes and additions. Read Chapter 17 for some things you can do in GeoCities to make your page more interesting.

Chapter 17

Jazzing Up Your Web Page

· ·

In This Chapter

▶ Livening up your page with funky animated icons

▶ Adding a cool voice greeting to your page

▶ Counting the number of visitors to your page

· ·

Some people just can't get enough of a good thing. Helloooooo . . . I'm talking about us — you and me. I thought we'd be satisfied with the page we have. But nooooooooo! We want more, don't we? We want to make our pages seem like we're pros. We want people to look at our pages and say, "This one's set up by someone who knows HTML inside out, upside down, right and left, and every which way around." Don't we? So let's get started.

You can do lots of things to make your pages look really, really good. You get to add a cool graphic, a pretty nifty little counter, and a voice greeting in this chapter, but you're going to want to do more, without a doubt. You see three or four more of those HTML tags mentioned in Chapter 16, and you get an idea about how to use them in a Web page. You can do lots more things with your pages without asking the old folks for a raise in your allowance! Heck, after you finish this chapter, you can start charging your friends — maybe even your parents' friends — to code their Web pages! (Sounds cool, huh? That's what they call it when you build a Web page — you *code* a page.)

Adding Animated Icons

How about adding some icons to your Web page? I thought you'd like that. The icons you get to use are courtesy of Stepping Stones, the cool folks who create cool icons and are gracious enough to let us use 'em. Do you think we oughta send them a thank-you note? If you want to, send Chris a message at Chris@ssanimation.com. It never hurts to be nice.

Just as you wouldn't take something from your brother's room that doesn't belong to you (without first asking permission), it's not right to take stuff you find on the Web and add it to your home page without asking the author for permission.

All the text, the graphics, the sound clips, and the movies on the Web are owned by someone. They may make those bits and pieces of their Web pages available for anyone to use — or they may not. In many cases, it's not easy to recognize that a page is designed and built by a kid. In fact, some adults create some pretty bad pages and some kids do some very nice ones, so the owner of those bits and pieces may be just a bit put out to find his or her work on your kid's Web page. Better to supervise a bit and encourage your offspring-unit to use the graphics provided by Stepping Stone rather than to swipe some other graphics that may be more appealing and be copyrighted. Better safe than sorry. Who needs e-mail from lawyers?

On with the animation. You have only three steps to follow to add an animated icon to your home page:

1. **Copy the icon from the Stepping Stones Web page to your computer.**

2. **Copy the icon from your computer to your Personal Disk Space on the GeoCities Web server.**

   Your Personal Disk Space is a portion of the GeoCities Web server on which files related only to your home page are stored. You have 1MB of Personal Disk Space. See Chapter 16 to find out more about making your own Web page at GeoCities.

3. **Add a command to your home page file to display the icon on your Web page.**

Getting the icons you want to use

Stepping Stones has provided us all with some outstanding graphics files to use on our Web pages. It's a pretty simple matter to move them from his space at GeoCities to yours, so listen up. You *do* want to build your page faster than that jerk in third period math, right?

To copy the icon from the Stepping Stones home page to your computer, follow these steps:

1. **Start your browser and go to the Stepping Stones home page at** `www.ssanimation.com/gallery.html` **(see Figure 17-1).**

2. **Scroll down the page until you see several tables listing the available animated icons.**

3. **Click on any hyperlink to see what it does.**

   The SS Animation page displays an animated icon (see Figure 17-2)

4. **To view another icon, click on the Back button on your browser to return to the list of icons, and then repeat the process.**

5. **Continue looking at the icons until you find the one you want or until you get bored.**

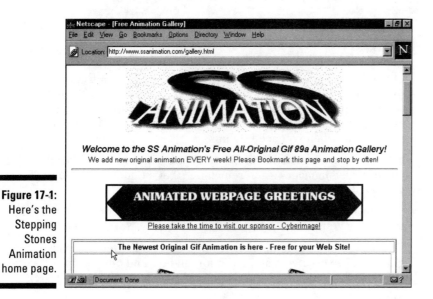

Figure 17-1: Here's the Stepping Stones Animation home page.

6. **Click on the icon you want and let it do its crazy back and forth routine.**

I kinda like that Welcome Morph one. You pick whichever you like but I'm going for the one in Figure 17-2.

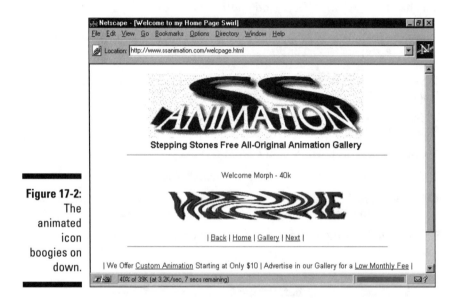

Figure 17-2:
The animated icon boogies on down.

7. **Create a folder just for images on your hard drive.**

Did I tell you I'm psychic? I can foretell the future. In my crystal ball, I see you downloading a whole bunch of these icons over the next few weeks. So here's a piece of advice: Create a separate folder on your hard drive for icons only. That way, your icons are all in one place and easy to find when you need them.

In Windows 95, you use Explorer to create a new folder. In Windows 3.1, you use File Manager — and remember that a folder in Windows 95 is called a directory in Windows 3.1.

I create a folder called (can you believe it?) Images. Now you're ready to pop the graphics into your Images directory. Nothing to it.

To get even more organized, you can create subfolders for your graphics. I've created a subfolder for .gif files and one for .jpg files.

8. **Move the mouse pointer to the icon and click on the right mouse button.**

A pop-up menu allows you to save the icon to your own computer (see Figure 17-3).

8. Move the mouse pointer to the icon and click on the right mouse button.

A pop-up menu allows you to save the icon to your own computer (see Figure 17-3).

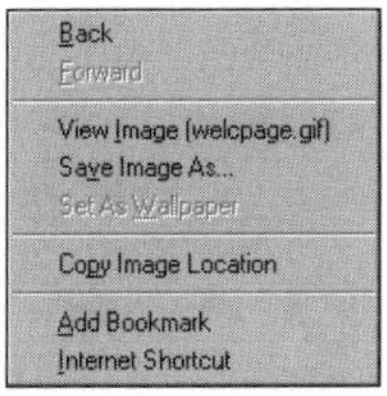

Figure 17-3:
Use this
handy pop-
up menu to
save the
icon to your
computer.

9. Choose Save Image As.

The Save As dialog box with the icon's name highlighted in the File name text box appears (see Figure 17-4).

Figure 17-4:
This icon's
name is
shortened
to
welcpage
in case
you're using
Windows
3.1.

10. Open the Image folder, open the .gif subfolder, and then click on Save.

The dialog box pops up with a filename (it's the filename Chris chose for this file — in my case, welcpage.gif.) The welcpage part is pretty obvious (yeah, yeah, I'm boring) — it's a Welcome to my Home Page graphic. Well, duh. The .gif part of the filename is the type of graphic file this is. Most browsers can easily display .gif or .jpg (or .jpeg) files. Other types of graphics files may require your visitors to have special plug-ins or special software to see them.

The .gif and .jpg formats are enough to entertain people; you don't need fancy graphics that make people go and get some stupid viewer they don't even want. (And if you make them leave to get something like that, they may not come back.)

Getting your icon from your computer to your Web server

To copy your icon from your computer to your Personal Disk Space on the GeoCities Web server, follow these steps:

1. **Open** www.geocities.com/Utilities/utilities.html **in your browser.**

   Now you're at the familiar GeoCities site (as shown in Figure 17-5) and ready to party!

2. **Scroll down the page and click on EZ File Upload Utility (see Figure 17-6).**

   Depending on the browser you're using, the upload utility may not be available, or may not work. It works nicely with Netscape, as you can see from the figures in this section.

Figure 17-5: The GeoCities Utilities page you come to know and love.

Click on this link

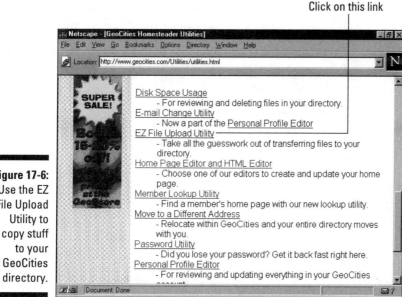

Figure 17-6:
Use the EZ
File Upload
Utility to
copy stuff
to your
GeoCities
directory.

3. **Scroll down the page until you see the PROFILE INFORMATION section (shown in Figure 17-7).**

   Whoa, this looks all too familiar from Chapter 16. Get used to it; you're going to see it again — several times in this chapter alone! If you already know the filename and the path to where the file lives, you can type it in and skip to Step 9.

4. **Fill the boxes with the information requested and then click on Browse.**

   Yes, you have to supply the info. What are you, a secrecy nut?

   You see the screen in Figure 17-8 if you're using Netscape when you click on Browse.

   Depending on what browser you're using, you may not have a Browse button. Some browsers don't let you browse for folders and drives, just Web pages. Crazy but true.

5. **Go to the folder where you stored the icons.**

   This sounds easier than it looks the first time or two. Doesn't look too familiar and sure isn't where you put that image file, is it?

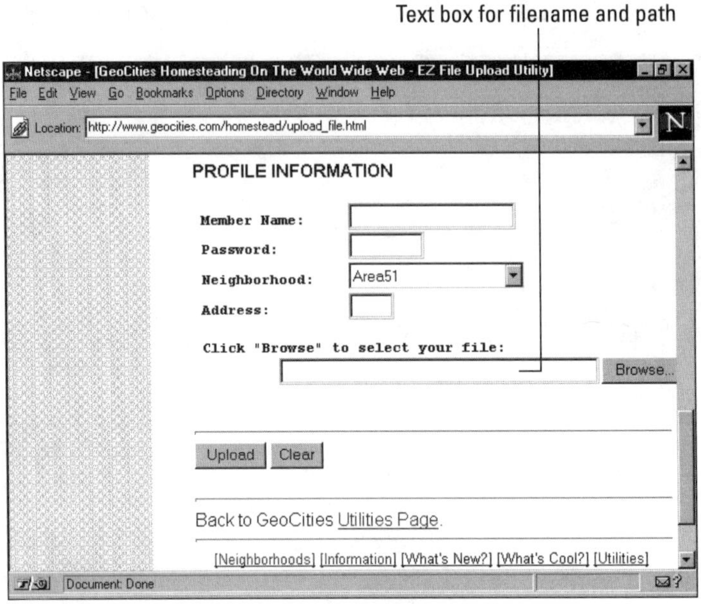

Text box for filename and path

Figure 17-7:
If you can
fill in the
path and
filename
here, pat
yourself on
the back
and jump to
Step 9.

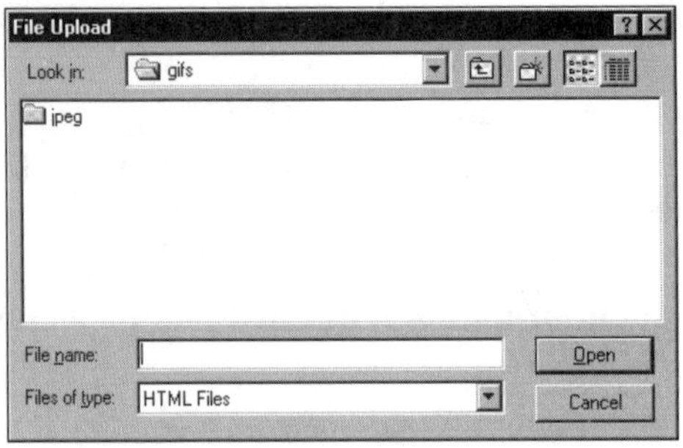

Figure 17-8:
This
window is
Netscape's
version of
the dialog
box.

6. **Use the arrow button to open the Look in drop-down list, and click on the icon for drive C.**

   Ah ha! The folder named gifs. Click and . . . ummmm, this is not a good sign — not good at all. It appears to be empty. But don't panic! Notice that the extension in the dialog box appears to be looking for files that end in .html. That's because you started this exercise from your browser and that's the extension of your Web pages.

7. **Click the arrow beside the Files of type box to open the drop-down list of file types. Click on the All Files (*.*) item (see Figure 17-9).**

   This section should display all the files in the current folder. Yes! Life is good! There's that elusive graphic file!

Figure 17-9:
Choosing to
display all
file types.

8. **Double-click on the file you want.**

Notice that the filename gets copied to the Browse box. Also notice the full name of the file. The .gif is part of the name. Remember that. You'll be quizzed on it later.

You could have saved yourself a lot of grief and just typed the filename in the PROFILE INFORMATION area. Do that next time.

9. **Click on Upload in the GeoCities PROFILE INFORMATION window.**

Before the Upload begins, you get that intimidating warning about entering an unsecure area.

10. **Click on Continue.**

If you entered your member name, password, and graphic name correctly, your file is uploaded a few seconds or minutes later! How difficult was that? You are rewarded by a screen like the one in Figure 17-10.

If you type anything wrong, you get a Sorry message instead. Check your spelling and type your password again, very slowly, very carefully! That pesky password is likely to give you fits if you get in a hurry.

11. **Follow the same procedure for all icons you want to upload to use on your home page.**

Putting a whole bunch of animated icons on your page isn't cool because then your page ends up looking tacky. Instead have just one or two, and change them every week.

Figure 17-10:
Yes! You
have your
very own
icon!

Getting the icons onto your home page

You're almost done. Hang in there a little longer. It's worth it. To add a command to your home page file to display the icon on your home page, follow these steps:

1. **Click on the <u>Utilities</u> link at the bottom of the page to go back to the GeoCities Utilities page (see Figure 17-11) and then scroll down and click on <u>Home Page Editor and HTML Editor</u>.**

2. **Scroll down the screen and fill out the PROFILE INFORMATION section.**

   You're getting good at this. You probably can fill it out in your sleep now, can't you?

3. **Click on the Choose Your Editor Here button, which displays the screen shown in Figure 17-12.**

   Speaking of editors, mine is pretty smug about her spelling skills. She tried to tell me that *accommodate* has two *m*'s . . . uh, I guess it does. Oh, like she never misspells annytheng. (If you wonder what I'm babbling about, look carefully at Figure 17-12.)

4. **Select Basic Personal Home Page Editor.**

   Remember this from Chapter 16? Right! Click on that circle beside the editor so that it turns dark.

Figure 17-11:
Use this
page to get
to the editor
screen for
your home
page.

Figure 17-12:
The Basic
Personal
Home Page
Editor is the
editor of
choice.

5. Scroll down the page.

The filename should be Index, and .html should be selected.

6. Click on the Goto Selected Editor button (see Figure 17-13).

You're now ready to edit your home page to put the icon on it.

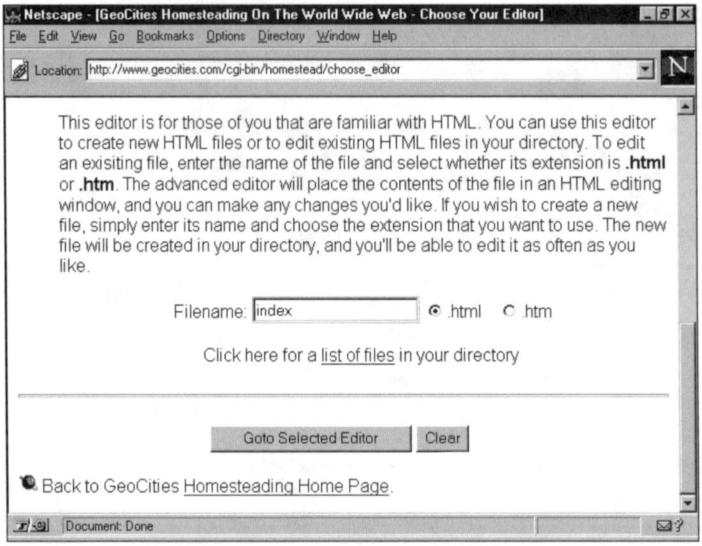

Netscape - [GeoCities Homesteading On The World Wide Web - Choose Your Editor]

File Edit View Go Bookmarks Options Directory Window Help

Location: http://www.geocities.com/cgi-bin/homestead/choose_editor

This editor is for those of you that are familiar with HTML. You can use this editor to create new HTML files or to edit existing HTML files in your directory. To edit an exisiting file, enter the name of the file and select whether its extension is **.html** or **.htm**. The advanced editor will place the contents of the file in an HTML editing window, and you can make any changes you'd like. If you wish to create a new file, simply enter its name and choose the extension that you want to use. The new file will be created in your directory, and you'll be able to edit it as often as you like.

Filename: index   ⊙ .html   ○ .htm

Click here for a list of files in your directory

Goto Selected Editor   Clear

Back to GeoCities Homesteading Home Page.

Document: Done

Figure 17-13:
Yep. We were here in Chapter 16, too!

7. Scroll down the screen to the Body Text section.

8. In the Body Text section shown in Figure 17-14, type this:

```
The Word Player is just moving in and hasn't really
   unpacked yet.

<p>

<center><IMG SRC=welcpage.gif></center>

<p>
```

If you uploaded something other than the Welcome Morph named welcpage.gif, replace the welcpage.gif with the name of your image file. Remember, no mistakes or a hundred lashes in the town square!

In case you're curious about what you just typed, the <p> starts a new paragraph. The <center> centers everything after it until the browser reaches the </center>. Oh, yeah. Those things with < and > are called *tags*.

9. Click on Create/View at the bottom of the page to see what your page looks like.

My page (okay, it's lame!) looks kinda like Figure 17-15 but morphs into a fuzzy changeable thing and then says, "My Home Page." Don't laugh! Well, don't laugh too long. Please. I'm old. You'll hurt my feelings. (For a minute anyway. I'll get over it.)

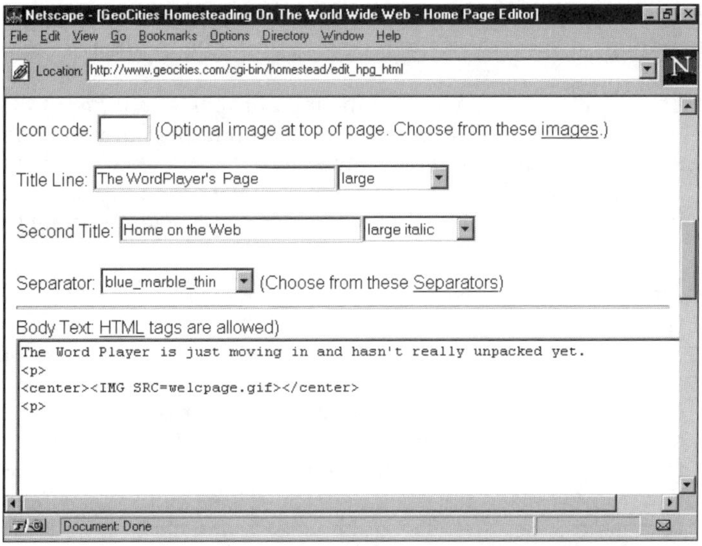

Figure 17-14: Adding the Welcome Morph icon with some opening text.

Figure 17-15: Here it is. It ain't much, but it's mine.

If you get a broken page or mosaic icon instead of the animated one you were hoping to see, any of the following could be to blame:

✔ You didn't type the name of the icon properly, you forgot to type one of the other characters such as ‹ or › on that line, or you added an extra space where you shouldn't have. Go back and check. If you see that you typed everything correctly, you may have typed the name of the icon in uppercase (*A*) instead of lowercase (*a*). The case of the letter makes a difference.

✔ Although you successfully uploaded the file to your Personal Disk Space, GeoCities hasn't updated your file list to account for the new file. Although this rarely happens, it's still a possibility. So try viewing your page again in a few minutes by clicking on the Reload button on the toolbar. If the icon *still* doesn't display, you crashed the entire GeoCities system and you're in trouble! No, I'm just kidding. Scared ya, didn't I? Perhaps your Personal Disk Space still hasn't been updated. So just make sure this is indeed the case. Go back to the Utilities page (use the History command to get there faster; choose Go and click on GeoCities Homesteader Utilities if you see it there). Click on Disk Space Usage. Fill out the PROFILE INFORMATION again!!! Click on View. You now should see a list of files in your disk usage listing, including the icon file you're trying to use. See whether it has the same name as the one you're using on your page. If it doesn't, make the necessary change on your home page. Then try viewing your page again. This little trick should work.

If you have pictures of your own in .gif format, you can upload them to your Personal Disk Space the same way. Then add the same command to your home page, making sure that you type the name correctly. These steps also work if you have JPEG pictures. JPEG pictures have the .jpg extension instead of .gif.

Counting the Visitors to Your Page

A *counter* automatically counts and displays the number of people who visit your page. The counter tells you how many times your home page is requested by someone's browser (including yours). Well, you can make it cheat, but it's kinda cool just the same. If you just sit there and click Reload on the browser's toolbar a bunch of times, you can run the counter up pretty good. Okay, so it's not scientific — it's still fun! And you don't have to tell your friends that you reloaded the page 4,234 times — I sure won't! Adding a counter is really simple; you just follow these two steps:

1. **Initialize the counter.**

2. **Add the counter command to your home page.**

The end. Told you it was simple! Seriously, though, the following sections explain these two steps.

Hold still, you counter. I gotta initialize you!

Initializing the counter doesn't mean that you put your initials on it. *Initializing the counter* simply means that you set the counter to zero so that it counts your first visitor as number 1, your second visitor as number 2, and so on. To initialize the counter, follow these steps:

1. **Go to the GeoCities Home Page at** www.geocities.com.

2. **Click on the Open button on your browser's toolbar.**

3. **Type** http://www.geocities.com/cgi-bin/counter/*member.* *password* **but replace** *member.password*, **with your member name and password.**

   So if your member name is **coolguy**, and your password is **abcdefg**, you type **http://www.geocities.com/cgi-bin/counter/coolguy.abcdefg**.

4. **Click on Open.**

   You should now see a blank page with the exception of a 1 in the top left corner of the page. The 1 means that you successfully initialized your counter (see Figure 17-16).

If you get a Server Error message instead of a 1, the probable reason is that you made a mistake in typing the command. Retype it and try again.

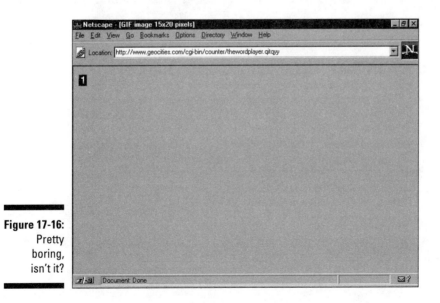

Figure 17-16:
Pretty
boring,
isn't it?

Don't you counter my command, home page!

After you've initialized the counter — well, really, it's more like you've started the counter for your member name — it's not going to do you much good until you add some code to it to run on your home page. To add the counter command to your home page, follow these steps:

1. **Get back to the editor.**

   By now, you're very familiar with the process, aren't you? Flip back to the "Getting the icons onto your home page" section if you need a refresher.

2. **Scroll down to the section titled Body Text and type this:**

   ```
   <p>
   You are visitor number <IMG SRC="/cgi-bin/counter/
      member">
   ```

   as the last line in that section (see Figure 17-17), but replace member **with your member name.**

   So if your member name is **prettygirl**, you type **<p> You are visitor number <IMG SRC="/cgi-bin/counter/prettygirl">**. The <p> in the command means that you want to start a new paragraph.

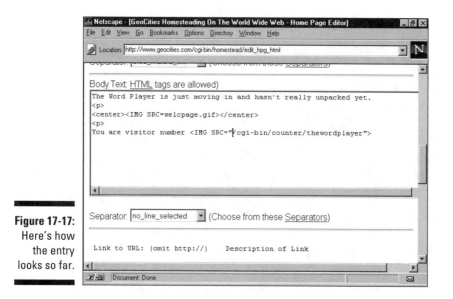

Figure 17-17: Here's how the entry looks so far.

3. Click Create/View.

Kabooom! You should see your counter. Check out Figure 17-18.

If you can't see the counter, click on Reload on your toolbar. That action usually fixes the problem. If you still can't see the counter, check whether you've made a typing error. If you didn't make a typo, maybe you didn't initialize the counter properly. Go through the initialization again. We'll wait for you. We've all made mistakes.

To check whether the counter is working properly, click on the Reload button a few times. Each time you do, the counter increases by one.

Adding a Voice Greeting to Your Page

GeoCities offers a really neat service called DialWeb, through which you can add a voice greeting to your page. However, this service is available only for a period of 30 days from the time you add it to your page. After 30 days, DialWeb costs you about 4 bucks a month. Now here's the important part, so listen up. **You should get permission from your parents before you use this feature.** If you don't, you could be grounded when the phone bill comes in next month, because using this feature requires that you make a long distance call to record your voice greeting. So ask before you use it. Oh, one more thing, you could even lose your Web privileges. Now *that* would be really sad.

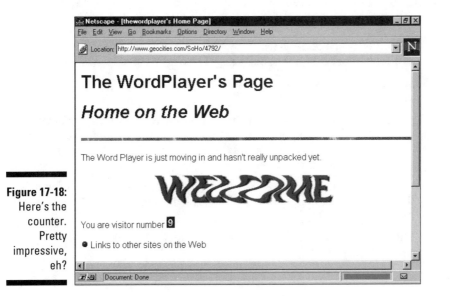

Figure 17-18: Here's the counter. Pretty impressive, eh?

You oughta know two things about the DialWeb feature. The first is that it takes a long distance call from most parts of the U.S. to use it. The second is that the feature costs money after the 30-day trial offer. I don't own stock in GeoCities, and I don't benefit from promoting this service in any way. I just think it's a neato feature, one that very few if any home page providers give their users. So at least try the free offer. It's really rad. But if you still think this is a sales pitch, perhaps I can interest you in a better deal. You see, I have this piece of prime real estate . . . .

Adding a voice greeting is a three-step process, each of which is explained in the sections that follow:

1. **Get a DialWeb ID.**

2. **Add the DialWeb code to your home page.**

3. **Record your message.**

To listen to your message after you've recorded it and it appears on your home page, you'll need the RealAudio software, which you can download from the RealAudio Web site. See Appendix B for installation instructions.

Get a DialWeb ID

DialWeb makes its home at GeoCities, too, so you don't have to go far to make use of their service. (You *did* get permission, right??) You'll have to wade through the screens and the rules and regulations before you can use this feature, but not just everyone has a voice message on their Web page, so it's worth the frustration! To get a DialWeb ID, follow these steps:

1. **Go to the DialWeb registration page at** `www.geocities.com/ dialweb/dialweb_home.html` **(see Figure 17-19).**

2. **Scroll down the screen and click on "I'm interested — So what's the deal?"**

You see a screen that outlines the terms and condition (that's lawyer talk for "we have our rights and you better pay attention"). *Read* this part! If you haven't gotten permission yet and you're not sure this is a good idea, don't go further!

3. **If everything looks pretty okay and you do have permission for this little experiment, click on "I'm Ready, Let's Get Started at the bottom of the page."**

The Registration page appears (see Figure 17-20).

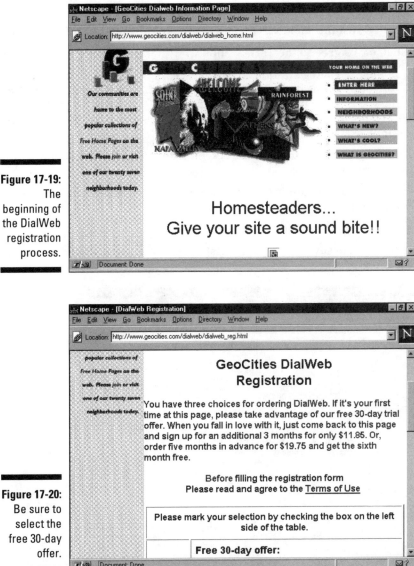

Figure 17-19:
The
beginning of
the DialWeb
registration
process.

Figure 17-20:
Be sure to
select the
free 30-day
offer.

4. Click on the Free 30-day offer option.

5. Scroll down the same screen and complete the member information.

6. Click on I Agree to the Terms, Submit.

You then see a Registration Complete! screen containing important information for using DialWeb (see Figure 17-22). This screen shows the code you need to put on your home page, and also your DialWeb ID and PIN number, which appear at the bottom of the screen. You can't record your message without these two numbers.

7. Choose File⇨Print to print the screen when this page is complete in the browser window.

The information on this screen is also sent to you as an e-mail message, which you should get right about . . . now!

8. Go check your mailbox.

The message saying that your registration is complete should be there.

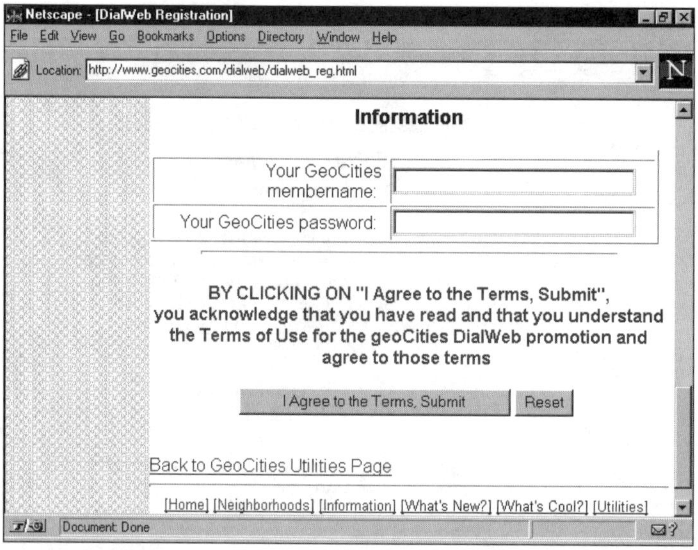

Figure 17-21:
Are you *sure* your parents okayed this? Just checking one more time . . . .

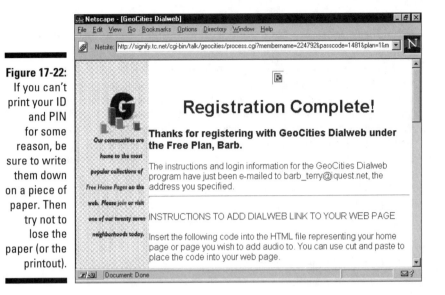

Figure 17-22:
If you can't print your ID and PIN for some reason, be sure to write them down on a piece of paper. Then try not to lose the paper (or the printout).

Add the DialWeb code to your home page

Next, you have to add some HTML code to your home page. Don't worry. You don't have to know it; you don't even have to type it. To add the DialWeb code to your home page, follow these steps:

1. **Using the mouse, highlight the lines shown in Figure 17-23 and then choose Edit⇨Copy.**

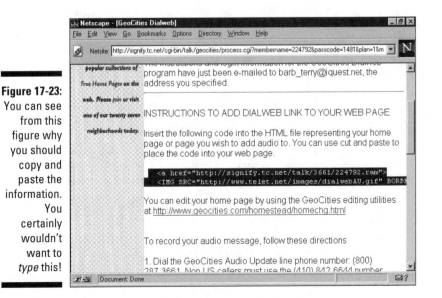

Figure 17-23:
You can see from this figure why you should copy and paste the information. You certainly wouldn't want to *type* this!

2. **Open your home page using the Home Page Editor, go to the section titled Body Text, and click once with the right mouse button on any blank line.**

   This action tells the editor where to paste the two lines of code that DialWeb wants you to include on your page. More HTML stuff. It looks complicated — but it's not. The first line is simply a reference to the file you're going to make at their site when you call them. (You did save the instructions they sent in your e-mail message, right? Good!) The second line is a reference to the DialWeb logo graphic that they want you to show on your page (so that other people will use their service). Just stick this info in the body text of your home page. Where? Ohh . . . at the top, at the bottom, wherever you like at the moment. You can move the code whenever you feel like it.

3. **Choose Edit⇨Paste.**

   The two lines should now appear wherever you had the cursor when you chose this command. (Bad location? Try Edit⇨Undo.)

4. **Scroll down the screen and click on Create/View.**

   You should see the DialWeb logo on your page. Because you still haven't recorded your message, clicking on the logo results in an error message. If you don't see the logo, click on Reload.

Record your message

So now follow the instructions they sent you in that e-mail message. This is not physics here. Just follow these steps:

1. **Dial the phone number they sent you — a basic no-brainer.**

   You get a really boring recorded welcome message that tells you to put in your six-digit ID. Mail message, remember? Right! That ID.

2. **Give your passcode.**

   You also can find it in that mail message. I hate to tell you this, but your identity has been reduced to a bunch of numbers.

3. **Record your voice message for your home page.**

   Don't record a boring "Hello, how are you?" kind of message. Let it be something interesting — a joke, a riddle, your pet barking, whatever. That's one way to make people keep coming back to your page.

4. **Press the # on the phone's keypad when you finish recording your message.**

   I know that you know where the # is, but for those who don't . . . it's on the last row — right beside the 0 for Operator.

5. Listen to the recording about how to play your message back.

They're boring instructions, but they work — if you listen.

6. Check out your message.

You can decide whether you like what you've recorded. I can't hear it, so you're on your own.

7. Hang up when you're finished.

Duh. Not too tough.

The GeoCities site has a ton of information on the kind of stuff you can do to liven up your home page. Look at the pages of some of the other members to get ideas. If you like something on someone's page and want to know how it was done, send the member a message. People are always flattered when their stuff gets appreciated by others and are always willing to help. It doesn't hurt to ask. That's how you discover cool stuff . . . keep asking questions.

Now get back to downloading more icons.

Dull Web sites don't get visited often or repeatedly. If you want people to keep coming to your site, be sure to update it as often as you can with new icons and information. BUT . . . don't do it until your homework is finished!

PART VI
The Part of Tens

©RICHTENNANT

"Ronnie made the body from what he learned in Metal Shop, Sissy and Darlene's Home Ec. class helped them in fixing up the inside, and then all that anti-gravity stuff we picked up off the Web."

In this part . . .

This part has two chapters in it. The chapters are a source of information which parents and kids need to ensure that their adventures in cyberspace remain enjoyable and don't turn ugly. Although the information is at the end of the book, the chapters contain tips and guidelines that are applicable throughout the book.

Chapter 18

Ten Things You Should or Shouldn't Do on the Web

• •

In This Chapter

▶ Never, ever, EVER give out personal information

▶ Never arrange to meet anyone in person without a parent's permission

▶ Never send a nasty message, thinking it can't be traced back to you

▶ Never respond to a nasty message if you get one

▶ Never use foul language in a chat room

▶ Never go where you aren't supposed to

▶ Keep newsgroup and mailing list replies short when you can

▶ Avoid responding to chain letters

▶ Read the FAQs

▶ Grow with the Web

• •

*T*he Web has changed the way we live and play, the way we spend our free time, and the way we talk with others. The Web offers good things, and the Web offers bad things. The good definitely outweighs the bad — more than 10 to 1. But the bad, if left unchecked, can really ruin your day and make your Web experiences unpleasant. This chapter gives ten things you can do to get rid of the bad and make your WebVentures truly enjoyable.

Never, ever, EVER give out personal information

Let's say you're at a mall, just hanging out with your friends, and a guy comes up to you and asks you for your phone number, address, and so on. You don't know this guy from Adam. Would you give him your number? Like, duh!! Of course not. Why then would you give it to someone on the Web? You can't even see the person who asks you for information on the Web. At least in the mall you can see the guy.

Can you tell whether the person you're chatting with in a chat room or the person who sent you e-mail is a *really* a guy or a girl? The person could be a 45-year-old icky, smelly, yucky guy who hasn't showered in days and who is just pretending to be a 10-year-old girl, saying he likes to play with Barbie dolls. It's easy. He just signs his name as *Sarah, Age 10* or something like that. No one can tell who he really is. So be smart. If a person asks you for your phone number, or your address, or *anything* personal about you that you aren't comfortable with sharing, you don't need to get scared or anything. Just politely tell the person that you will first ask your parents and then send it. You shouldn't be scared, because you never know, the person asking could really be a 10-year-old Sarah asking — just because she wants to be your friend. In that case, you'd be pretty embarrassed if you got paranoid, alerted the cops, who busted down Sarah's door one evening while her mom was cooking dinner, and took her father away (like they do on the TV show *COPS*), in his tank top and ugly boxer shorts. The headlines on the 10 o'clock news would be something like "A 45-year-old man by the name of Sal was apprehended by the police for claiming to be a 10-year-old girl named Sarah on the Internet." Little would anyone know that the dad couldn't stand being around computers, couldn't type to save his life, and would rather be poked in the eye with an ice-pick (hate it when that happens) than log on to the Internet. The moral here is to not get scared and paranoid when someone asks you for personal information. Instead be strong and tell them you'll get back to them later.

Never arrange to meet anyone in person without a parent's permission

The Web is a truly wonderful place where you can have loads of fun, learn a lot, and meet really nice people. But sadly, many people hang out on the Web just to take advantage of kids and do them harm. If you follow a few simple rules, we can help put these jerks outta business. Never arrange to meet anybody face-to-face without getting permission from your parents first — even if the person says that he or she lives in your own neighborhood, right around the block from you. You never know who you're going to meet. Remember the story of Little Red Riding Hood and the big bad wolf who dressed up as poor ole Grandma? Well, times have changed, but a lot of wolves are still out there. This is a very serious matter and shouldn't be taken lightly. Just go to the Heidi Search Center at `www.halcyon.com/alt.missing-kids.gifs/heidi.html` if you really want to see what I'm talking about. There you'll find pictures of over a thousand kids who're missing. So if you want to meet someone, the first thing you do is tell your parents about it. Be smart and you'll be safe. Remember . . . you, smart; they, jerks.

Never send a nasty message, thinking it can't be traced back to you

If you think you can send nasty, anonymous messages to strangers and not get caught just because nobody can see you, wake up and smell your pet's litter box. Phew! Now that's a smell that'll knock your socks off. Every e-mail message leaves behind a trail as clear as a polar bear's footprints in the snow. The message can be traced right back to you in a matter of minutes.

Never respond to a nasty message if you get one

When a dog barks at you, do you bark back? Uhhhhhhhh . . . NO!!!! Because if you do, you might be mistaken for a dog, too. So if you get a nasty message in the mail, don't send one back. But you don't need to be scared either. Just call your parents right away and show them the message. They'll know what to do. Remember, messages can be traced back to the sender.

Never use foul language in a chat room

In chat rooms, usually an adult is watching everything that everybody types. So if you use foul language, you can be certain that it's not going unnoticed. If it's the first time you're caught, you'll be warned. You won't get a second warning. You'll be automatically thrown out of the chat room and will never be let back in again.

Never go where you aren't supposed to

If you come across a Web site that requires a password to get in and you know you don't have one, don't try to break into the system intentionally by using illegal means just because some jerk told you it works. Now this may sound far-fetched to you, but a whole bunch of 15-year-olds got themselves into doggy dudu by being too smart for their own good. Hear this and hear this well: Breaking into a computer system is a big, I mean B-I-I-I-I-G, crime! It's just like breaking into someone's house. Do you think the cops will believe you if you said that you were just trying to see if your neighbor, old man Oscar, was home? I think not. Similarly, if you tell the cops that you were just trying to see how smart you were and find out whether you could crack into a Web site, but you meant aaaabsoooolluuutely no harm, you're in for a big surprise. God help you if the judge at your hearing is the guy from *My Cousin Vinny*.

A *hacker* is someone who's curious about the nitty-gritty stuff that makes computers work. A hacker doesn't intend to do anything illegal such as breaking into a computer system to steal information for wrongful purposes. A *cracker* is a someone who likes to break into computer systems to steal information and possibly damage the system. Hacker — good; cracker — bad.

Keep newsgroup and mailing list replies short when you can

When posting a reply to a message on a newsgroup or on a mailing list, keep your messages short and to the point. If the message you're replying to is lengthy, don't include the entire message in your reply if all you have to say is, "Totally, dude. I agree with you totally." That's a sheer waste of space and computing power. At any given time of day, millions of messages move around the Web. You don't want to add to that number if your message is not worthwhile. So keep your messages short and simple.

Avoid responding to chain letters

Every once in a while you'll get a chain letter in your mailbox. A *chain letter* instructs you to forward the same letter to five or ten other people. The letter says that if you do, you'll get good luck, but if you don't, you'll be hit by bad luck. Let me tell you something. I get a chain letter at least once every month. I trash them right away. Chain letters are a waste of your time and others' time as well. And if the sender was so concerned with your well-being, how come he or she didn't send you a thousand dollar check with the letter? Now that would be *real* good luck, right? So go ahead and forward the letters — forward them to the TrashCan in your mailbox.

Read the FAQs

Most mailing lists and newsgroups have a list of FAQs — *Frequently Asked Questions*. Take the time to read this list. It contains, well, the frequently asked questions about the mailing list or newsgroup. Doesn't take a rocket scientist to figure out that one, does it? Before you post a question, read the list of FAQs. It probably contains the answer to your question. People on mailing lists and newsgroups don't like to answer the same questions over and over again, especially if it's clear that the person asking the questions hasn't made the effort to read the FAQs.

Grow with the Web

The Web is growing at a breakneck speed. Every week the Web has something new. Even though keeping track of all the new stuff is difficult, you should try to learn at least one new thing about it every few weeks. That way you'll truly enjoy your cyber cruises. Home pages and chat rooms can keep you excited for only so long. After a while, they get boring. But if you make an attempt to use the new technology that enters the Web every week or so, you'll have much more fun and excitement. So don't just cruise the Web, *use* the Web as a learning tool, and make the most of it.

Chapter 19

Ten Questions Parents Frequently Ask about the Internet

*E*ven though millions of people all around the world flock to the Web every day, 99 percent of the world's population doesn't have a connection to the Web and hasn't heard of it. To them, the Web is something you see in a house that hasn't been cleaned in a long time. Others have heard the hype but are too terrified to join. If you belong to either of these two groups, this chapter is for you. People often ask or are afraid to ask the following ten questions about the Web. Read through the questions; they provide an insight into the craze that is the World Wide Web.

What is the World Wide Web?

The *World Wide Web* is a vast network of computers spanning the globe. The Web is part of an even larger network called the *Internet*. The Web is very easy to use, and you don't need to know much about computers to use it.

The coolest thing about the Web is that you move around it by clicking on words or pictures — not by typing strange-looking commands thought up by a programmer.

So what's the fascination with "a really vast network of computers"?

The fascination is that the Web is a network on which all the following exist: a huge library in which you can find almost any information you're looking for, a village square where you can meet people, a bookstore in which you can get the latest newspapers and magazines, a forum for discussing ideas and getting solutions to problems, a video arcade in which you can play all kinds of games, a laboratory in which you can perform experiments, a record store in which you can listen to music, a phone booth that lets you call all over world, and a mall in which you can shop till you drop. The Web has much more to it, but I think you get the idea. And here's the kicker — all this is available through your computer.

Will the Web make my child smart?

NO! If someone told you that, they lied — or at least exaggerated. The Web is not central to the learning experience — the three R's are. They always have been, and they forever will be. The Web is just one of many tools you can use to enhance the learning experience, but cruising the Web doesn't make a kid any smarter. In math class, for example, it's not the kid with the most expensive calculator who necessarily gets the high score; it's the kid who understands the problem and then uses the calculator effectively. The Web is such a tool. It will never substitute for a child's creativity.

I have heard bad stories about the Web. Are they true?

You're probably referring to all the easily available adult-oriented material to which we wouldn't want our kids to be exposed, right? Well, let me ask you this: When was the last time you went to a bookstore? Did you go to the magazine rack and take a good look at the magazines on the top shelf? What did you see there? Adult magazines, right? Does the presence of adult material make bookstores bad? Absolutely not. The number of good books in a bookstore outweighs the bad ones 1000 to 1. Adult-oriented material has been readily available in bookstores for years, but you've always offered your children the good things and warned them of the bad, trusting that they'll be able to tell the difference and make the right choices when they're older. The Internet and the Web are no different. You should follow the same precautions in using the Web as you do in other aspects of life.

I'm still uncomfortable. Are there any other precautions I can take?

Sure! Tools are available that restrict access to all areas on the Web that are unsafe for kids. When these tools are in place, they will not let your child get to those areas even accidentally. The tools are software programs that function as *filters*. They work hand-in-hand with the browsers you use to cruise the Web: the programs filter or stop any indecent material from being *downloaded* (or copied) to your computer. The CD enclosed with this book has a few of these software filters on it. Appendix A introduces you to some of the filters.

What's this thing called a virus that my friend caught on the Web?

A *virus* is a piece of software code that is created with malicious intent. Like a flu virus that you can catch unknowingly, a software virus is also caught unknowingly. It usually hides among good clean software. But when you run that good software on your computer, you inadvertently run the virus program, too. The virus then can destroy the data on your computer.

You can prevent a virus from attacking your computer by taking simple precautions.

- ✔ **Use virus-detection software.** By running virus-detection software periodically, you can usually find and eliminate a virus from your computer. Like a flu virus passed around from person to person, a software virus is passed around from disk to disk or when you download a virus-infected file from the Web. Always check disks and programs before you use them.

- ✔ **Back up your data regularly.** If you maintain backup copies of data, you always have them to fall back on. Almost everyone I know who performs backups religiously does so because they have lost data to a virus or a hard-drive crash at one time or another. How does that go, once bitten . . .

332 The Part of Tens

My neighbor's kid ran up a huge bill using the Web. How can I prevent that from happening?

Your neighbor's kid was probably using a service that charges for Web access by the hour. You can run up huge bills that way. The CD enclosed with this book provides information and software to connect to AT&T WorldNet Service, a Web access service provided by AT&T. The service charges a flat monthly fee — about 20 bucks a month. That's it. You can use AT&T WorldNet Service 24 hours a day all month and not be charged a penny more than that.

I hear I can make lots of money on the Web. Care to tell me how that works?

I would if I knew. Very few people, if any, have made money from the Web. Everybody just has a plan, a very good plan they say, that they want to sell you. If you buy it (it usually costs $19.99 — too good to pass up, right?), the only person making the money is the person selling the plan.

What's this thing I hear about credit card fraud on the Web?

Frankly, your credit card account is more susceptible to fraud when you make regular purchases at the store than when you make purchases on the Web. Think about it. When you sign a receipt for a credit card purchase at a store or for dinner at a restaurant, do you ever ask for the carbon sheet that separates your copy from the store copy? Of course not. What do you think happens to that sheet? It goes in the trash, at which point anybody at the store or restaurant has access to it. That sheet has all the information anyone needs to commit fraud. Isn't that just asking for trouble? Or how about when you use the credit card to make a reservation or purchase over the phone. Do you always whisper into the mouthpiece? I think not. You get my point?

I agree that the possibility of fraud on the Web is real, but the major credit card companies have joined hands with major software manufacturers to come up with software that makes fraud extremely difficult. So before you start worrying about fraud on the Web, start asking for the carbon sheet at stores. You can find documented cases of people going through a store's trash for the carbon copies and using them.

What do I do if my child receives unwanted and really offensive material?

If you receive offensive material, the first thing is to not get scared. If someone tries to send offensive and unwanted material or messages, don't reply, but do save a copy of the material or message. You can then do any or all of the following:

✔ Ask your Internet Service Provider (AT&T WorldNet Service, for example) to trace the message using the sender's e-mail address.

✔ If you know your way around the Web, you can directly contact the postmaster or Webmaster at the address from which the message was sent and alert her or him to the message. If the nasty message you receive was sent by JohnDoe@address.com, for example, the postmaster's address is usually postmaster@address.com. The Webmaster's address is usually webmaster@address.com.

✔ You can always alert the police. These days most police units have cyber-sleuths on their force who know just what to do in such cases.

Index

• *G* •

• *H* •

IDG BOOKS WORLDWIDE, INC. END-USER LICENSE AGREEMENT

4. **Restrictions on Use of Individual Programs.** You must follow the individual requirements and restrictions detailed for each individual program in Appendix B of this Book. These limitations are contained in the individual license agreements recorded on the disk(s)/CD-ROM. These restrictions may include a requirement that after using the program for the period of time specified in its text, the user must pay a registration fee or discontinue use. By opening the Software packet(s), you will be agreeing to abide by the licenses and restrictions for these individual programs. None of the material on this disk(s) or listed in this Book may ever be distributed, in original or modified form, for commercial purposes.

5. **Limited Warranty.**

   (a) IDGB warrants that the Software and disk(s)/CD-ROM are free from defects in materials and workmanship under normal use for a period of sixty (60) days from the date of purchase of this Book. If IDGB receives notification within the warranty period of defects in materials or workmanship, IDGB will replace the defective disk(s)/CD-ROM.

   (b) **IDGB AND THE AUTHOR OF THE BOOK DISCLAIM ALL OTHER WARRANTIES, EXPRESS OR IMPLIED, INCLUDING WITHOUT LIMITATION IMPLIED WARRANTIES OF MERCHANTABILITY AND FITNESS FOR A PARTICULAR PURPOSE, WITH RESPECT TO THE SOFTWARE, THE PROGRAMS, THE SOURCE CODE CONTAINED THEREIN, AND/OR THE TECHNIQUES DESCRIBED IN THIS BOOK. IDGB DOES NOT WARRANT THAT THE FUNC- TIONS CONTAINED IN THE SOFTWARE WILL MEET YOUR REQUIREMENTS OR THAT THE OPERATION OF THE SOFTWARE WILL BE ERROR FREE.**

   (c) This limited warranty gives you specific legal rights, and you may have other rights which vary from jurisdiction to jurisdiction.

6. **Remedies.**

   (a) IDGB's entire liability and your exclusive remedy for defects in materials and workmanship shall be limited to replacement of the Software, which may be returned to IDGB with a copy of your receipt at the following address: Disk Fulfillment Department, Attn: The World Wide Web For Kids & Parents, IDG Books Worldwide, Inc., 7260 Shadeland Station, Ste. 100, Indianapolis, IN 46256, or call 1-800-762-2974. Please allow 3–4 weeks for delivery. This Limited Warranty is void if failure of the Software has re- sulted from accident, abuse, or misapplication. Any replacement Software will be warranted for the remainder of the original warranty period or thirty (30) days, whichever is longer.

(b) In no event shall IDGB or the author be liable for any damages whatsoever (including without limitation damages for loss of business profits, business interruption, loss of business information, or any other pecuniary loss) arising from the use of or inability to use the Book or the Software, even if IDGB has been advised of the possibility of such damages.

(c) Because some jurisdictions do not allow the exclusion or limitation of liability for consequential or incidental damages, the above limitation or exclusion may not apply to you.

7. **U.S. Government Restricted Rights.** Use, duplication, or disclosure of the Software by the U.S. Government is subject to restrictions stated in paragraph (c) (1) (ii) of the Rights in Technical Data and Computer Software clause of DFARS 252.227-7013, and in subparagraphs (a) through (d) of the Commercial Computer — Restricted Rights clause at FAR 52.227-19, and in similar clauses in the NASA FAR supplement, when applicable.

8. **General.** This Agreement constitutes the entire understanding of the parties and revokes and supersedes all prior agreements, oral or written, between them and may not be modified or amended except in a writing signed by both parties hereto which specifically refers to this Agreement. This Agreement shall take precedence over any other documents that may be in conflict herewith. If any one or more provisions contained in this Agreement are held by any court or tribunal to be invalid, illegal, or otherwise unenforceable, each and every other provision shall remain in full force and effect.

The World Wide Web For Kids & Parents CD-ROM Installation Instructions

The World Wide Web For Kids & Parents CD-ROM contains software for both Macintosh and Windows users. Not all software works on all platforms, so be sure to read Appendix C for complete program information, system requirements, and essential information before you install programs.

Note: You don't have to install all the programs provided on the CD. Just install the programs that appeal to you.

To start the CD using Windows 95, follow these steps:

1. **Insert the CD in the computer's CD-ROM drive and wait a minute to see if the CD starts up automatically.**

   If the CD starts, the first thing you see is the IDG license agreement.

   If nothing appears after a minute or two, your computer is saying, "Me want icon." Click on the Start button, choose Run, and type D:\INSTALL.EXE in the Run dialog box, substituting your CD-ROM drive letter for the D, and then click on OK. The CD sets up an option for you to use — free of charge. Then choose Start⇨Programs, select the new IDG Worldwide group, and select the World Wide Web icon. Then continue with the steps that follow.

2. **Accept the terms of the IDG license agreement.**

   Nobody's gonna twist your arm. If you don't want to accept the terms, be that way — but we'll miss you. If you *do* accept the terms, you're in for a lot of fun. The happy Dummies family CD kicks in and makes using the CD a breeze.

Note: When you're ready to use the CD again, you either just pop the CD into the drive and let it do its thing, or if your computer is the finicky kind that needs an icon, use the Start menu to open the IDG Worldwide group and select the World Wide Web icon.

If you're using Windows 3.1, your computer needs an icon. Just follow these steps:

1. **Insert the CD in your CD-ROM drive.**

2. **In Program Manager, choose File⇨Run.**

3. **In the Run dialog box, type D:\INSTALL.EXE.**

   Substitute your actual CD-ROM drive letter if it is something other than D.

4. **Click OK.**

   The *World Wide Web For Kids & Parents* icon is installed in Program Manager in a program group named IDG Books Worldwide.

Note: To use the CD, open the IDG Books Worldwide program group and double-click on the *World Wide Web For Kids & Parents* icon.

If you're using a Mac, just pop the CD into the CD-ROM drive and double-click the World Wide Web icon. The interface runs without another word.